# HOUSE PLANTS

## How to Keep 'Em Fat & Happy

Linda Finkle-Strauss

# HOUSE PLANTS
## How to Keep 'Em Fat & Happy

Illustrated by Pam Carroll

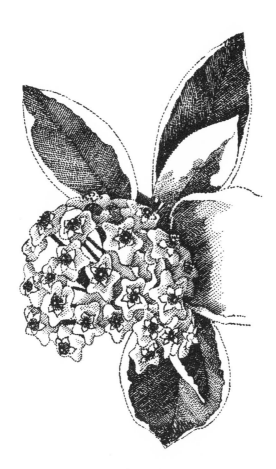

McGRAW-HILL BOOK COMPANY

New York · St. Louis · San Francisco
Toronto · Mexico · Düsseldorf

Book design by Lynn Braswell.
Illustrations by Pam Carroll.

Copyright © 1977 by Linda Finkle-Strauss.

1234567890MUMU7832109987.

**Library of Congress Cataloging in Publication Data**

Finkle-Strauss, Linda.
   House plants.

   Includes indexes.
1. House plants.   I. Title.
SB419.F513    635.9'65    76-16104
ISBN 0-07-021007-1
ISBN 0-07-021008-X pbk.

for Steve, Jessica, and Zoe

# Contents

# CONTENTS

# HOUSE PLANTS

How to Keep 'Em Fat & Happy

# Introduction

This house-plant madness started for me four years ago. I moved with my husband from a splendid, wild ranch in Humboldt County to the big city, San Francisco— glimmering golden jewel by the bay, but city nonetheless. And suddenly a longing began to grow. Throughout the years we were in Humboldt County I'd had a burgeoning vegetable and flower garden and a small orchard to contend with, I had remained quite sane in the house-plant department with a single treelike coleus in the front parlor. But in San Francisco I began to feel barren and lonely. I soon found myself planning absurdly complicated errands all founded upon the unspoken desire to be caught waiting for a bus right outside a house-plant store; my purse sprouted a small scissors and plastic bag for taking ivy cuttings on the way to the mail box, and the only grocery store whose prices I found bearable boasted dozens of potted herbs between the lettuces and green onions. One pot of parsley led to another and on it went.

Now the house is crowded with plants, and there's the good, rich, kindly smell of wet soil in the early mornings; friends and visitors are either of the same mind as I or else they make jokes about the tropical rain forest up here. It doesn't matter to me at all. Whatever direction your eyes choose they are filled with dancing green visions: the gentle arch of fern fronds, the proud outline of my crazy Chinese evergreens, or the joyous glow of light of a superb coleus. I wake up in the morning to the kindly smell of wet soil and think I'm in Rousseau jungle-garden-heaven. It's not the country, but it isn't half bad.

Who knows what brings on this craving for the green stuff? Poking around with indoor plants has become a fantastically popular hobby. Or, more than a hobby, a mounting need. Perhaps in our collective unconscious there is a great longing for return. We city dwellers are sharply cut off from our agrarian past, our souls, nurtured for centuries by a close contact with nature, are seeking to reestablish that bond, to put down new roots. Caring for indoor plants, for any living creatures, brings great peace to the spirit. Running soil through your hands and mixing it together and smelling its clean, wet richness is a remarkable balm. There's a great feeling of success that comes from following a plant's growth, shaping it into more beautiful healthy forms, propagating new plants from it, and having it around for a long time as a robust friend—a success to be heartily enjoyed. We are fortunate that satisfaction lies so close at hand. One thing is sure: never argue with satisfaction.

What do you need to grow plants well? Confidence is at the top of the list. It's easy to do a good job and be known as a green-thumb mystic. The key is a lot of confidence and common sense and a little bit of knowledge—about how plants grow, what they need, and when to do what you're supposed to. And don't be afraid. Everyone kills off a plant or two (or ten) at first. New leaves unfold and old leaves drop off; all are part of the same whole, an amazing process of growth. You will grow by improving your skills and learning better ways to care for your plants (that's the whole hope behind this book) and your plants will grow as the centuries have taught them to and be beautiful, healthy, and fine.

It's an odd thing. Plants, like all growing creatures, respond terrifically to joy and an easy confidence and very poorly indeed to pain and fear. Kind words and music, laughter, and even companionship—all are part of what you are able to provide. Perhaps it's merely that when you're around them a lot and thinking positively of your ability to do well by these green friends, you are more attentive to their needs and more consistent in your care. Or perhaps, as recent research studies suggest, there is physical and scientifically measurable change in response by plants to positive or negative energy around them. My guess is that both are true, each only a different way of looking at the same reality. Folk medicine and laboratory research have always benefited from each other's wisdoms. So can you.

Do it all—the words, the thoughts, the music—as gushingly as fits your own nature. I'm not exactly one for long, soul-searching conversations with my plants or turning on the radio for them when I'd rather have the house quiet, but I love them dearly and their response continues to be steady, lavish growth. Remember two things: One, that plants are unbelievably rugged and filled with a will to survive and, two, that you're growing them in your house for your own enjoyment and satisfaction. Don't grow plants you don't like or plants that need certain conditions your home can't possibly provide. No one can grow all plants well. The same house or apartment just cannot be all things to all creatures (green ones, four-leggeds, two-leggeds, and otherwise). You'll get a good understanding through the chapters of this book of which plants like what conditions, which are the easiest ones to start with, and where to go from there—so grow what you can grow well, grow A LOT of it, and wallow in your pleasure and success.

Let's get closer to the ways to do all this. You may have heard a great many contradictory quick bits of advice about house-plant care. Don't worry about them. The primary force that wrenched this book past the stage just when it was just a grandiose idea was the memory of my own confusion when I first tried to learn more about plants. It seemed that everyone was willing to tell a part of the story and no one the whole. It's easy to get little odds and ends of free advice. ("Don't touch the leaves of that piggyback; he hates to be touched!" "Never mist in the morning; it ruins the plants." "Always water before noon; night watering brings on rot!") All of these vehement but casually offered bits of information are founded in fact. But none of them tells the whole story behind misting or watering or whatever. What I always wanted to know was the foundation behind a piece of horticultural habit so I could know how to vary the thing and what I was really doing and what the plant had to do to meet me halfway. For instance, African violets like high humidity; misting is a great way to increase humidity, but fuzzy-leafed plants may rot if water rests on their leaves. And what does high humidity mean? Are there other ways to provide it besides misting? Or is there a way to mist without getting the leaves wet? And can't fuzzy leaves ever get wet without rotting—hey, wait a minute, how about when it rains in their native forests or whatever? And that's where you're left. Incomplete advice brings on more confusion than you were stuck with when you started. There are easy, common-sense answers to all of these maddening contradictions.

The best way to start is with a full understanding of how a plant grows and where its strengths come from; then to take a look at each process involved in caring for a plant—watering, providing humidity, fertilizing, repotting, soils, pots, the works—and truly understand what you are trying to accomplish when you do all of these things; how the plant responds to each; and what are the alternatives to the usual methods. It's at this point that you are finally able to see where common sense enters in and all the feelings of helpless confusion begin to fade.

There's yet another factor to consider that isn't often discussed: each plant is an individual. Much as you can learn a great deal about how to take care of plants in general, any rule will quickly be broken by an extraeager giant or a wobbly fellow who still hasn't decided that growing is worth all the trouble. Just as people have their oddities in relation to health, so will plants. You may do something that I warn vehemently against and a particular plant may still thrive. This plant may be much the same as the person who gets four hours sleep every night, doesn't believe in raincoats, loves to sit reading in a nice refreshing draft, and never has been sick in his life. You certainly shouldn't worry about it, nor should you badger the happy fellow into a semblance of textbook normalcy. The very best you can do with your plants is start out on the midline of informed advice and then, as your eyes and sense of touch and experience become more sensitive, you will begin to see the nuances and variations of the general rules. Perhaps that's all that the famous "green-thumb" mystique entails; you choose to become more sensitive to the signs and language of the growing world and a new two-way relationship of communication begins. Individual plants will begin to throw you hints as to how to better your skills. It's at that point that a craft becomes an art, you are constantly learning and your tasks cannot become stale. It's also at that point that gardeners—both of the indoor and outdoor varieties—become hooked for life.

# 1

# The Basics *of* Good Care

Before you can begin to make good sense out of the various cultural requirements of house plants, it is important to understand how a plant grows and does its work.

## The Pattern of Growth

You take a look at a plant and your first impression is of the foliage, all that stuff on top. It's what you bought it for, it's what you're looking at it for, but it is not the key to health and future well-being. The health and consequent beauty of the foliage is primarily dependent upon the health of the root system. The roots have a complex job to do: they grow, move out into the soil, search out water and nutrients, absorb them, and begin to carry this nourishment up cell by cell through the stems and leaves of the plant. If anything interferes with that process—the pot being too small and the roots cramped, the soil exhausted of nutrients and the plant not fertilized to make up for it, water not available because you suddenly got busy or the soil flooded because you suddenly got overenthusiastic—then the roots suffer, and that incredible process of transport of nourishment slows down. Leaves then drop and the plant is on its way to looking pretty bad. Your job as a plant tender is to see that nothing interferes with the roots' ability to do their miraculous, unthinking, complex job. It is toward that end that so much time will be devoted here to talking about soils, repotting, watering, fertilizing, and the like. Always keep in mind that you're after healthy roots—they are essential for beautiful foliage.

*Now here's another bit of knowledge to seize upon before we move along; I'll come back to this one again and again, but take a good look at it now. A plant grows primarily at its tips.* This is true both of the foliage and the roots, and it's the most important aspect of understanding toward keeping your plants in a beautiful lush state. More energy goes into the new leaves coming out at the tips of each branch than into any other spot along the stem. That "energy" can be measured in a laboratory as a high concentration in these new leaves of a special group of chemicals, which are manufactured by the plant and called the growth hormones (or auxins). You may prefer to think of it that way or you may just keep in mind that the newest, fastest growing parts of any being are the ones that take the most nourishment, concentration, and energy.

The root system grows by following the same pattern of terminal growth. At the edges and tips of the roots, new growth is constant. Tiny roots begin branching off from the main roots; these get bigger and new branching roots grow from them, and the process continues. These new roots are called "hair roots." They occupy most of the energy of the plant in regard to the root system, and the entire mass of proud and eager foliage aboveground depends upon these tiny fellows for water, nourishment, and health. The hair roots are the ones who are doing all the work: the most active growth, as well as the moving out and searching through the soil for water and nutrients.

And once acquainted with these all-important hair roots, we run smack into an explanation of a few old mysteries. One is that you can kill a plant overnight by letting it stand in a full saucer of water: root rot may begin and bring on the collapse of the entire plant. I'd always found that one nearly incomprehensible: an entire plant from two inches of water! And then there's that one about killing a plant by applying a fertilizer solution that's too strong; one slip of the teaspoon and you've "burned the roots," the plant is suddenly dying. Both are impressive catastrophies, but easily understood and avoided if you've got the hair roots in mind. The plant depends completely upon their good health and ability to work. But they are all fairly small, tender, and vulnerable; that is the key. They can rot quickly and they can be burnt by a strong chemical solution. One overwhelming catastrophe and they all go at once; the plant is suddenly left without any system for seeking water or nourishment. It is unlikely indeed that the plant will be able to sustain itself long enough for a whole new crop of hair roots to grow. On the other hand, if the hair roots are healthy, which they usually will be, they are *turgid*, every cell is filled with just the right amount of water, they look eager and stretched out and taut. And, naturally, that look of turgidity is the look of health for the entire plant.

I hesitate to toy with the grand leap toward anthropomorphisms and plant world-views, but it will serve you well to define a plant's life and health by its ability to do work. The look of a healthy plant is that of active, eager, vibrant work. The stems are strong and supportive, leaves are lifted up and turned toward the light, the veins in each leaf are well defined and actively engaged in moving the water and nutrients up from the roots and out to all parts of each leaf. Drooping, curled, or limp leaves do not display turgidity; they indicate that the plant is not able to do its work and is less than perfectly healthy.

This work that a plant does is a miraculous cycle. Water and nutrients are absorbed by the roots and transported up through the plant to all the stems and leaves. Meanwhile the energy from the sun is converted into glucose through the process of photosynthesis in the leaves and then transported downward through all parts of the plant, cell by cell, finally reaching the tips of the roots. It is with that stored energy from the sun that a plant is able to grow; to synthesize its own chlorophyll, pigments, hormones, vitamins, fats, proteins, starches, DNA, RNA; produce seeds, flowers, the whole works. But without the water brought up out of the soil by the hair roots, photosynthesis could not take place; water, if you will remember, is one of the required compounds in the process of photosynthesis.* Perhaps I'm threatening you with memories of eighth-grade botany lectures; all I can seem to remember from those days is throwing sunflower seeds and raisins down the aisles, staring out the window, and then reprimands after class. If only I had listened then. And yet, it doesn't matter. Nobody's asking you to make RNA or flowers. All you have to do is see that water is available and nothing interferes with that total process of growth. The plants know everything there is to know about it. What comes next is the little stuff that we get to do.

## Your Jobs

### FRESH AIR

Plants require fresh air at all times. You may notice after a big party—when the room was crowded with people and smoke hung in great clouds—that the plants look sad and a little bit done-in themselves. Leaves are slightly limp, neither looking bright nor eagerly supported. The reason is a lack of oxygen. You need to see to it that you have good ventilation in your home. That means opening the windows every day. You aren't aiming for a gale wind, just a gentle recirculation of the air. Beware of the window that opens and admits a cruel freezing chill on a plant that minutes before thought it was in the radiator-heaven tropics. Always avoid drastic changes of any kind in plant care. The watchword is consistency. Plants are unbelievable cha-

---

* *Photosynthesis*: happens in the chlorophylls: food is made: Carbon dioxide + water + light → glucose + oxygen ($6 CO_2 + 6H_2O$ + energy from sunlight → $C_6H_{12}O_6 + 6O_2$)

    *Respiration*: happens in the mitochondria: food is used: Glucose + oxygen → carbon dioxide + water + energy ($C_6H_{12}O_6 + 6O_2$ → $6 CO_2 + 6 H_2O$ + energy in food calories)

meleons in their ability to adapt to change but they only do so and retain their loveliness if the change is gradual. Sometimes all that is needed is a couple of windows opened a few inches at the top to refresh the air and aid everyone's good health.

Beware of strong wind. You'll understand the danger if you've ever stopped to look at clothes hanging out on a line to dry on a very windy day. The wind whips the water from them in fast rough gusts. The same thing happens to leaves. Water is forced out of the foliage much faster than it can come up from the roots to replace that loss. The result is a plant with limp, dry leaves and an appalling look of total collapse. The soil will probably still be wet. So don't water it. Move the plant out of the wind to a fairly dim recovery spot. Wait a while and the roots will have a chance to bring up the needed water and everything will be fine again. But take care that this doesn't happen more than once or twice; there are very few plants that can endure this type of abuse without losing some leaves and therefore looking worse for the wear.

Beware too of gas fumes. Long before your nose picks up on the danger, leaves may blacken and drop. Sometimes shoots become dwarfed, they branch repeatedly and new leaves continue to be small; other plants may refuse to flower and begin a slow decline. If you have any reason to suspect that gas is leaking in your home, check it before you suffer any plant loss. You can call the utility-company service department or try a few tests of your own. Bring home a healthy, potted tomato plant from the nursery; if there is gas in the air, its leaves will droop and discolor within the day. Or bring in some fresh-cut carnations; gas fumes cause the petals to curl inward and look like they've folded up for the night.

## CLEAN LEAVES

Even if there is fresh air in the room, nothing very good has been accomplished if the plant's leaves are dirty. The pores that cover the surface of the leaf are there exactly for the purpose of absorbing needed elements from the air. Your job is to keep those leaves clean and pores unclogged so that the plant can proceed uninterrupted with its work. Washing the leaves regularly is the best approach. Every time you take your plants to the sink or bathtub or wherever to water them (and more about that later), you should wash off the leaves. Anything that puts out a strong force of water will be a good tool. That can be the sprayer attachment for washing the dishes or a special sprayer bottle from a nursery or beauty-supply store or auto shop. I've found one wonderfully handy bulb sprayer that's available at a few plant stores and through several seed catalogues.* Or a watering can would do well if it has what's called a "fine rose," the round thing with all the little holes in it, attached at

---

* See appendix for a list of seed, plant, and bulb catalogues.

the end of the spout. What you're looking for is anything that puts out enough water to actually coat and wash off the leaves in a quick and easy way; the little spray bottles or brass atomizers for misting put out such a gentle spray that your thumb muscles give up long before a single leaf is really clean.

And so you wash. Pay good attention to the undersides of the leaves as well. There are pores there too. Indeed, it is on the undersides of the leaves that most of the insects who bother house plants first decide to roost. An added advantage of regular leaf washing is that you dislodge and send these fellows down the drain while they are still small and few enough that they haven't done much damage. For the extralarge plant who stands as a permanent and very heavy guest in the corner, you can occasionally set down newspapers and do just the same. Or you might prefer to wipe off the leaves (underneath too) with a soft, damp cloth.

People sometimes ask about the white spots that look as if they were accidentally splashed onto the leaves; these are often seen on plants just brought from a green-house. And splashed they are. There is a white shading compound used in green-houses to cut down the amount of sunlight the plants receive during the brightest days of summer or at any time of year if the plants grown are lovers of the shade. The shading compound is applied to the inside surface of the greenhouse glass and drips or gets splashed over the plants. It is not harmful, just strange looking, and repeated water washings get rid of it. If you're in more of a hurry than that, try washing it off with water and a mild soap (a soap, not a detergent—use Ivory or any biodegradable product you have); then wash off the soap and the plant will be fine.

There are two other important considerations to discuss. The first is the relationship between wet, just-washed leaves and sunlight. You must *never* put a plant which has water on its leaves back into its old familiar spot if sunlight might shine directly on those leaves. Similarly you must never do your leaf washing at the sink or bathtub if the day is gloriously bright and sunlight is streaming through the window and onto the plants. Sunlight shining on a single drop of water heats the water and magnifies in intensity, burning a hole right through whatever is beneath it. You will occasionally see a plant that has perfectly round little holes in its leaves; these were most likely caused by the sun shining on droplets of water on the leaf surface and that's the situation you are trying to avoid. It's also something to beware of with many philodendrons and other members of the aroid family. They do an amazing trick which is called guttation. This occurs when the roots have brought up more water to the leaves than can be transpired or evaporated into the air. The leaves get rid of that extra water through tiny specialized pores usually found at the edges of the leaf, and small droplets of water appear as if from nowhere. It's only common sense that whether the water drops come from your sprayer, the plant's pores, or a leak in the roof, you'll have to make sure that sunlight doesn't turn them into magnifying glasses and burn holes. So be careful.

The second important consideration leads toward taking a better look at the old bugaboo about water on hairy-leafed plants. While it is a perfectly justifiable bugaboo, a little better understanding of the factors involved will allow you to replace fear with common sense and to vary the rule somewhat when you have to. Most of the plants which have little tiny hairs covering their leaves are native to the tropics. The purpose of those hairs is to conserve moisture; they prevent water from evaporating out of the leaf into the hot air. The hairs serve a protective purpose and make it possible for the leaves themselves to be more tender and beautiful than they could be if they had to do the whole moisture-conserving job by themselves. (The cactus has resolved a similar, albeit more intense and dry, heat problem by developing its calloused, impervious outer surface and prickly spikes.) The hairs on plants will also act to conserve moisture if water is splashed onto the leaves. The hairs hold the drop of water in, make evaporation very slow, and where the water drop remains, that tender beautiful leaf may begin to rot. So you don't want to do too much leaf-washing of these plants. Generally, it isn't necessary. The hairs also act to repel dust and oils and the leaves just don't need such frequent cleaning. You can do a good job with a soft dry cloth or medium-sized watercolor brush and simply dust them clean. But if they are excessively dirty, you can use a firm spray of water to clean them well. You only need to be sure that they remain in a well-ventilated, warm but unsunny spot until the leaves have a chance to dry. The lovely plants which have those little hairs include African violet, gloxina, the hirsute (or hairy) begonias, and purple velvet plant. Piggyback is an odd one because, although it has the little hairs covering its leaves, it is native to the North American Pacific coast and gets drizzled on through most of the cold part of the year. Dump the theories and spray or mist piggyback to your heart's content; just don't get cocky and forget to watch out for sunlight on the wet leaves.

There are several leaf-shine products on the market which I would not recommend. Check the label; most of them have an oil base and that oil remains behind looking glossy, as only oil can, and clogging the pores of the plant so that they cannot maintain health as nature intended. Some people also talk about washing the leaves with milk and rubbing them to a shine. Here again the glossy look is probably achieved from the butterfat which would be glimmering at the expense of clogged pores. I do know that once you use milk, the plant looks much drearier as the milk wears off than it did before you began. You are locked into a lifelong chore; that one's not for me! It seems crazy that people would want plants to look shiny beyond their natural healthy glow.

I sometimes imagine an overwrought public-relations lady from the Shiny-Leaf Company, dressed to the teeth for the occasion—bush hat, khaki safari jacket, giant boots laced to the knee, parasol—with a bevy of strong male natives behind her. She is walking through the Amazon jungle and clicking her tongue in dismay at the twenty-foot philodendrons who have never known civilization and Shiny-Leaf. She has the natives climb to the top of each vine and polish the leaves to a "glossy, hard brilliance." They take photographs; these then appear throughout the world in the next edition of the *Shiny-Leaf Illustrated Star*. She is offered the presidency of the company but declines, deciding instead to take her crusade to Africa, the West Indies, Sumatra, Borneo, the World. I'd rather leave her behind.

## HUMIDITY VERSUS DRY AIR

Most of the hairy-leafed plants come to us from the tropical regions of the world; so do most of our other nonhairy favorites. The list of origins reads like an exotic travelogue—Java, Sumatra, Brazil, Guatemala, Borneo, Tanganyika—places you'd head for wearing a white linen suit and hoping to meet up with Sidney Greenstreet and a bottle of gin. What this means is that most house plants like a lot more humidity than our homes usually provide. These tropical natives are rugged creatures and will certainly thrive, making a house resemble a lush green jungle, but only if we meet their need for moisture in the air.

There are two primary plant signals that the air is too dry. The first of these is that a plant develops *brown leaf tips*. This browning happens only at the tip or edge of the leaf and indicates that this smallest most delicate part of the leaf (or frond— ferns suffer greatly from this malady) ventured bravely out into the world and met up with air that was excessively hot and dry. Water was then quickly evaporated from the leaf, most dangerous at the narrow tip, and browning resulted. That brown area is simply dead. If you wish, you can cut it off for the sake of the plant's appearance. I prefer this to leaving the odd mixed green/brown effect. Either cut the leaf tip straight across or try to duplicate the contours of a healthy leaf. There will often be a little browning again where you cut, so you cut that off and that's the end to it—*if*, in the meantime, you've corrected the low-humidity situation.

The second sign of the air being too dry is *lower-leaf drop*. I might as well stop now and admit it: lower-leaf drop is a symptom of just about everything. It indicates: overwatering, underwatering, overfeeding, underfeeding, the air being too dry, the pot being too small or too large, the light too intense or too dim. The immediate sense of dismay you feel when encountering this awesome fact is tempered somewhat by an understanding of why this is true. It all goes back to that guiding principle I talked about in the section on patterns of growth: that a plant grows primarily at its tips. Whenever a plant encounters a situation of stress, it will continue to send the same full quota of nourishment to the new leaves at the tips and will make up the difference by dropping older, lower leaves. That's why there exists the classic less-than-ideal picture in our minds of the leggy specimen: several strong main branches come up from the soil and bear at their tips a beautiful showing of healthy new leaves; the lower parts of those branches, however, are bare. The total look is something more akin to the lollipop trees of our childhood drawings than it is to a nurseryman's well-grown ideal. When you bought the plant it looked very much like the ideal. If you pay good attention to consistent humidifying, watering, fertilizing, repotting, and the like you will prevent the plant from having to make those lower-leaf sacrifices in the face of stress and your plant will maintain its beautiful shape. If, however, you are now sitting looking at one of your favorite plants that in recent months has taken on more and more of the sacrificial pompon look, do not despair; in the next chapter I'll go through ways to repair the damage.

There remains only one untied end in regard to lower-leaf drop and your attendant dismay: if the cause could be low humidity, under- or overwatering, the pot size, under- or overfeeding, the light being too bright or too dim, or all of the above —how in the world do you know which to change? Like all practical questions discussed out of context and in an abstract way, the answer is much simpler than it looks. *You know!* You're never worried about overwatering and underwatering at the same time. You know which side you're pushing and the leaf drop is a sign that you've pushed too far. The same goes for pot size, light, fertilizer, and humidity. Use your common sense at all times; it's the best tool you've got when it comes to plant care. But if you still have trouble second-guessing the cause—you can't decide between overwatering and underfeeding for example—resort to the scientific method. Cut down on the watering for the first week; if the leaf drop hasn't stopped, then fertilize with a well-diluted solution. You should not try everything at once. Use the process of elimination and allow for recovery from one source of trouble before you toy with the next.

Now let's get back to humidity. There are lots of ways to provide more of it. How many you choose to use depends on how dry your home is, what you can set up and then be consistent about, and what kinds of plants you like. Ferns need high humidity; cacti thrive where it's hot and dry; most of our stand-by house plants do beautifully in between. While we are discussing humidity, consider this: increasing the relative humidity in your home *does not* mean adding water to the plants. While standing behind a sprayer bottle, thumb pumping up and down and bottle aimed at the begonia, one definitely has the notion that the water vapor is a direct aid to instant health and that the begonia should look as much better as your thumb is tired. That's not what's happening. What is happening is that when the air is humid, when the air is already holding a good deal of water vapor, the plants do not lose as much water from their leaves through evaporation. By increasing the relative humidity in your home you are decreasing the rate of water loss from the plant's leaves. It is that rapid water loss to dry hot air that brings on brown leaf tips.

So let's consider the ways to increase relative humidity. I'll start with the least effective and move on toward the most:

(1) *Pans of water on radiators:* You simply put a lot of water around the room, in pans on the radiators or near the heater, or in drinking glasses set in between and around your plants. The water evaporates and you fill up the pans again. That provides more water vapor that's gone into the air and the humidity is somewhat higher.

(2) *Group plants together:* Plants benefit greatly from each other's company. It's a delightful truth that the more plants you have in one room, the better they all do. The reason for this is largely the increase in humidity. Once you have twenty plants in a room there is *a lot* of wet soil: water evaporates into the air from that soil and the humidity goes up. A grouping of six or seven plants on a small table makes a beautiful and humid growing area. The only thing to be wary of is that you don't get greedy and cram too many in one small spot; all plants need elbowroom, so that air can circulate freely on all sides and balanced growth can occur in all directions.

(3) *Spray foliage when watering:* Although not at the top of the list of effective ways to increase humidity, leaf washing certainly adds water to the air around a plant. You're washing leaves for other important reasons anyway, but it's encouraging to know that as the water evaporates from the leaves, the humidity problem is somewhat improved.

(4) *Dry wells:* This is a great method and, if you have a hot, dry house as well as a passion for ferns, pay closest attention to the list from here on. You set up a dry well underneath each plant or at least under those that have shown they're suffering in the dry air. First you find a deep tray or water-holding saucer; hopefully it's a hand-painted Italian porcelain antique, but a plain, deep saucer or a soup bowl from a thrift shop will do just as well. You fill the tray with an inch or two of clean pebbles. You stand the plant in its pot on top of the pebbles and pour water into the tray. That's a dry well. The water level must remain just below the top of the pebbles. You keep filling it up as the water evaporates. The purpose of the pebbles is simply to raise the pot out of the water. Remember you must never let a plant sit directly in water for fear of inviting root rot. With the dry-well set-up, a great deal of water evaporates into the air in the immediate vicinity of the plant that needs it the most. Even ferns with dozens of brown-tipped fronds soon become beautiful again as the new growth emerges and does not have to contend with the old dry-air problem.

(5) *Misting:* Little brass or plastic sprayers are inexpensive and available in plant shops and bargain basements and even the grocery store. Suddenly misting has come into vogue. You can use one of these small and specially designed misters or an old (well-rinsed) Windex spray bottle or anything you can find that puts out a light, fine spray of water. You walk up to your plant, spray a fine mist into the air all around it, and go back to reading your book, playing your piano, or yelling at your dog. That extra bit of water in the air right around the moisture-loving plant is a great boon and, if done regularly, brown leaf tips become a thing of the past. You do, however, want to remember all the cautions about water on leaves and sunlight burning holes

through water drops. This is probably the reason that the "never mist in the morning" rule cropped up; the rays of the morning sun are strong indeed. But misting is beneficial at any time and particularly at those times when the house is warmer and the air consequently extradry; if you have central heating that goes on with a vengeance before breakfast, mist in the morning by all means. Better to try other means of raising the humidity for hairy-leafed plants, though; getting *their* leaves wet on a regular basis is best left to the experts, though you may be one soon enough yourself.

Consistency must be taken into account before you decide on misting as your path to humidity heaven. It you aren't able to mist every day and are only hoping to try it on a hit-or-miss busy schedule, look to the other methods listed that will take less time but provide humidity in a more dependable way. Consistency is fundamental to proper plant care. The flip-flop changes are the bad ones for plants. Plants adjust slowly and well to one set of conditions. If suddenly the next day things just aren't the same, they will adjust to the new conditions too, but at the expense of lower leaves or of brown leaf tips, and beauty is sacrificed again to survival. Plants are rugged, determined creatures and can adjust to a wide range of humidity, light, and watering situations; all they ask is a little consideration. What a plant does by way of adjusting is actually to change the number and kind of epidermal cells in its leaves or fronds (the proper name for the foliage of ferns or palms). When the air is dry, there are many tough protective cells in that outer layer. As the humidity increases, these protecting cells decrease in number and size and that's a look that appeals to us; it is softer, deeper, a more vibrant but more delicate green. Then suddenly the humidity drops and those more delicate tissues suffer; they can't change back that fast. It's a matter of degree. The most beautiful plants are those grown in consistent relatively high humidity. But your plants certainly will remain attractive at a moderate humidity level if they don't have to deal with a person who relishes the highs and sudden lows. I have a friend who mists four times a day, every single day; I hardly mist at all. His plants are unbelievably lush; his house resembles a crowded and exciting tropical forest; his begonias have leaves eight inches across. But I have too many other things to do—I have a husband, babies, dogs, cats, and a dozen other interests—and my time is too precious to me to use an hour of it parked behind a Windex bottle. His ferns outshine mine by five to one—it's okay with me. I'm crazy about my ferns anyway and I've solved the humidity problem with enough other devices that the fronds show brown tips only on the driest days. Be a realist and make *your* choice.

(6) A *humidifier:* Now for solving the humidity problem, there is nothing like an electric humidifier. There are basically two types of humidifiers. The first is the kind that I had when I was a child; hot steam and the Vicks Vap-o-Rub smell would spurt out whenever someone got a cold. This type of humidifier heats the water and sends out steam to build up the water-vapor content of the air. The second is a cool-vapor humidifier and it is the one Dr. Spock is recommending for the little ones today. It operates on a fan principle; the water is blown out in tiny particles, there is

no heating of the water and the vapor comes out cool. This cool type of humidifier is slightly more expensive, ranging with size and quality from about four to twenty dollars, but it is a better investment for the sake of the plants than a hot-steam humidifier. The reason for this is that the hot steam raises the temperature of the air and that increase in air temperature is not desirable. The explanation for that lurks behind the notion of "relative humidity."

*Relative humidity* is the relationship between how much water is in the air right now and how much more the air can still hold. So 15 percent humidity means the air is only holding 15 percent of the water vapor that it could. The air will continue to accept water vapor and the plants will continue to lose it from their leaves until that relative humidity figure moves to the 100 percent mark. Obviously you are not aiming for 100 percent relative humidity in your house; that would mean indoor rain. Between 30–50 percent is good for everybody: people have fewer dry-nose and throat complaints, plants have fewer brown leaf tips, everybody's happy. You can buy a small relative-humidity gauge at a hardware or nursery-supply store and keep track mechanically for a while until you get a good sense of what feels right.

What feels right and how much extra water vapor you need to add to the air will vary. The first variable is how dry your house is to begin with. I don't have a tremendous humidity problem since our flat has steam heat; the radiators start clanking and puffing and, because the valves aren't as tight as they should be, great gusts of steam come shooting into the room. That is a moist kind of heat. Electric wall heaters and gas furnaces make for much drier heat; open fireplaces and wood-burning stoves are the driest of them all. Your nose and skin know it and the plants know it too. Depending on your situation, you will have to decide how much humidity work there is for you to do. Some of the newer home-heating systems have a humidifying element attached to the furnace so you simply adjust it to the relative-humidity level you desire and occasionally refill the water tank; the next time I go shopping for a new heating system, that is definitely the one I am going to choose.

All of this talk about heat in relation to humidity is not accidental. There is a direct relationship between the relative humidity of the air and the temperature of that air. As air gets hotter, the molecules expand and each molecule can hold more water vapor; that, of course, means that the relative humidity goes down. In fact, for every twenty-degree increase in the temperature the relative humidity is cut in half. That explains why brown leaf tips and dry noses are such a problem in winter. You walk into the house after being away all day; it's freezing and you turn the heat all the way up. Within a half-hour, the temperature goes from forty-five up to seventy-five degrees and the relative humidity drops from 40 percent to 15 percent. That's a giant reduction in relative humidity but your feet haven't even warmed up yet. So the heat stays on all or most of the night and the humidity remains very very low. That means trouble for the plants.

Winter is a particularly difficult time for them for this and other reasons. With the shorter days of the year, less sunlight reaches the plants. They are naturally growing much more slowly than they did in spring and summer. So any stresses in their environment are more costly; new leaves just don't come surging forth so fast to make up for losses. You also don't keep the windows open very much although that would be beneficial by bringing in moist, fresh air. I've adopted the Japanese country custom of opening the windows every morning for at least an hour, come rain or come shine, and it makes a wonderful difference; neither do I feel like a martyr any-more. Americans live in a foolish dream world in regard to winter heat. If you keep your house temperature down slightly from what you've always thought was essential and cozy, you will have more humidity in the air.

All of your plants are not humidity-crazy but as winter begins and then pro-gresses, you see which ones are and to what degree. The first month that the heat goes on full force, the marantas (prayer plant) and fittonias (nerve plant) and ferns develop brown tips; the next month it's the Chinese evergreen and false aralia; the next it's the spider plant and dracaena and palm. You don't need a list; a daily inspec-tion will tell you when the dry-air tides have turned. At that point you need to step up your humidifying efforts. You get out a scissors and cut off some brown tips and see that they don't need to reappear.

## OXYGEN IN THE SOIL

Oxygen must be available to all parts of the plant for proper growth. After you've taken care to provide proper ventilation and keep the leaf surfaces clean, you have no more worries about plenty of oxygen being available to the foliage. But what's happening in the root ball is another story. Without some effort on your part, the oxygen in the soil is soon driven out by the effect of water being repeatedly poured through from the top. When a cutting is potted for the first time or an established plant is repotted, great care is taken to choose a soil mixture that will be porous, that can be pressed firmly into contact with the roots and still retain a buoyant texture so that the soil will be able to hold air throughout. As the plant grows, the roots spread out. They generally move downward in the pot and then begin to work in a circular way so that the bottom two-thirds of the pot is soon filled with roots. The roots them-selves act to hold air spaces in the soil. As the soil dries out in between waterings, all the tiny holes and spaces between particles of dirt lose the water that once occupied them and air takes its place. Then you water again and the air is driven out—often you'll see tiny bubbles come percolating up—and the cycle begins again.

During those in-between watering times when oxygen returns to the soil, it is able to return plentifully and quickly if the soil is loose and light. The roots make it easy in the bottom two-thirds of the pot; they hold the soil apart and the air just naturally moves in. The only problem usually occurs in the top section of the pot. Here there are no roots to hold air spaces and counteract the force of continual overhead waterings. The topsoil often becomes hard packed, almost solid, and less conducive to fine healthy growth. Your job is to do something about that.

Whenever you see that the top of the soil has become too tight and unyielding, you must loosen it. Take a fork and go in with the tines right up against the inside edge of the pot. Push down gently and then push in toward the plant. Doing it this way—with the tines of the fork against the edge of the pot—you're sure not to damage any roots that are growing high. Go all around the pot until you've come full circle. Then it looks all soft and crumbly. And you're done. The entire operation takes about thirty seconds, yet it greatly aides the plant's ability to grow. It's a good idea to check topsoil whenever you water. If you find it hard, wait until the next day to do your aeration tricks; soil that's handled when soaking wet dries more like dirt clods than like the textbook crumbly ideal.

## *LIGHT*

The light that a plant receives is all-important. Too much is no good; too little is just as bad. Unfortunately however, it is impossible to discuss light in a general way that would be helpful for all plants. You, after all, want to know where to put your new grape ivy. The illustrated index, beginning on p. 151, will give you specific suggestions for each plant. It's good to know, though, that the rules aren't hard and fast. Most of the long-time favorites enjoy their reputation for reliable pleasure because they are adaptable. They can thrive in an impressively wide range of light conditions. One kind of light will be their super ideal and, in that light, they will be spectacular; yet they will also do very well in something less than that ideal and you will still be able to enjoy them. Very few of us have greenhouse growing conditions in our home and we must do the best we can.

It is also helpful to know that in the city the classic descriptions of "exposures" don't mean as much as they might. I have yet to see two windows with a western exposure that are exactly alike; how much sunlight your plants actually receive depends on so many things: the size of your windows, how heavy or light the curtains are, how close the building next door is, if you live on the top of a hill or just under one, if yours is the notoriously foggy neighborhood or the famous sunny one and on and on. For instance, a northern exposure is supposed to offer only low-level general light; but in my house in San Francisco, with two giant bay windows which face north and only a hilltop park for an across-the-street neighbor, the light is incredibly bright and lasts all day long. I keep my best coleus plants in those windows and they exhibit the vivid colors only present in coleus when the light is very strong. Western light also has a dozen different meanings in San Francisco. A western exposure right by the beach provides a blistering hot window on long summer afternoons, whereas western light on Telegraph Hill doesn't mean nearly the same thing; so many hills have blocked the direct rays of the sun that the light is diffuse and far more gentle.

It is far better to develop your own sensitivity about light and use your eyes well than to rely on any reference book. Ask questions in stores and read about plants and their specific needs, but then just walk around and take note of where you see specific plants doing extremely well. Try to sense the quality of light where they are growing and compare it to the next best thing (or better!) that you have at home. Also be sure to note in that mental catalogue of Strangers' Loveliest Plants whether the plants remain where they are winter and summer and, if so, whether they stay beautiful all year long. Often a Boston fern hung in a shop window in November remains magnificent only until the lengthening days of April or May; then the direct sun hits and fronds begin to brown and that plant jumps off the list.

The most useful classifications are those that deal with the quality of the light rather than the direction of it. They are: (1) *Bright Direct Sun:* The windows that get this kind of light usually become very hot as well. That heat can be a problem. Your choice of varieties for a hot sunny spot will be limited—unless of course you've become a cactus fan. (2) *Bright Indirect or General Light:* There is no direct hot sun but abundant spill of light from overhead. This is a prime location and will satisfy all plants that like a lot of light. You'll have extravagant foliage and flowers too. (3) *Average Indoor Light:* This means the light quality of a room interior if there is bright light from windows nearby. The great majority of house plants do well by this situation—which is lucky since most of us have more of this than any other. (4) *Poor or Dim Light:* The long hall with one small window, the basement apartment, or the room interior without help of good light from nearby windows—all of these are included here. There aren't many plants that will do well in dim light, but take heart; there are some.

When you get a new plant and bring it home, you've got to put it someplace. You've asked at the store and have been told some kind of vague category of light as what you're aiming for. You put the plant into the spot you think fits that light requirement and wait. Extra attentiveness is essential at this point in order to detect the earliest signs of discontent. There are several things you're watching for. Reactions to lower humidity and a different intensity of light are of primary importance. You do not need to take all your meals with the plant; just check in on it once a day or so.

*Here are the signs of too much light: Sun scald* appears as small irregular patches of yellow-to-brown dryness on the surface of the leaves. It is similar in cause to the holes burnt by sun through water droplets, but whereas the burn holes are perfectly round and go all the way through the leaf, sun scald patches are slightly irregular in their borders and their surface looks tough and parched. *Burnt leaf edges* also might appear; this is the same problem as brown leaf tips (caused by air that is too hot and dry) but here it is carried to a drastic extreme. The edges of the leaves are brown or black and they sound crinkly and crumble off when touched. That tissue is simply dead, burnt by the hot sun. A less intense reaction than sun scald or burnt leaf edges is seen in a generalized *shriveled appearance* to the leaves. This looks and feels much like sun-burnt or wind-burnt skin on a human being. The leaves are contracting slightly as they become dehydrated; they become drawn up in an effort to reduce leaf area so that evaporation will slow down. *Leaves that curl under sharply* are also doing so as a protective reaction against the dehydrating effect of the sun (or sometimes wind). *Constant wilt* is another indication that a plant cannot tolerate its extrasunny spot. If the plant is not in a pot too small for it (see section on repotting), there is no reason why it should wilt daily. If that wilt occurs during or right after the intense period of sunlight in its particular window, you can guess that the plant simply isn't able to bring up water from its roots fast enough to replace what has been lost through evaporation, and you should move the plant to a less demanding location. *Bleaching of the leaves* is an odd-looking development that arises from too much light. You most often see the extremes of this case in the laundry or beauty-shop window where a once lovely dieffenbachia or sansevieria looks bleached out, almost white, from the sun. It isn't a yellowing but a paler and still paler version of the original green. You may never have noticed it before, but once you have this possibility in mind as you walk through the city, you will suddenly stop and see a plant that looks for all the world as if someone threw it in with the wash to be bleached.

*Here are the signs of too little light: Poor growth* is the first. If a plant is receiving less sunlight than it needs, it cannot manufacture enough food energy to continue to grow. It will simply stand still and be unable to put out new leaves. This is often seen as a *lackluster quality*; the green is not vibrant, the stems are a little slack, new leaves are few and far between. Sometimes, however, *elongated stems* are your first clue to a deficient light condition. The stems lengthen considerably in a search for better light. They attempt to stretch out and get the leaves, the source of food manufacture, closer to the sun for greater efficiency. *Flowering plants may fail to flower.* Every house plant we know (with the exception of ferns) produces a flower. Most of them need such great intensity of light, however, that they only do so in their native outdoor environment or in the intense sunlight of greenhouses or the artificial-light set-up of special nurseries. But if you have a plant that is supposed to bloom indoors and it won't and nothing else is amiss—humidity, time of year, or pot size—your guess should be that it needs slightly better sunlight. *Loss of green color* can also be a sign. This is very different from the bleached, whitened quality from too much sun.

With too little light, the green color moves toward a sickly yellow cast. You needn't worry about the distinction anyway because too much light and too little light are never concurrent threats in the same window. The worst fear from deficient light is that the *limpness and lackluster quality may finally become rot*.

My notes tell me that at this point I am to "allude to the Big Circle," and indeed I will. In the next section on watering, I will discuss more fully the relationship of water to general growth. But you can easily imagine what takes place: the sunlight is very poor; photosynthesis is held down to a minimum since one of the main basic ingredients, the energy from the sun, is missing; the plant is hardly working or growing at all; little water is lost through the leaves or used in growth; water remains in the soil, unused but occupying all the air holes; the roots finally are exhausted with their static maintenance existence and inability to find oxygen, and root rot begins. Root rot is seen as a dark brown, almost black quality that begins at soil level on the main stem. It progresses rapidly upward and, once begun, it is almost impossible to stop. The best preventive technique is caution with watering, even underwatering, and providing adequate light. If you suspect root rot, give the stem a pinch at its base. If it is healthy, it will be firm and resist your fingers; if root rot is present, your fingers will push through the mushy, hollow stem and meet.

Armed with this basketful of signs of light problems, you should be able to correct any difficulties quickly. It is true, however, that any plant goes through a period of adjustment to you and the conditions in your home. This critical period is usually over in a matter of a week or two. By then you should be well established in a routine of proper watering and you've also found the best light for the plant. You can relax now and simply enjoy its growth and beauty. But understand that the plant came to you from a greenhouse or nursery with conditions there a far cry from what it finds in your house.

Boston fern and coleus present striking and frequent examples of this sensitivity to changed growing conditions. You bring home a resplendent lush Boston. Its fronds are fat, long, and a beautiful dark, dark green. You hang it in place (more on how to select that place in the section on ferns) and suddenly find that the new fronds come out thinner, smaller, and a much paler green. You shouldn't be so surprised. Remember that in the greenhouse it was probably grown in moderate to low light intensity and with staggeringly high humidity to make up the difference. As it comes home to you and finds more sunlight available, the number of chlorophyll cells in each frond decreases; the plant doesn't need so many because with this great abundance of a basic ingredient it can make the same amount of food energy with a fewer number of cells. Since chlorophyll supplies the green color to a plant, the green fades when the chlorophyll cells are less densely packed. The fronds aren't as fat because they need to protect themselves from the lower humidity. Plants are conservative creatures; they quickly cut back on extravagance and lushness when their environment becomes more severe. If you want greenhouse-specimen ferns, you will need to keep the light down to moderate or low levels and the humidity way up. If you fall short of your ideal, enjoy your ferns anyway; maybe next year you'll move.

It's a similar problem to find the right conditions for a coleus. You fall in love with a coleus; it has huge leaves, the colors are intense, the shadings are exquisite, and there's an almost iridescent quality to the brightest areas. It looks *so* good you can hardly believe it's real and that *you* can buy it for seventy-nine cents. You bring it home—most of the leaves drop off within a few days and the ones that do come back display lots of green with only pale accent color in the center. Plants like this are grown in intense light in the nursery; there's no possible way for them to maintain that extravagance of color at your house unless you, too, can offer great light intensity. The beauty of colored-leaf plants (coleus, croton, iresine) is similarly dependent upon the relationship between light available and the number of chlorophyll cells in each leaf. The colored pigments that make these plants look so fancy are present at all times. When the sunlight is sufficient for good growth but is not quite fantastic, the plant manufactures a large amount of chlorophyll and this green masks the more unusual reds, oranges, and yellows. As the light intensity increases, fewer chlorophyll cells are needed and beautiful colors shine through.

You can see that the same plant will do well in a variety of light conditions, though it may take on a slightly different appearance with each. One aspect of the change is due to the modified density of chlorophyll cells. Another is the development of an outer protective covering to the leaves. Given this phenomenal ability of plant cells to modify into needed forms, a plant can adapt well to changing conditions. We then benefit and have a certain plant to enjoy even though the textbook says it probably won't make it. The only thing you have to keep in mind when you're testing these limits is to keep the change gradual. If you go to the beach for ten hours the first day of summer, you'll be a very sore lobster that night; but gradually work up to your body's ability to protect you from the burning rays of the sun and you finally can stay out safely all day. The similarities here between you and your plants aren't so far-fetched; we're all creatures of the same planet if not precisely the same mold. For instance, Swedish ivy is one of the most widely adaptable plants I know. But if you take a potful from a dim interior setting and place it on a hot sunny window seat, you will soon see all of the classic signs of too much light; sun scald, burnt leaf edges, instant wilt, the whole works. Instead, spend a week or two gradually moving it closer to its desired destination, three or four days at each intermediate spot. If at any time you see signs of distress, quit there; this plant is putting up a billboard that says "I just can't go no more."

Depending on the physical problems involved in this gradual change you might want to adjust your tactics. A hanging plant for a very sunny window might be your problem. In that case, hang it just after the brightest time of day for that window; continue to take it down for the fierce heat and put it up just after; or pull a curtain for those few hours; or use whatever other alternative Rube Goldberg device you can think up to keep it from being scorched the first week out. Continue this program of extra protection for at least a week, gradually increasing its exposure after that. Or if you have to work and the weekend is the longest experimental period you have, be sure to introduce new plants to potential problem spots on Friday or Saturday and keep an extraclose watch for as long as you can.

The same general idea is the one to follow moving plants from bright to dim locations. It's easier because the effects of too little light appear more slowly and you don't have to race in the door by 4:18 to pull the drapes closed. It may take weeks or even months for the signs of too little light to surface. Again, make the transition a gradual one and keep a sharp eye on plants growing in dim corners; if they go for a long period without much sign of growth, be extra careful to hold back on watering and thus prevent root rot.

If you have a problem spot to fill—a window that's extraordinarily bright and hot, a bookshelf above a radiator, or a dim hall—the first thing to do is check the plant index and try to find the ones that need the least amount of convincing. There is really no substitute for choosing the right plant for the right place; it's the *only* sure-fire way to get fabulous, healthy results. Or you might want to work with artificial light for the totally dark bathroom or as a supplement to natural light for your dim, long hall. Then, as a last resort, try the forced-adaptability game with the plants that show a wide range of growing conditions. Just remember to be patient and gentle. I've had good success growing plants near a radiator for a month or two at a time; I do the best I can to increase humidity for them—dry wells, misting, occasionally a humidifier. Then they either adapt and remain there happy forever or I move them to a recovery spot and bring someone else in for the trial by fire.

One thing to keep in mind is that young plants adapt far more willingly than do their staid, entrenched elders. This appears to be true of all species on the globe. I have several coleus plants doing well—not superbly, but well enough—in a scorchingly hot, bright window; these all began there as cuttings and, while their colors are astounding, their leaves are neither as large nor as tender as those on similar coleus plants at the opposite end of the room. They began there as early as possible and they've done their best; and, since I'm not yet ready to open my heart to cacti on that window seat, their best is just fine with me.

## WATERING

*Questions about watering come in all shapes and forms.* "When should I water my angel-wing begonia?" "How many times a week for a small fern?" "How about that giant snake plant I just bought?" The answer to all is exactly the same: you water *each* plant when that plant needs some water. However discomforting and vague that advice might seem, it's the only real answer I can give. The idea is simply this: Water is only one of the elements needed for growth; you don't give more water until you can see that the plant has been working well and growing—thereby using the water that you gave it the last time. Overwatering is a far more serious threat to the plant's life than an occasional mistake in the overly dry direction. A slight drying out of the soil in between waterings is, in fact, essential to proper root growth.

The roots' job is to seek out water and absorb it; that slight drying-out period is a great impetus to new root growth. It is also essential that water evaporate from the tiny spaces in between soil particles so that air can reenter the soil and be available to the roots.

How much water a plant actually needs and uses depends on a great many factors, factors which also vary from time to time. The *age of the plant* is important. Young creatures usually grow at a much faster rate than old folks. They are doing more work and they need more of everything, water included. The *type of pot*—clay or plastic—is another important factor. Obviously, more evaporation will take place through the walls of porous clay. The *size of the pot* makes a difference too. You repot a plant and add about an inch of fresh soil all the way around the old root ball; in a four-inch pot that's not a great deal of extra water-holding soil, but in a ten-inch pot it is a considerable reservoir. The larger the pot the less often you are likely to have to water. And then *the weather* affects your watering chores tremendously. In summer when the farthest thing from your mind is folding up the picnic and rushing back home to water, the plants suddenly need your help the most. The sweet, balmy air and warm wind is wonderful but it's also drying out their soil. The light is fantastic and they are growing apace; the roots are busy and the soil is soon dry. But in winter, when bright sun is scarce and growth is the poorest, the plants hardly need to be watered at all. Just when you are stuck inside in a storm and would be happy to turn on some romantic music and float about playing the Guardian Angel with watering can, your watering chores reach their least time-consuming point. Winter is, in fact, a *resting period* for most plants. With the shortening of the days and the increasing number of gloomy ones, photosynthesis comes nearly to a halt. At times like these when work is minimal, water will last in the soil a long, long time. Take heed that the plant is on vacation and don't try to follow your old watering schedule now. It is conversely true that there are periods of *sudden spurts in growth*. When the weather first warms up in spring and days begin to lengthen, the plants all go crazy in proletarian delight and water requirements take a sharp jump. This also happens when a fresh batch of buds forms on a plant that flowers in one giant spurt. Flowering involves a tremendous expenditure of plant energy and you'll find the water needs following suit. You will also see the impact of *special locations or native habitat*. It is only common sense that a plant sitting in an ultrabright window will be growing faster and using more water than a plant in a cooler or less bright location; the plant in the bright spot will be losing more water through surface evaporation as well.

The *native-habitat* business can be best seen in a remarkable quality known as succulence. Plants that originate in the desert or arid plains have adapted over the centuries to infrequent rainfalls. They are capable of storing water for long periods in their succulent, fleshy, swollen tissues; the outer surfaces of their leaves (although some look far removed from what you would ordinarily call "leaves") have modified to be tough and closed and most unamenable to surface evaporation. Cactus is the supreme example of succulence. Many other cactus relatives show a similar quality —jade plant, snake plant, or donkey tail. Swedish ivy shows a degree of succulence; so does the wax begonia; African violet has leaves that are slightly fleshy and adapted to this water-storing ability. Any plant which exhibits succulence will need less water than the average and to the degree that it is super-succulent it will need less and less. On the other side of the fence are the ferns, which have very limited surface devices to retard evaporation. House-plant ferns are native to moist, tropical forest regions and, as such, have learned to rely on constant plentiful rainfall for their water supplies. They are delicate and their foliage is finely cut. They are dependent on frequent waterings. You will even be able to see the differences among ferns in their water needs by how finely cut that foliage is; the more extravagant and lacy the pattern of the fronds, the greater will be the need for water.

These tidbits of foreknowledge are useful aids when it comes to watering, but again, as with all other elements involved in plant care, you unearth all the abstract advance information you can and then feel your way to each plant's happiest state through direct experience. *Take as a general rule that you water each plant when the top half-inch of soil in the pot looks dry and feels almost dry.* So you begin to walk around the house sticking your finger in pots and feeling for wetness. Wet soil will stick to your finger in crumbly bits; dry soil won't. I know a great many plant enthusiasts who are compulsive soil feelers; they walk into someone's house and, before they know what they're doing, they've backed up to a particularly beautiful plant and have one finger surreptitiously checking the soil. There are far worse social aberrations and it is a fine way to get a firsthand feeling for how moist a successful grower is keeping a particular plant. You can also develop an extra sense of your plants' needs by keeping track of the weight of their pots. A pot full of wet soil is very heavy; dry soil in a pot feels foolishly light, as if there were nothing there at all.

I am a soil feeler myself, but the method of weight testing is also enormously appealing. It bespeaks that delectable refinement of the senses by degree, rather than number or prescription, that accompanies any tactile art. Your spirit is made finer by the subtle and improving quality of your choices. Plant tending is like that. You may keep plants alive by a stark schedule and a general method. But growing *beautiful* plants is a smooth, gradual art—ultimately unquantifiable. There exists no state of final perfection. An ugly, bedraggled specimen of today may be beautiful next season by your constant and improving care. But even the most perfect plant requires that you maintain and even better your abilities as it continues to grow, change shape, and undergo its other natural changes. But come away from musing to return to the watering can.

Given the general rule that you are ready to water again when the top half-inch of soil looks dry and feels almost dry, I can make that a bit more specific. *Ferns* need to be kept evenly moist, just slightly wetter than the general rule. *Most flowering plants and those with colored leaves* (coleus or croton, for instance) are right in the middle. *Green-leafy plants* stay healthiest if you move to the dry side between waterings. All of this makes perfect sense if you consider how much work the plant is doing. Ferns have the hardest job of all in relation to their water supply. They can't survive too many mistakes in the watering department since they have so much surface area from which water can evaporate and so few protective methods for conserving moisture. Then come the flowering and coloring capabilities as extra jobs added on to normal growth. Then the plain green beauties who are the least ambitious but most reliable of all.

*All of these general indications and factors influencing water needs will not tell you when to water. They will only help you understand what you find out through your fingers.* Keep the general rule as your standard—that you water when the top half-inch of soil looks dry and feels almost dry—and forget about an ironclad schedule. You will understand more and more of the subtleties and variations as the months pass by. Your ability to anticipate watering needs will develop along with your experience and familiarity with new kinds of plants. So you travel once around the house in the morning and check to see who needs to be watered. Each day you water the plants who need it.

Now choose your method: I take all the plants to be watered to the sink or bathtub. Although it's generally both. Then I fill up a watering can or pitcher or jar. A watering can is best, one with a "fine rose"—that round blob with all the tiny holes which attaches at the end of the spout. The rose gently disperses the water as it falls and that's good. When you use a pitcher or old fruit jar, and especially if you're lazy and pouring from some height, the force of the water forms a deep trench or sinkhole where it first hits the soil. Gravity being what it is, the water rushes to that lowest point and all goes down there; when that happens, you really can't be sure that the entire root ball is getting wet. Hence the advantage of the fine rose.

You also want to be using water that is room temperature or slightly warmer. Don't use cold water; there are many plants that so strongly resent this Spartan treatment that their roots take on a chill and leaves keep coming up with black spots on them for months to come. Feel free to use the water right from the tap unless it is *very* heavily mineralized. If that's the case, draw it the evening before and let it stand twelve hours before you use all but the sediment. Rainwater is naturally the best to use, but the plants understand that it's a modern age and we all must make compromises. As for me, it will be an exceedingly long time before I turn to collecting bowls of rainwater for watering my plants.

Watering can ready, you then gently fill up the space of the top inch or two in the pot with water and let it seep through. Once it's gone down, you do that again.

The plant is watered. You should be sure to see that water comes out the drainage hole; then you know the plant has gotten what it needs. At this time you can also wash the leaves with a sprayer, check for topsoil aeration, and remove dying leaves. Remove leaves the first day you notice they are beginning to go; yellowing leaves will not get better. The same energy that is going into keeping them alive might just as well go to healthy leaves who have a future. The bathtub and sink are ideal for leaf washing with gay abandon. To my mind, the advantages of clean healthy leaves and the subsequent finer growth far outweigh the bother of carrying the plants back and forth. You can leave the plants where they are to drain thoroughly, which means at least twenty minutes to be sure. You tote them back to their home spots at your convenience or when the next person who intended to take a really quick shower has just undressed and begun to bellow. That person will, however, usually agree to help carry some of the plants.

It is also possible to water your plants right where they are. It depends on your situation and what's best for you. A giant house and a tiny sink or a bathroom with only a stall shower make this alternative sound superior in every way. The only advantage lost is that of liberal leaf washing (and associated water play) but if you're careful to keep the leaves clean with other methods, your plants will be just fine. All that you need underneath each plant is some sort of glazed saucer capable of holding an inch or two of water. You simply fill up your watering can and walk around the house. Fill up the top inch or two of space in each needy pot and let the water run through. Come around again in a few minutes and check the saucers. If a plant has absorbed all the water you gave it and there's no excess in the saucer, add a little more; you will soon learn how much each plant needs. It's important to be sure that you've watered the soil thoroughly each time. That's not all. Here's the *most* important part. No more than thirty minutes later—fifteen is better so you're sure not to forget—go back and empty *all excess water* out of the saucers. It is essential that a plant never stand in water for long periods of time; that can bring on root rot and the rapid death of the plant. As long as you are faithful about going back and emptying the saucers, you are allowing the plant to be watered well and to be drained thoroughly and this method is every bit as good as walking back and forth to the bathtub. Pick what's best for you.

There's a third method which is called bottom watering. It means exactly that. You set a potted plant into a saucer or bowl or giant cooking pot and pour water into the outer container. The water level should be about halfway up the side of the plant's pot. And then you wait. The water will be drawn up through the drainage hole and absorbed by the soil—through capillary action. You wait until you see that the topsoil is wet; that means that water has been absorbed throughout the pot—it moves by levels—and that the rest of the soil is now thoroughly wet as well. With a small plant this can take five minutes; for a giant plant with a densely tangled root system, it may be an hour or more or overnight. Whenever it happens, you then take the pot from the water and set it on the drainboard to drain thoroughly before it gets carted back home.

Bottom watering is a particularly useful method for several special watering problems. One of these special cases is that of fuzzy-leafed plants. In talking about leaf washing, I discussed the potential difficulties present in getting water on fuzzy leaves, particularly leaf rot and spotting. If you can be extra careful about not splashing, you may certainly water fuzzy-leafed plants from the top; but bottom watering is a good way to safeguard these plants against your human frailties. This is also true for several plants that do not have fuzzy leaves, but whose leaves form natural cups at their base. Spider plant is probably the most familiar of these. Many begonias also grow from one central point. Each stem has a slight curve to it and as it arches up from the base, a tiny cupped shape is formed. If you water from the top with a liberal splashy hand, water may become trapped in that cup and encourage rotting of the leaves or central crown of the plant. Feel free to water from the top if you intend to be careful; it's not an impossible task.

Bottom watering also becomes extremely useful for watering extralarge plants. You can simply set a giant beauty into your pot-roast kettle or dutch oven, water it from the bottom and thus be sure that it is watered well. The problem with extralarge plants is that their roots are often thickly tangled and growing irregularly in their pots. So when you water from the top and even then when water comes out the drainage hole, you cannot be certain that the whole mass of soil is evenly wet. The water might have passed through one area very quickly and another area not at all. With bottom watering you can see these variations and wait until they correct themselves. One side of the topsoil may become wet long before the other. In that case you wait until the dry area can catch up and you keep this new information firmly in mind. Next time you repot the plant you will want to loosen the soil and ensure more even drainage; in the meantime, you remember to give the dry and thick side time to get plenty wet.

Thus even with small plants, bottom watering is an excellent method to check for uniform drainage. If you have your doubts about a certain plant and wonder if water is passing equally through all parts of the soil, or if the soil might be so hard packed that water is interminably slow in its travels, try bottom watering and see what you can find out. Soil that is extremely hard packed is not conducive to good root growth and you may want to repot the plant right away.

The last special case to be made for bottom watering is perhaps the most important one. When, quite by accident I'm sure, you have a plant whose soil has become unbelievably dry, you should bottom water it. It's an odd thing but, when you water a superdry plant from the top, you'll find that the water rushes through immediately and little or none is absorbed. The water finds quick passage through the many air holes in the soil, and the soil itself has no time to soak it up. When the soil has dried out thoroughly, it shrinks away from the sides of the pot leaving a pronounced air space which the flow of water will follow first. A friend of mine who owns a plant store in San Francisco reports that customers call him daily with the same confusion: "My Boston fern just won't take any water. I water it every day and every drop rushes right out. I think my plant is dying. It looks just horrible!" He then advises them to mix themselves a strong relaxing drink and meanwhile offer that ailing fern a refreshing opportunity to experience bottom watering. All will soon be all right. Part of the reason for this difficult situation is that the ingredients of house-plant soils are specially chosen for their ability to retain air and to resist the temptation to absorb excess moisture. I will discuss this all more fully in the context of choosing and mixing soils, pp. 35–40. Suffice it to say for now that you must remember this quality and opt for bottom watering whenever the soil is particularly dry.

There still remain two important aspects of watering that I must make clear before moving on. Forgive me if it suddenly seems that watering is the only aspect of plant care I am willing to discuss. There is a great deal to be said about watering and rightfully so. Properly understood and properly practiced, watering your plants as they need to be watered will make a remarkable difference in their health and beauty. The reason is simple. Watering is the most frequent element of care you have to provide. If you water thoughtlessly—without heed to when the plants have actually used up the water from last time and then need more—you are bound to induce periods of stress. That stress may either be soil that remains too dry to supply needed moisture to the roots or it may be soil that is continually so wet that air is unable to return to the soil and oxygen is therefore unavailable to the roots. In either case, the plant must make do with less than optimal growing conditions and it will do what plants have done for centuries when subjected to a stress condition: lower leaves will drop so that the requirements of the newer leaves, those closer to the actively growing tip of each stem, will be met in full. Whichever the cause, that plant will have lost lower leaves and be much less attractive for it.

Consistency is the key to successful watering. I have suggested a number of ways to go about the whole operation. Pick the ones that suit your schedule best and then be scrupulous about sticking with them. I'm not saying that the whole plant population will collapse or go on strike or start yelling obscenities if you lapse now and again. But the closer you come to being a meticulous Head Gardener in your watering chores the more confidently and extravagantly your plants will grow.

Plants are truly fantastic in their ability to adapt to changing conditions, but they do not remain beautiful if those changes present themselves with undue regularity. They merely remain alive and almost well. The pompon look of healthy tip growth and bare lower stems usually indicates an inconsistency in care; particularly in watering. A touch of realism is prerequisite to this goal of consistency and its attendant extravagant success. Too often we plant enthusiasts assume that we have enough botanical love within us to encircle the world. No shopping excursion is complete until a new plant is admired, paid for, and carted home. This is fine if you have few other responsibilities; though it doesn't seem to work for very many people for long. While there may be enough love, there is rarely enough time. Soon you realize that there are choices to be made—either the plants suffer or you drop some other obligations, or else you keep the size of your friendly plant population within reasonable bounds.

Life being what it is, I have now disciplined myself to walk through plant stores with my hands in my pockets; I am only allowed to do *that* much if I've left my purse in the car. Lavish your care on the plants you already have; increase your collection only when you're sure you can take care of the newcomers equally well. It is not the activity per se of caring for plants, but the attendant grace of doing it excellently that enlivens our spirits. As Kurt Vonnegut, Jr. would say, "And so it goes."

It is commonly acknowledged that more newcomers kill plants by overwatering than by any other bit of ignorance or naive abuse. *Here's what overwatering is and is not.* You can water a plant from the top and pour water through, then again, and again, twenty times if you like; that is *not* overwatering so long as you then let the plant drain thoroughly and do not water it again until the soil has begun to dry. *Overwatering is watering before the plant has used the water you gave it last time. Overwatering is also letting a plant sit in water for an extended period of time so that the soil never has an opportunity to dry out.* "Accumulated" or "standing" water is one of the great taboos in plant care. The reason for this, as I've said before, is that healthy growth depends upon a slight drying-out period in between waterings, both to give the roots an impetus for new growth and to allow water to be used up or evaporated from the tiny spaces between the soil particles. In this way air can return to those tiny spaces and be available to the roots. There are some plants which can actually grow in water but their root system must go through rigorous adaptation in order to do so. And from my experience, they all grow more rapidly and more beautifully when planted in soil and allowed a minimal drying-out period between waterings.

Here are the signs of overwatering: (1) *Lower leaves yellow and drop off*: you understand that one well enough by now. (2) *Leaf tips turn brown*: this is one of the peculiar paradoxes of plant growth. Air that is too dry may bring on brown leaf tips. Especially with plants which are subject to dry-air problems, these brown leaf tips will be much worse if you aren't watering often enough. So with plants of this nature you can sometimes control the brown-tip problem by watering just a bit more often; as of course you can do more directly by increasing the humidity in the room. But here is the paradox: brown leaf tips can also indicate watering too often, watering before the roots have had a chance to do their own water-finding-and-absorbing work. This is frequently a problem with spider plant and several others with great water storage systems for their roots. The roots of a spider plant look like enormous white icicle radishes. They are able to store enough water for the plant for considerable periods of time; you will rarely see a wilted spider—no matter how dry the soil. This is true of other plants with water-storing abilities—cacti, succulents, dracaenas, most members of the fig family, the large philodendrons, and others. Many of these plants will develop brown leaf tips if the watering can comes around too often. If you find a plant browning at the tips, ponder first the likelihood that the air may be too dry; that is a far more common complaint. Then look to the possibility that it is a plant that has adapted to long periods of dryness and that you are watering too often. (3) *A clay pot that is always dark:* if you have many plants in standard unglazed clay pots and one of them is always much darker than the rest, there is a strong possibility that the plant residing therein is being watered too often. The logic is simple: the plant is not using the water you're giving it and the excess remains in the porous clay, hoping for a miracle of instant evaporation. It's one of the benefits of clay pots that they allow you this clue as to how the plant within is faring. Pick up on the clue and water that plant less often. (4) *A clay pot that feels slimy:* the slimy feel is often merely a prelude to the appearance of green stuff growing on the outside of the pot. That green stuff is algae and it is only able to take hold and live there because the clay pot has extra moisture available that the plant doesn't use. It is related and similar in effect to the white stuff you often see on pots, but that is from excess fertilizer and I'll discuss it in the next section. Beautiful as the formations of algae often are, you should wipe them off—a terry-cloth or paper towel works well—and then water the plant a little less often to keep the algae from reappearing. If they do come back, wipe them off again. They don't do any direct harm to your plants, but they do block air holes in the pot. So what was once a porous clay pot with the ability to send excess water out and bring needed oxygen in through its side walls becomes a nonporous clay pot—and irregularly so. The loss in quality of growing conditions is not an earth-shattering one. I know many satisfied home growers who longingly await the beautiful appearance of these growths and would *never* wipe them off; needless to say, most professional growers simply don't have the time to don a starched lab coat and walk up and down the rows with a stack of fresh terry-cloth towels. Take your choice; it's a little bit better for the plants if you allow no hangers-on.

## FERTILIZING

There is no doubt that fertilizing occasionally is an essential part of house-plant care. Whereas a plant growing outdoors has falling leaves and organic debris to feed it and earthworms and other tiny soil creatures to condition its soil, the plant indoors grows forever in a closed environment; it's in its pot and that's all there is. So you're the one who's going to feed it.

But beware: there's a far greater danger of overfeeding than of underfeeding. Good potting soil begins with everything in it that the plant will need. When a plant is newly repotted, it won't need fertilizer for some time. Only once its roots have begun to move toward the edge of the new pot will it have begun to exhaust the nutrients in that fresh soil. Keep in mind that a plant must actually expend energy to absorb new food. If the food is truly needed, fertilization will bring on a grand rush of new beautiful growth. But if the soil already abounds in nutrients the plant may actually suffer from your overzealous, albeit loving, approach.

I fear for the little creatures of all species who are entrusted to those of us humans who interpret feeding as pure love. Take as sufficient testimony the number and variety of cat-food commercials on television and you begin to appreciate the extent to which we affluent Americans wheedle, beg, urge, and cajole our loved ones toward their food. I recall one singularly lovely feline who began life as a tough character on the streets of Berkeley but has since moved up into the ritzy New York high-rise set. There she has convinced her new people that the only choice for dinner is peach ice cream! Jump into that game with a crafty cat, folly though it may be; but don't do it to your plants.

Keep in mind that you don't want to rush natural growth. When I buy a new house plant, I soon become intensely attached to it. I can envision even the smallest three-inch dracaena ten years hence as a ceiling-brushing giant. But I don't try to speed that growth with fertilizer. Healthy growth is always a balance of proper light, rich and porous soil, sensible watering, repotting, and fertilizing as it's needed. You can't be successful with crash programs in any of these realms. Plants from irresponsible nurseries whose growth has been sped up by intense lighting and constant light-level feeding are beautiful indeed when you first see them; but take one home, watch most of the leaves fall off, and you begin to wish the nursery *hadn't* been trying to dazzle you with its seventy-nine-cent wonders.

*Voilà!* So now you are sufficiently filled with religion and exhortations and will fertilize wisely and well. The next thing you want to know is what fertilizer to use and how often to use it. What are you looking for in a fertilizer and how do you read the labels for what you want to know?

Plants depend upon a steady supply of nitrogen, phosphorus, potassium, calcium, sulfur, magnesium, boron, iron, zinc, copper, sodium, and other vitamins and minerals. All but the nitrogen, phosphorus, and potassium are considered trace elements (they are needed only in minute quantities) and, as long as you are using a good potting soil, you need never worry about replenishing them. But the nitrogen, phosphorus, and potassium—otherwise known as N, P, K, or the Big Three—are used by the plant in much greater proportion. Before a plant needs repotting, its soil will have been exhausted of these most important nutrients. Here's what they do. *Nitrogen (N)* is responsible for green leafy growth. It helps to produce strong growth of new shoots and leaves. Its availability is essential to the production of chlorophyll cells. An overabundance or imbalance of nitrogen may even induce a flowering plant to turn to lush, green growth and abandon its flowering habit. *Phosphorus (P)* is credited with supporting proper flower production and other sexual affairs such as fruits and seeds. Its availability leads to strong root development and properly stiff stems. *Potassium (K)* is generally considered the "quality element." Through its effect on the chemistry of sugars and starches it is credited with working for greater plant-cell health and therefore general resistance to disease.

On any bottle of plant food, you will find a three-number figure with dashes between each number. Those three numbers express the relative strengths of the nitrogen, phosphorus, and potassium—as N-P-K—and therein lies the most important quality of the fertilizer.

Fish emulsion, which is a highly popular and effective fertilizer, is primarily nitrogen; its N-P-K code on the label is 5-1-1. That's fine for green, leafy plants. But feed fish emulsion to a plant you love for its flowering beauty and you will be rewarded with lush green growth which arrives at the expense of the flowers. The flowers will soon be small, few, or entirely absent. Fish emulsion is an excellent organic fertilizer for all plants with green or colored leaves, but just not for flowers. You can, for instance, feed it to coleus plants with great success since, if it does inhibit their flowering, that's fine too. But what you need for your indoor floral garden is something that falls under the gardener's notion of a "well-balanced fertilizer." A balanced fertilizer is simply one in which the N, P, and K are in more equal proportion to one another. That might be 10-10-10, or 3-3-3 or any combination of similar strengths. If anything, the middle number, the P or phosphorus, should be high. 10-15-10 is a figure commonly found.

There exists a bit of a controversy in the plant world over the choice of fertilizers. Some excellent growers insist that only a well-balanced fertilizer will do for all plants. They contend that feeding a high-nitrogen fertilizer, such as fish emulsion, to green leafy plants will eventually result in weak support systems, poor cell formation, and the like. I haven't been able to find any evidence or research reports which would support this theory. It's simply hard to say. I've done a bit of experimenting on my own plants and remain satisfied with the formula of fish emulsion for the green giants and the well-balanced fertilizer for those which promise to flower. Travel far along the road of individual growers' preferences in feeding and your head begins to feel woozy and wobbly. You won't go wrong with the simple two-way choice I've suggested and if you want it even simpler than that—you're a natural-born conservative—you can always buy just one well-balanced fertilizer and use it successfully for all. There is clearly a place for an Adelle Davis of indoor gardening that is waiting to be filled. It's frustrating indeed when you attempt to find information about house-plant nutritional requirements. There are volumes of research findings on improving wheat yields and other agricultural wonders, but the territory of the potted parlor palm remains untraveled.

Fertilizers are packaged in all forms. You don't need very much. The small tins and bottles are fine and three dollars' worth should last a year or more. Most fertilizers come as liquid or granulated powders which you dilute with water and then water into the soil on your appointed combination feeding-and-watering rounds. Some are in the form of a tablet which you bury in the soil; the food is then released slowly each time you water. This same method of slow release is found in another type of fertilizer that comes in the form of tiny, opaque, yellowish balls. These are scattered over the surface of the soil and finally become transparent when all their strength has been dissolved and watered into the soil. You most often see these tiny balls on the topsoil of plants in nurseries or public gardens. This fertilizer is an excellent one but rarely stocked in neighborhood retail stores. Sometimes confused friends ask me about a newly purchased Boston fern which was accompanied by instructions not to fertilize; they assume the man at the plant store was either vicious or crazy. Usually, however, a little poking around in the soil reveals a slow-release fertilizer. Follow your fancy when it comes to choosing the form of the fertilizer. It is the N-P-K ratio that determines how valuable it will be for your plants. Whether you prefer to dilute, bury, or scatter is most likely just a throwback to your architectural inclinations from the sandpile days.

The next question is how often should you fertilize. A general rule is to feed foliage plants who are growing at an average or "moderate" clip once every three months. Plants who are particularly slow growers can wait until five or six months have gone by. Flowering plants and young, ambitious, fast-growing plants and crazy, ambitious fast growers of any age may be fed as often as every month or two. The idea is the same as with all aspects of plant care; your greatest successes coincide with your development of a constantly improving sensitivity to provide stuff for the plants as they *need* it. The more work and growth a plant has done, the more of everything it will require, fertilizer included.

Make a schedule for yourself. If it's a three-month schedule, mark off the calendar so that on a certain week you fertilize all plants as they come up to be watered. I find it helpful on those weeks to stick toothpicks or wooden markers into everybody's soil; I remove the marker as each plant is fed so I don't loose track of who ate and who didn't. I tried sticks of spaghetti one time after a futile cupboard-ransacking mission which revealed no toothpicks; that was most unfortunate since spaghetti goes limp and then promptly dissolves in the moist soil, and I urge us all to be more professional in the future. If your plant collection is quite varied in age and size and flowerability and your fertilizing schedule appears complex, try writing down the dates on small wooden plant markers. (Use tongue depressors or popsicle sticks or whatever else the Handy Housewives' Hints column in the newspaper might reveal. No doubt, as with all their suggestions, the "possibilities are endless"!) Keep those marker sticks permanently in the pot's soil. If, however, you rebel totally against any system or calendar regularity, there is one type of fertilizer so dilute that you may feed it at every watering. I've used this method quite happily for some of my flowering plants, and as long as you follow the directions and keep it quite dilute—and also watch for the signs of overfeeding which I'll discuss shortly—it's an excellent choice for the busy or the vaguely organized.

Now for some important precautions and never-to-be-ignored admonitions. *Follow the dilution directions* on the package to the letter. If you have any doubt about the measurement, be conservative; make the solution weaker. There's a tremendous danger of actually burning the root hairs with a fertilizer that's too strong. Those tiny root hairs are vulnerable indeed to this type of chemical burn and if they all succumb at once to your overly loving touch, the plant will look painfully sad the day after—either all the leaves will droop way down or there will be a violent attack of leaf drop. Either it will take weeks to return the plant to its old healthy prefertilized self or it may never return at all. The risks are far too high. Don't take the chance; always go for overdilution. *Be wary of package labels* when it comes to deciding how often to fertilize. Remember that the fertilizer manufacturers make the most money when you use the most fertilizer. Capitalism thrives by its own rules and, as even the most trusting soul soon discovers, those rules do not emphasize consumer economy or public service. In addition to those dangers already mentioned, too-frequent feeding can bring about the build-up of fertilizer salts within the soil, so that even if your original dilutions were correct, too-frequent applications will do the final damage. This is an easy situation to avoid. Follow my advice about a schedule for fertilizing and don't be more liberal until your direct experience with individual plants gives you reason to strike out on your own. If you think that you've already saturated a plant's soil with fertilizer and that a build-up of salts might be a problem, there's an easy remedy: pour six times the pot's capacity of water through the soil. That will leach out most of the stored nutrients and excess fertilizer. *Never fertilize a wilted plant.* It is only when the hair roots are healthy, turgid, and strong that proper absorption of the fertilizer can occur. If the soil is excessively dry or the plant is already showing signs of wilt, it's an excellent bet that the hair roots as well are suffering from that lack of moisture. Adding fertilizer on top of their present woes is a foolhardy idea. You run a sure risk of burning the roots or forcing the plant to absorb far more fertilizer in solution than it can use. In this case, water the plant first—bottom watering is most likely your choice because of the wilted condition—and then add fertilizer solution after the plant has been thoroughly watered, perked up, and well-drained. *Never fertilize a sick plant.* The logic here is much the same. Fertilizer will not correct an ill that was caused by something else; it does not matter whether that was lack of water or an attack of aphids or spider mites or sun scald or troubles with a leaf-hungry cat. If you have a sick plant, isolate it, discover the cause of its misery, and find a way to make it well (see chapter on doctoring, pp. 104–117). But don't expect a vigorous dose of vitamins and minerals and unguents to remedy all ills. You are in fact likely to do considerable damage to the hair roots when they are in a weakened state of poor health. *Never feed during the winter or a major rest period.* When a plant is taking a well-deserved rest from the intense activity of spring, summer, and fall, don't burden it with extra food. The sunlight in winter is at its weakest ebb, photosynthesis slows down, growth slows down, watering is no problem, and added fertilizer is completely wasted. If it has any effect at all, it will be harmful. You risk increasing the accumulation of chemical salts in the soil or blocking the needed air passages in the sides of the porous clay pot as these excess salts leach out through the walls. Nearly all plants experience a major rest period during the winter, initiated by the decreasing intensity of the available sunlight. A plant may also undergo a major rest period initiated by you—for instance, when you change its location from a bright to a dim spot. Flowering plants usually take a rest period, either instead of the winter rest, or, more often in addition to it, when they have completed a fantastic, quick outburst of blooming. During any of these natural and needed vacations, fertilizer is unnecessary and may even be harmful.

You can take this as a cue for the best way to establish a *fertilizing schedule*. Forget about winter. When spring arrives, begin to watch for the first stretch of warmer, clearer days and the happy response of your indoor plants. There will be a marked revival and spurt of growth; leaves reach upward, new shoots appear, buds form. Fertilize then—and three months later for summer and again in the fall. That's the general idea. This procedure works with great simplicity and success for 90 percent of your plants. The special cases can be easily remembered.

One last word about nutrition and the possibility of practicing a bit of recycling on the side. I am often asked about using compost, eggshells, tea, coffee grounds, vegetable cooking water, and other readily available sources of natural fertilizer for potted-plant soil. In general I feel that the savings both in fertilizer money and in ecological pride are not worth the risk. Compost is likely to contain bugs, worms, and bacteria that will play havoc in the enclosed environment of a pot. Though beneficial agents in the great outdoors, they need to be avoided here. In addition to this risk, there is that of impaired drainage when you add any solid matter to the top of the soil. It may pack unevenly and prevent water from passing through and thus preclude uniform growth. It is best to stick with the organic and manufactured chemicals here.

## SOILS

No plant lover is afraid to water, but many are afraid to repot. A bustling business has developed in recent years in those plant stores which will repot plants for their more skittish customers. The *bête noire* of "root shock" keeps many folks on the overly anxious side of this easy task. In the next section we will turn to repotting, when to do it, how to do it, what to watch for, but first you will need to know about soils. Mixing your own house-plant soil is a quick and easy job—a little messy, but so is making dinner.

You can use the prepared packaged soils that are now available everywhere. You will find them at garden-supply houses or dime stores or grocery stores or even some department stores. I prefer to improve these a bit or make my own more economical mix.

There are two basic types of prepackaged soils. One is a dark, dense, sandy soil; the other, often referred to as African-violet soil, is a lighter-weight mix with lots of perlite (the white stuff) in it. I find the straight sandy soil too heavy for general use. It tends to pack down quickly and drive air space away from the roots. Its dark color also makes it difficult to tell at a glance when a plant needs more water. The lighter mix is excellent, porous, and rich in organic material. It is, however, far too expensive and unnecessarily beefed-up for most common house plants. Its use demands more frequent waterings because of that extralight texture.

The easiest way to improve these alternative shortcomings is to *mix the two soils, half and half*. This offers the best of both possible worlds and makes a fine general-purpose soil. When puttering around like this you can then vary the mixture a bit to suit your purpose. I might go toward more of the heavy, sandy soil in midsummer and for my extra-fast-growing plants; I am sure that their roots are aggressive and impervious to rot and I would appreciate the lightening of my watering chores. I go more amply toward the African-violet soil during a harsh winter or for more fragile creatures when I want to guarantee optimum air-holding capacity in the soil. You can obtain the same fine, general-purpose soil by bypassing the African-violet mix. This is the way I prefer for my own use and its cost is quite reasonable. Shop by telephone and find a plant store that sells perlite and vermiculite in bulk. Buy a giant-sized sack of the sandy soil. *Mix three parts sandy soil, one part perlite, and one part vermiculite* (mixing by volume, not by weight!). And you're done.

Either one of these simple soil combinations will fill the bill for what I call Standard Indoor Potting Mixture. Refer to the discussion of individual plants in the illustrated index for specific advice.

Whenever you're mixing soils to use immediately in repotting, you mix everything together thoroughly. You might as well use your hands from the beginning since they'll not stay clean very long anyway. Then wet the soil. You'll have to work the water in well—very much like adding the last scoop of flour to bread dough—since the perlite and vermiculite resist the water and prefer to float. Your goal is to have the soil thoroughly moistened without any excess water at the bottom of your mixing bowl (or spaghetti pot or whatever). If you have it too wet, add more soil or wring out the excess by handfuls and transfer the handfuls to another container. You can test for the perfect degree of wetness by squeezing some soil in your fist. You should not be able to wring out *more* water. When you open your fist, the ball of soil should sit there and begin to crumble just slightly when you touch it with your thumb. If it won't crumble at all, you've made a dirt clod and that's no good; it's too wet. Add more dry soil and try again. If it falls apart as promptly as the pressure is released, the soil is still too dry. You add a bit more water, test again, and you are ready to repot.

Good house-plant soil must have a light, porous texture. Indeed, such a texture is more important than the richness of the ingredients. The enclosed environment of the indoor pot ensures that the soil will not be wasted away or nutrients leached out by the rain. What is there to start with will last well. And you will in fact be adding fertilizer from time to time. The water-holding and air-holding abilities of the soil are its chief requirements. The light, porous texture ensures that it dries out evenly and without great delay, thus allowing oxygen to return to the soil for proper root growth. The roots naturally hold the soil particles apart. The roughage in the soil also helps to keep it from packing down. When soil is soaking wet, those minute air spaces are occupied by water instead. As the soil dries out, air can return and the roots remain healthy.

## REFERENCE LIST OF BASIC SOIL INGREDIENTS

Few indoor gardeners choose to mix their own soils from scratch. But most of us toy with the idea from time to time, so I have included this listing of the basic soil ingredients to help you to better your understanding of soil combinations. There is no universal mixture, no alchemical formula, no final state of perfection. Soils are combined from basic natural ingredients which are readily available and inexpensive. Loam, humus, leaf mold, peat moss, and manure are the organic materials that compose the soil where plants grow in nature. But indoor gardeners have adapted this soil more closely to their own purposes by the addition of perlite and vermiculite, both inorganic materials. These peculiar-looking minerals guarantee against waterlogging and hold open the air spaces within the soil. Even when wet they do not easily compress, and their extreme lightness is much appreciated when you are carrying a sizable potted plant to the kitchen sink.

1. *Loam* is fertile pasture topsoil, rich in sedimentary material. It is a naturally occurring mixture of clay, silt, and sand. *Sandy loam* merely means that the sand is in greatest proportion.

2. *Humus* is the organic portion of the soil, richly nourishing to plant life, and made up of partially-decayed organic matter, most notably leaves.

3. *Sand* used in potting is known as "sharp sand," with sharp rather than smoothly ground edges and the particles larger than those of fine beach sand. Sand found along a river bar, builder's sand, or aquarium sand are all suitable. If builder's sand is used, it may have been washed with ocean water and be too salty; just to be on the safe side, put a hose in a bucket, fill the bucket with sand, turn on the hose, and wait for ten minutes until any salt water has washed out.

4. *Leaf mold* is a common source of humus in the soil. Leaves are gathered, packed

together, wetted, and turned frequently until they have decomposed to a flaky but not crumbling state of decay. The leaf mold is often pressed through a wire-mesh screen to remove the largest, more stubborn pieces. A few twigs and irregular bits remain and serve to lighten the final soil texture. Leaf mold will vary in its acid reaction in the soil according to the type of tree the leaves came from.

5. *Peat moss* is the dense moss used in potting soils. It is composed of *sphagnum moss* (a long-stranded variety) and other types of mosses which have already begun to decompose and pack down. Peat moss is relatively inexpensive and distinctly acid in its reaction in the soil. Both sphagnum and peat moss have extremely good water-holding ability and are rich in organic elements, particularly nitrogen.

6. *Manure* is manure, most notably from the cow. Poultry manure may be used, but only at half-strength in order to prevent burning. Manure tea, a liquid fertilizer, is made by combining manure and water in a bucket until a light amber solution results; the plants are then watered only with that solution. Dried and pulverized manure is widely available, and is either incorporated into a soil mixture or applied dry to the soil surface (one tablespoon for a six-inch pot) and scratched in before the plant is watered.

7. *Crushed brick* or *rubble from unglazed clay pots* or *sandstone* is used to provide a porous, gritty, and light soil texture for cactus plants. The pieces are smashed with a hammer to sizes no larger than a small pea.

8. *Osmunda fiber* is a tough wiry material which is actually the root mass of the osmunda fern. Osmunda fiber is famous for the fact that it has long been the preferred medium for potting orchids. However, growers are now favoring chopped fir, pine, and redwood bark as more economical and more easily manageable materials.

9. *Charcoal* is often used as a filtering agent in soils or planting schemes. Potting charcoal is sold at nursery-supply houses and many neighborhood plant shops. Aquarium charcoal, untreated briquets, or fireplace survivors may be used. The pieces should be about the size of lima beans.

10. *Bone meal* is a valuable aid in increasing the nutrient level in basic potting soil. It is an excellent source of phosphorus and has a slow-release effect.

11. *Vermiculite* is valued in potting soil for its lightweight, highly water-absorbent, but firmly porous qualities. It is a micaceous substance and may be seen whenever you notice an iridescent reflection from pot soil on a sunny day.

12. *Perlite* is volcanic ash that has been expanded by high heat to yield a lightweight, firm, spongelike rock.

13. *Limestone or whiting* is available in powdered form and is sometimes incorporated to offset the overly acid condition of highly nitrogen-enriched soils.

# A Variety of Soil Mixtures

| | STANDARD | SANDY | EXTRARICH | HUMUS-RICH | ACID | SPECIALTY |
|---|---|---|---|---|---|---|
| | **most plants** | **cacti** | **bulbs** | **begonia, fern, African violets, tropical** | **woody plants, azalea, gardenia, camellia** | **orchids, bromeliads** |
| **basic indoor soil mixture** | 2 loam<br>1 humus<br>1 sand | 2 loam<br>2 sand<br>1 cr. brick | 2 loam<br>1 humus<br>1 manure | 1 loam<br>1 humus<br>1 sand | 1 loam<br>1 peat moss<br>1 sand | 3 bark<br>(osmunda, fir)<br>1 leaf mold |
| **variation 1\*** | 3 pkged. soil<br>1 vermiculite<br>1 perlite | 3 pkged. soil<br>1 vermiculite<br>1 perlite<br>3 sand<br>1 cr. brick<br>  or clay<br>  rubble | 3 pkged. soil<br>1 vermiculite<br>1 perlite<br>2 humus<br>1 sand<br>+B\*\* | 3 pkged. soil<br>1 vermiculite<br>1 perlite<br>1–2 humus/<br>  leaf mold | 3 pkged. soil<br>1 vermiculite<br>1 perlite<br>3 peat moss<br>1 leaf mold | 2 pkged. soil<br>1 peat moss<br>1 sand |
| **variation 2** | 4 loam<br>2 leaf mold<br>2 sand<br>1 manure<br>+B\*\* | 1 loam<br>1 sand<br>1 leaf mold<br>1 cr. brick<br>+B\*\* | 3 loam<br>1 leaf mold<br>2 sand<br>+B\*\* | 4 loam<br>5 leaf mold/<br>  peat moss/<br>  humus<br>1 sand<br>1 charcoal<br>1 manure<br>+B\*\* | 2 loam<br>1 leaf mold<br>2 peat moss<br>2 sand<br>1 manure | 3 leaf mold<br>1 sand |
| **variation 3** | 2 leaf mold<br>1 sand | 1 leaf mold<br>2 sand | 4 loam<br>2 leaf mold/<br>  peat moss<br>3 perlite<br>+B\*\* | 2 loam<br>2 humus/<br>  leaf mold<br>1 sand<br>1 manure<br>+B\*\*<br>+charcoal<br>  (2 C./peck) | 2 loam<br>1 leaf mold<br>1 peat moss<br>1 vermiculite | |
| **variation 4** | 1 loam<br>1 peat moss/<br>  leaf mold<br>1 sand | 1 loam<br>4 sand<br>1 peat moss/<br>  leaf mold | | 1 peat moss<br>2 leaf mold<br>1 sand | | |
| **variation 5** | 2 loam<br>1 leaf mold<br>1 peat moss<br>1 vermiculite<br>1 Tb. whiting<br>  (limestone/<br>  qt. dry soil) | 2 loam<br>2 humus<br>2 sand<br>2 cr. brick<br>+B\*\* (1 pt./<br>  bushel)<br>+ lime (2 C./<br>  bushel)<br>+ wood ashes<br>  (2 qts./<br>  bushel) | | | | |
| **variation 6** | 7 loam<br>3 peat moss<br>2 sand | | | | | |

\*variation 1: packaged soil refers to the basic humus-rich, dense, and finely textured potting soil available in bulk.

\*\*B = Bone meal: add at the rate of 1 teaspoon per six-inch pot or, for volume mixing, one-half cup per peck (eight quarts) of dry soil.

## STERILIZING SOIL

All soil to be used for house plants *must* be sterilized. The presence of bacteria and other tiny creatures wreaks havoc in the enclosed environment of the potted plant. Commercial soil is sterilized before it is packaged and this convenience is not one to be taken for granted. You can, however, sterilize your own soil if you've decided to play chef—with personally gathered leaf mold or river sand or whatever. The commercial technique makes use of high-pressure steam and is the most effective. For home sterilizing you can purchase formaldehyde preparations from greenhouse- or garden-supply firms. These chemicals do the job although once treated it may take up to a week or more before the soil can be safely used for plants.

So most home mixers resort to the kitchen oven. Soil is spread out in baking pans, baked for an hour at 180 degrees, cooled, and stored in a dry, bugproof location for later use. However, the odor of dry baking soil can be overpowering and the low temperature of 180 degrees risks being ineffective. Here is an alternative, odorless approach: Place the soil in pans and wet it thoroughly; work in the water until it oozes up between your fingers at the slightest pressure. Bake the soil for one hour at 275 degrees. It is "ready" when the entire mass is steaming, and when any odor is noticed (if at all). Cool the soil and allow it to dry until it cracks. Next press it through a hardware-cloth mesh (#4 or #6) screen to regain a light texture. The soil may then be stored in a dry, bugproof spot.

## POTS AND REPOTTING

You have a plant that needs repotting and the first thing you need is a pot. Choosing the right pot is half the job in encouraging healthy roots. And that is important; the roots, as you remember, wield most of the power for the plant's consequent growth and good looks. For the time being we will discuss only those pots with a drainage hole. You can pop a plant into just about any container but nonstandard plantings will be discussed in a later chapter.

The first decision you must always make is between clay and plastic. Great controversy continues to rage on this issue and it seems a bit silly, with more heat than light on the subject, as my father would say. Each type of pot has its advantages. I'm sure you can grow equally beautiful plants in either a glazed or a porous container if you understand the varying qualities and modify your habits of care to suit each situation. The classic clay pot is, I must confess, my favorite. This is largely a matter of aesthetics and traditional taste. I do love the way they look, the way they feel, and the way they smell. The basic horticultural advantage offered by the terra cotta pot is its porosity. Air can pass in through the side walls and therefore more oxygen is available to the roots. Excess water and fertilizer salts can pass out to make their appearance as algae or white salt crusts on the side walls of the pot; the plant is then rid of the undesirable elements and you are made aware of the conditions that encouraged them and that you can correct. You will, of course, clean the sides of the pots as these green and white spots appear to maintain the porosity of the walls. The only danger done by these often beautiful formations is that they block the air spaces of the pot and, worst of all, do so unevenly. It is another advantage of clay pots that the water normally passed out through the side walls has a general humidifying effect in a room full of plants. Another slight advantage of clay is its insulating and cooling effect. This allows for fewer extremes in temperature at the root level—which is beneficial; particularly during hot, dry weather.

A plastic pot, although not famous for good looks, has much to recommend it. I sometimes prefer plastic pots for their light weight. When you get past the six-inch size, weight becomes a substantial factor. Plastic pots are securing a great place for themselves, especially for hanging plants. Weight is important and so is the fact that their side walls will not allow water to pass. Hanging plants need more frequent watering than quiet sitters; air passes on all sides of and underneath the root ball and evaporation is rapid. A plastic pot always helps cut down on your watering chores. The main disadvantage of plastic or glazed pottery or any nonporous medium is that you lose a little bit of your leeway against overwatering. Rot is more common in non-porous pots. There is, however, a popular new set-up quite helpful in minimizing this danger. A plastic pot, with not just one but several drainage holes, clamps into a plastic saucer by little pressure pins. Any excess water flows into the saucer and the plant's roots are saved from wet feet. (For this very same reason, it is also best when potting in plastic to use a thicker layer of drainage material, rocks, or shards in the bottom of the pot.) The disadvantage of minimal air passage to the roots can be remedied partially by more frequent soil-loosening sessions with your fork and by more liberal use of bottom watering so that the soil does not pack down as fast.

The size of any pot is measured by the diameter across the top. You probably have noticed that pots vary in their depth. The *standard pot* is as deep as it is wide. This is the depth that is right for most house plants. A *fern pot* (or azalea pot) is more squat; the depth is three-quarters the top diameter. Ferns and azaleas tend to more shallow roots and these pots have been developed to accommodate them. A *bulb pan* is only half as deep as it is wide. This, obviously, is suitable for planting winter and spring bulbs. Any *saucer* that is used—for simple overflow or set up as a dry well—should be of the same top diameter as the plant's pot.

As you are probably most able to infer, the pot size is chosen to suit the plant. You are always attempting to house a root system in a container that corresponds to the root system's present size and shape. Some of the many strange varieties of pteris ferns have an unusually deep root system; these plants would do best in a standard pot. You might use an eight-inch bulb pan for housing two bushy young pteris ferns that each arrived in a four-inch pot. I also have a fondness for planting marigold or pansy seedlings in a wide bulb pan; six or eight small plants make a colorful grouping and the bulb pan is an appropriate size for their communal home.

When repotting, your choice is most often quite simple. A plant gets moved up into a pot one size (one inch) bigger than its previous container. Or, if you are repotting a plant out of its "point of purchase" five-gallon tin can and it is not root bound, you stick with the same size and merely make the planting more attractive. If you are grouping several plants together, simply estimate the pot size to give each plant nearly the same growing room that it would have had as an independent. Upon occasion, you might be going to a pot size that is smaller—if, for instance, the roots have been waterlogged and you are jumping in to save the plant before all the roots have died away, or if you are cutting the plant's foliage and root system back toward a more ideal size. However, the latter job, called "root trim," is not central to the art of repotting so I've saved it for a fuller discussion in chapter 2.

One last word about pots. They must be clean and dry, and new clay pots must be soaked before you can use them. The clean-and-dry aspect makes perfect sense. If old roots and bits of mud are blocking the pores of a clay pot, its famed air- and water-flow characteristics have disappeared. Even plastic pots must be clean at the beginning to ensure that any bacterial or fungus organism that bothered the former occupant will not harass the new one. You may find it necessary to go at clay pots with a wire brush or steel wool in order to remove all old crusts. Don't be shy; get them as clean as you possibly can, rinse them well, let them dry thoroughly and they are ready to use again. Heed my warning that the pots are dry before you plant in them, inconvenient though that procedure may be. A plastic pot can be dried with a dish towel, but a clay pot must be allowed to dry in the air. If you pot directly into a wet clay pot, a thin layer of mud is formed by the soil in contact with the inside walls. The pores are blocked by the mud and any hair roots that grow into it will be severed when you attempt to remove the plant for potting next time. New clay pots must also be soaked before they can be used for a peculiar, although perfectly common-sense, reason. If you have had any experience with the firing of pottery, you will appreciate that the high temperature required for kiln firing makes the newly fired clay unbelievably dry. I have a cat who enjoys teasing herself by licking at new clay pots; it's rather difficult to second-guess pussy cats but I imagine she likes the fact that her tongue sticks to the pot. The clay is parched and bone-dry; it will absorb water immediately upon contact. If you plant directly into such a new pot, the water from the soil and roots will rush headlong into the clay walls and your ability to offer perfect growing conditions will have evaporated as well. So you soak the pots; submerge them completely in bathtub or sink and let them sit there for several hours. You will see bubbles rising like crazy in the first few minutes as the water stampedes the air out of the porous clay walls. After a few hours, let the pots dry in the air and they are ready to be used.

All awaits in readiness. How do you know when to repot your plants? There is a basic pattern of growth that the roots follow and, with an understanding of that pattern, you are better able to anticipate their needs. As always, root growth develops by hair roots from a larger root, in a constantly branching and expanding system. But here I am speaking simply about the direction of that growth in regard to the shape of the pot. Root growth proceeds downward in the pot through the center; the roots then work outward in a circular movement to the sides of the pot. A snug fit is achieved after a month or two of residence in a proper-size new pot, with roots extending throughout the soil. It is this snug fit that precedes optimum root development. The roots behave best if they are in close contact, cell by cell, with the particles of the soil. The constant branching of hair roots from main roots continues in whorls and eventually there are more roots in the pot than soil to grow in. It is only at this point that the plant is said to be "root bound." When the pot's soil has been exhausted—both of space and nutrients—the point of no return has been reached. Growth will then be hampered by the pot's size and it is your job to do something about that. (There are some plants, such as impatiens or geranium, that prefer to be root bound and will react with a violent shudder if you try to do them a good turn; but these are special cases and their peculiar tastes will be noted in detail in the illustrated index.)

The signs of a root-bound condition are varied, but easy to spot: (1) If you suddenly find yourself watering a plant almost daily, begin to suspect it has outgrown its pot. When you follow the practice of watering a plant by need rather than by schedule, you are able to keep good track of the plant's changing requirements. If the need for water increases dramatically and there is no other good explanation at hand—such as a new crop of flowers or a sudden heat wave—you can guess that the pot contains mostly roots and that there is no extra soil to hang on to tomorrow's supply of water. (2) A sudden halt in growth may also indicate a root-bound condition. If this is the case and you can find no other reasonable explanation—a seasonal rest period or miserable gray weather or adjustment to a new location—check on the possibility that the plant is root bound. Look for other of the signs or turn it out of its pot if necessary to check. (3) You might also stop to investigate if you observe a plant looking ridiculously out-of-proportion to the size of its pot. The plant should be generally twice—or at the most three times—as high and broad as its pot. Past that, the plant and pot take on the look of ludicrous partners. In the case of an exceptionally large plant, such as a mature palm or a full-sized *Ficus benjamina*, this might be just fine. If the plant is growing well and no other signs of suffering are noted, you will not be easily tempted to repot a six-foot plant for the sake of proportion and the Golden Mean. But for younger and smaller plants, the idea of visual proportion will be a great aid to you in your attempt to anticipate when repotting is required for optimum uninterrupted growth. (4) When new leaves come out tiny and do not soon increase to expected size, you must suspect a root-bound condition and plan to repot quite soon. The decreasing leaf size indicates that the soil has been exhausted. Hair roots are now unable to grow to full size and the new foliage growth follows suit. You must plan to repot soon because the tiny leaves will never come to full size if the plant does not find some more root room. Daily watering is merely an inconvenience but the damaged hair roots must be allowed to repair themselves while still young or the blight will be more than temporary. (5) When roots peek out the drainage hole, you are sure they are looking for more "elbowroom." It is not the most sophisticated of signals but one which sneaks up on you the majority of the time. Most plants are still quite healthy when they send out drainage hole scouts and you have time to assemble your materials and get to work. (6) As in any stress situation, a root-bound condition will bring on lower-leaf drop. Lower-leaf drop can be remedied but it is a tedious and minimally rewarding task. So don't wait for this lamentable look to appear.

At any time you can simply turn a plant out of its pot to check the roots. Do this if you suspect a root-bound condition from any of the signals listed above. I'm afraid I tend to ignore the possibility as long as I dare; I would rather climb into the wing chair with a good new book than to assemble my courage and tools for an afternoon of repotting. But once the decision is made it's a joyous affair of mud and mess and the promise of healthy new growth. If what you see after turning the plant out of its pot is a tightly tangled web of roots, the plant is definitely ready for a roomier home. If you can see plenty of roots but they don't look all that crowded, simply pop the plant back into its old pot, firm down the topsoil, and return to your book. If, however, the soil begins to crumble and reveal a root system that looks barely adequate to the job of filling the pot, consider the possibility that a smaller pot is required. This is particularly suspect if foliage growth has been poor or exceedingly slow. You remove the excess soil and repot into a better-proportioned container. Remember that a moderately snug fit for the roots will bring on the best growth results.

With a root-bound plant you have one obvious choice, and that is to repot it. You might possibly choose to trim the roots and return the plant to its former pot; but that is more a matter of controlling or arresting growth, and the technique will be described in chapter 2 with other plans for shaping and pruning. The more generally useful approach is to ensure continuing growth and to "pot-on." Potting-on is a fine-sounding professional term and British indeed. It merely means to repot and choose a pot one size larger than was previously used. There is a definite danger in "jumping" pot sizes. Because of the roots' undeniable preference for cozy contact with the soil and inside walls of the pot, you will achieve a large-sized plant much sooner and with a much more beautiful result by going step-by-step through the different sizes of pots than you will by starting the young plant in the six- or eight-inch pot it will eventually need.

There are several difficult conditions which can develop from jumping pot sizes. One is that the roots grow like crazy in their new roomy pot. They rush out to the side walls in long direct threads, then back again to fill up the pot before they begin to circle the walls. The foliage growth is reflective of the root growth both in quality and shape. The scraggly long growth of the roots is echoed by the leaves and stems and the result is not attractive. It is also possible that the soil in an oversize pot will turn sour. The root growth will proceed at a normal pace. Where the roots are present in the soil they will act to hold air spaces between the soil particles. However, in the outer inch or two of soil that the plant does not yet need there is nothing to hold the air space. Repeated waterings soon pack down the outer soil and it readily turns sour and useless. When roots do move into the outer soil, growth is labored or rot is invited. And then there is a third possible negative result. This is the most unreasonable and it is simply that the plant refuses to acknowledge its new environment and will not grow. It is often the case that the hair roots have failed to direct themselves outward into the new soil; they prefer to backtrack in the tightly packed Old World than to venture so far to distant horizons. You will simply have to repot again, this time making sure that the pot size is in proportion to the size of the root ball.

The procedural steps in repotting are simple. I happen to find it quite thrilling to plunge my hands into moist dirt and mess around for an hour or two. By the way, once you're adept at the whole procedure, repotting one small plant need not take more than five minutes. Work at your own secure and comfortable pace. Have everything you will need already assembled: soil, new pots, pieces of old broken pots (professionally referred to as "shards") or large pebbles for drainage, a sharp knife, scissors, watering can, leaf-spraying bottle, whiskey (for you), chocolate cookies, whatever. You try to be well prepared and then work quickly and surely. Beware that roots accustomed to dark, cool, moist soil go a bit crazy when exposed to our dry and grueling outer air. If the telephone rings in midpot, either don't answer it or have a wet cloth handy to throw over an exposed root ball.

Do not, however, let the old bugaboo of "root shock" deter you from this loving task. Imagine, if you will, how much better the plants will do once settled in their new homes, and envision great spurts of growth that will soon follow. Then: (1) Place several pieces of broken clay pot over the drainage hole. You put them concave-side down so that the water will naturally fall over and down. Those shards prevent the soil from clogging the drainage hole and ensure against waterlogged soil at the bottom of the pot. You may use pebbles or small rocks for this drainage layer, but be sure they are clean and sterile. This means buying the packaged chunky white rocks at a plant store or pouring boiling water over your own collection. (2) Place an inch or two of soil over the drainage layer. Press it down gently but firmly with your fingers and make sure it is level. (3) Remove the plant from its old pot by turning it upside down; have your fingers straddled across the topsoil at the base of the plant to support the root ball. One sharp rap of the pot against the edge of the table and it naturally slips out into your hand—or should. I have always preferred to hit pots rather than rap tables so I give one strong thump on the bottom of the pot with the base of my hand. (A good friend, however, has pointed out that few people can hit pots with the same casual vengeance that I can.) So choose whatever you like. If nothing else works, take a small sharp knife and go around the pot separating the root hairs from the inside wall with a steady scraping movement. Or stick your finger or a

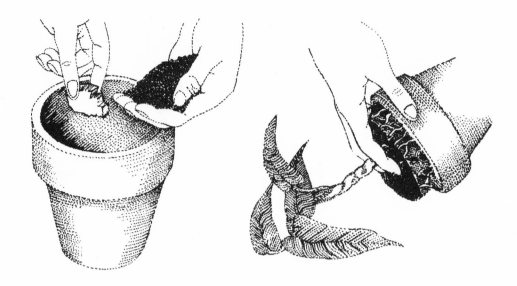

chopstick through the drainage hole and give a firm push on the old shard. (4) You now have an upside-down, root-bound plant in your hand. Remove any old clay chips or pebbles that may have become wrapped up in the tangled roots. Then turn the plant upright, take hold of the root ball, and gently roll it between your flat palms. Old loose dirt will fall away and you will be softening the root ball. This allows tiny air spaces to return to the soil and serves to loosen the texture of the hard root-bound ball. Brush your fingers along the surface very gently to loosen and direct some of the hair roots outward. You do not want to change the firm, flowerpot contour of the root mass; you are merely trying to make the surfaces more open and the roots quite willing to move outward into the new soil. It is an uncommon but miserable situation when a root ball is so tightly bound that, even when repotted, the root hairs refuse to grow into the new soil. A little light finger work and you're assured of success. (5) Set the plant on top of the added inch or two of soil in the new pot. Make sure that it sits level and that the surface of the soil is as high as you want it to be. You will soon be adding a little more topsoil over the former surface. When you are finished, the topsoil level should be about an inch below the top edge of the pot. (6) The most important part of repotting is the addition of new soil around the sides. Your goal is to have the texture and firmness of the soil equal throughout. You have loosened the old root ball and will try to approximate that degree of density in the new soil. Add new soil by dribbling in a small handful at one side; then go to the opposite side, then a quarter turn, then the final opposing side (or east, west, north, and south). You are doing this to keep the old root ball from tipping against the weight of the added soil. With even but firm pressure, push down on the new soil with your fingers. Some prefer to knock the pot down on the table; the traditional professional method is to use a small stick to tap down the soil. Whichever method

you prefer, remember that your goal is a firm but spongy feel to the soil. The soil must be in solid contact with the roots, and large air pockets within the soil are disastrous. Roots that grow into an air pocket will simply cease to grow. (**7**) The first addition of soil probably brought you a third or halfway up the pot. Then fill in the rest of the soil to within an inch of the top of the pot. Tap down the dirt with gentle, even pressure. Check that the surface of the soil is level and smooth and loose. You're just about finished. (**8**) The plant should next be watered—either gently from the top or by bottom watering. The purpose of this libation is not to provide water—water isn't needed at this point; the soil was already moist—but to check the drainage and spray the foliage clean. You watch with eagle eyes as the water level descends. Any dips or troughs or holes that develop must be filled in, and the soil around them tapped down. You are hoping that the water goes down evenly and at a moderate pace. If it rushes through in one quick gulp, the soil is probably packed too loosely; go back and press harder. If the water moves down so slowly that it is difficult to tell if it is moving at all, the soil is too hard-packed. Loosen it with a knife point or turn the plant out of its pot and soften the tight soil. (**9**) Correct any problem and check the drainage again by pouring water gently through. There just happen to be times when nothing will help a poorly handled situation in a potting job—the plant sits unevenly or giant sink holes develop each time you water. Take such a plant out of the pot and start all over again. You are doing it now, do it perfectly and then never worry about the plant's performance. (**10**) Remove any leaves or fronds that may have been damaged in the repotting process. Don't cheat; just cut them off with a small scissors. (**11**) Leave the plant to drain thoroughly. For the next several hours, you must allow it to recoup its forces in a cool, nonsunny spot before moving it to its permanent location.

# 2

# Keeping Your Plants in Shape

Now that you've come to understand all aspects of keeping your plants growing happily and in exuberant good health, you run smack up into your next task: how to keep that extravagant growth under control.

## Pinch, Prune, Cut Back, or Trim?

It is not only that a few impetuous young plants might soon grow you out of house and home, but that your ideal stance as a plant tender is one in which you constantly shape and guide that growth into finer forms. It is up to you to choose the direction in which you want a plant to go and then to urge it closer. There are those who prefer the anything-as-long-as-it's-natural look; and indeed I counted myself in that group until I finally got over my shocked delight that plants *do* keep growing . . . naturally. You must simply have in mind the final shape you want. You can buy a small coleus for forty-nine cents or a young *Ficus benjamina* for five dollars; then carefully examine the lush ten-dollar coleus and the tree-size eighty-dollar ficus. Constantly visualize those expensive and impressive shapes as your little plant keeps coming along. By pinching or pruning your plant's errant growth, you will soon have a giant masterpiece.

From the discussion in chapter 1 on lower-leaf drop, you can now claim to understand the pompon look. With a good understanding of pinching and pruning you can begin to correct that dastardly look and learn more about how to prevent it. You pinch to encourage a bushy, fuller shape and to force lower leaves to return and fill out bare stem growth. You prune or "cut back" to remove awkward or ugly tip growth and improve the aesthetic appearance of a plant; in cutting back you also procure a new cutting or two and generally get a chance to start over. Everyone needs a lot of chances.

## LEAF NODES

Pinching and pruning are key activities in maintaining beautiful plants. To understand how a quick pinch or snip can do so much good, you must first grasp the importance of the "leaf nodes" (or "leaf axils" or "growth buds"). A leaf node is simply any place along the stem where a leaf may emerge.

Obviously you can spot them where leaves now grow; those are the *active* leaf nodes. There are also marks on a stem that you can recognize as places where leaves, long since dropped off, did emerge. These are *dormant* leaf nodes. Dormant leaf nodes exist as well in many places along the stem that you cannot see. The dormant nodes represent a potential for leaf growth that has not yet found the power to break through the stem's tough outer covering. Occasionally you will notice a leaf node that is on the verge of becoming active; you will spot a light-colored raised bump pushing up against the tougher, darker-green tissue of the stem. Therein lies the power of pinching.

## PINCHING

Pinching is the way to make more leaf nodes active. And that's exactly what you want. A lush, bushy, luxuriously full plant means more leaves and less bare stem. The space along the stem between active leaf nodes is minimal; active leaf nodes come fast upon more active leaf nodes. The spots of bare stem where old leaves have fallen off show dormant nodes being forced to break through. When you pinch (Ah, "pinch"—that smug, insiders-only, jaunty word!) you simply go at the plant with your thumbnail and index finger and remove or "pinch off" the newest leaf or set of leaves on each stem.

There is no better tool than your thumbnail because you want to get those new leaves when they are still quite small. You want to pinch them out as soon as they are big enough to grasp, and do be sure you are getting them off *in toto*. You must wait until you are sure you are getting the entire miniature leaf or it will grow out and look silly with the tip half of it gone. The only thing that looks drearier than a pinchable plant that has not been pinched at all is one cared for by an overanxious pincher; the plant is studded with half-formed pygmy leaves.

It may appear odd that merely acting the aggressor on a quarter-inch of infantile plant life has such striking positive results. The cause of this phenomenon may be easily acknowledged if you hark back to the discussion in chapter 1 on the patterns of plant growth. An enormous amount of plant energy (food, water, hormone production, cell division, and so on) flows to the newest leaves at the tips of each stem. Plants grow primarily at their tips. If you simply remove those new leaves before they can use up their full quota of the plant's limited energy resources, that same energy is suddenly available for growth elsewhere. You remove the youngest, newest leaves. Growth is temporarily threatened. But fish gotta swim, birds gotta fly; the plant refuses not to grow. Leaves will push out somewhere else and you've achieved exactly the result you want: smaller expanses of bare stem between active leaf nodes. The entire process need not appear a novel twentieth-century insight. It is a natural back-up system for growth; animals do walk by in the forest and pinch or prune with a switch of the tail, trees fall oblivious to a young coleus below. If you can't grow up you grow out.

## BRANCHING

To be honest with you (not to imply that I haven't been until now, but, as my three-year-old daughter Jessie says, "I mean I'm serious *now*"), there are two ways that a plant can respond to pinching and I haven't found a way to predict which will occur. The first is that the plant will fill in lower spaces along the stem; that is, some dormant leaf nodes will become active. That's great. The second is that branching occurs. The new-leaf energy at the tip of the stem remains at the tip of the stem:

what was once the main stem with a new single leaf (or double-leaf set, depending on the individual plant) now becomes a main stem with a branch and a single leaf at the tip of that (or two branching stems each with a double-leaf set at its tip). One more paragraph and I'll describe the two simple variations of stem patterns, single-leaf or double, and the difference between pinchable and unpinchable plant forms. For the moment though, let's concentrate on your Grand Plan versus the whims of your plant. Primarily you need a Grand Plan.

## HAVE A PLAN

Suppose you are pinching under ideal circumstances: you have a young plant and you are determined it shall not go wrong. It is particularly important to start pinching from the cradle with plants that are ultrafast growers and therefore tend to get scraggly. Count coleus, wandering Jew, Swedish ivy, kangaroo ivy, plain green ivy, heart-leaf philodendron, purple velvet, pothos, and many geraniums among these. In this case, if you pinch while the plant is quite young and it branches, that branching is low to the soil and will only serve to provide a wider base and fuller look for the bushy, leaf-laden plant you want two or six months hence. Besides, your pinching may have already brought forth all the active leaf nodes the plant can bear and branching only makes the future look brighter. Keep on pinching and you will soon have a fantastically beautiful, full-blown gem.

On the other hand, if you are pinching to correct a lousy situation, you must have a more tenacious spirit. You have before you a coleus or a wandering Jew that has lost numerous lower leaves from past mistakes. Don't take it personally; if you have a fondness for coleus or wandering Jew, you will have myriad experiences with the bare-lower-stem dilemma. Initially you might decide how disastrous the situation appears. It is far more difficult to encourage dormant lower-leaf nodes to break through than it is to keep healthy lower nodes active from the start. You may decide to chop off the healthy tips into new cuttings and prune back the parent plant for a far smaller, more reasonable, fresh start. (Or if you have developed a keen resentment toward those extravagant bare stems throughout the months of lower leaves dropping before you knew why, you may do best to take tip cuttings, throw away the parent plant, and be on your way to new success with no love lost.) If you decide it's worth a try at pinching, here's how you go. You pinch out the new leaves on each stem. If the plant responds with dormant leaf nodes becoming active on the lower stem, that's terrific. The next time you see new tip leaves appearing, you pinch again. Just maintain your determination; you are in charge and you will not let the plant grow upward until you are satisfied with the quality of what's already there.

However, the plant may have a stubborn tip-oriented streak: it will not send its new-found energy to the lower stem but will branch at the tips instead. When you see that happening, pinch off both of the new branches. Keep right on doing that until you get the desired leaves filling in the lower stem.

I have one coleus that I have been wrestling with for two years. I had let it get much too long and leggy in the days when pinching was a mystery to me. Then like the new principal of a reform school, I set out to pinch. I pinched; it branched; I pinched again—for months. Finally one day a lower leaf node broke through. Another four months of pinching and the plant looked superb. A few months later we went away for several days; a surprise blistering hot spell hit San Francisco and we came home to find everyone in good shape but my pinched prize. It was a favorite in the first place because of its thin, delicate leaves; they were quite vulnerable to the intense heat, and all the lower ones were on the floor. I didn't quite feel I had the stamina to pinch for the rest of the calendar year; I made lots of cuttings and started again. This time with four main stems in the pot instead of one and much greater opportunity for a bushy look with a less combative style.

## WHO DO YOU PINCH?

There are some plants that are pinchable and some that are not. Obviously there must be something to pinch on a branching main stem. There is no point to removing the new leaves if there is no possibility for filling in lower leaves, or for branching. So don't pinch plants that grow in a single canestalk pattern (palm, false aralia, dracaena, dieffenbachia) or plants that grow outward from a center crown (African violet, spider plant) or from a shallow root mass (ferns). These plants generally take good care to maintain their older leaves if they are treated to the proper light, water, and soil.

The plants that are pinchable are those that grow in a branching-main-stem pattern. There are those that form two leaves at a time and those that only form one. Generally, the latter are thought of as vines, ivy the most common of these. In fact the popular names of many such plants allude to them as ivy even though they are not (*Plectranthus australis* becomes Swedish ivy, *Cissus antarctica* becomes kangaroo ivy, *Cissus rhombifolia* becomes grape ivy). The single-leaf stem has one leaf emerging from the main stem; more stem, another leaf on the opposite side; more stem, and up or down it goes. When these plants are pinched and branch, a single new stem comes off from the main stem. The double-leaf pattern simply shows two leaves at a time on opposing sides of the main stem; new tip leaves emerge in a pair. When branching occurs at the tip, each pinched leaf pair becomes a new branch and there are four leaves at an old two-leaf site. Both of these patterns are highly pinchable.

You should also plan on pinching out unwanted flowers. I tend to bristle when I hear coleus flowers referred to as insignificant. What gall for non-flower-producing creatures to scoff at this marvel of nature. Yet, with due respect, you may still decide to pinch some flowers. Flowering requires a tremendous flow of energy, the sexual determination to produce a quality crop for future generations. So, if your coleus begins to send up a flower spike and you are not yet fully satisfied with the leaf situation below, pinch out the entire spike and let the plant concentrate on what is already there. Pinching auxiliary flower buds is also a common practice with some plants, most notably chrysanthemums; extra buds are removed so that the one spared flower will be larger and more impressive. More specifics are mentioned in the illustrated index, under the entries for individual plants.

# Pruning or Cutting Back

Pruning, or cutting back, is a fabulously useful technique for improving a plant's bare shape or maintaining a desirable one. You might choose to cut back a plant if it has greatly exceeded what you consider its optimum height or breadth. You might also cut back to remove upper branches or stems that appear overextended, irregular, or scraggly. Naturally, in removing tip growth, pruning will also act to encourage branching and lower-leaf activity.

You do the pruning with a small, sharp knife or a topnotch scissors. If you use a scissors, it must be lightweight and supersharp—so keep it out of circulation and do not use it for general household cutting chores. For pruning an extratough plant you may need an outdoor gardening clipper or a frozen-food knife. Whatever the tool, its purpose is to make a clean, quick cut with no mangling damage to the stem.

You should make the cut on a slanted plane. *You cut just above a leaf node.* The reason for this is that you want the plant to have leaves at all the stem tips when you've finished; you are pruning for good looks and barren stems look silly on top. So you cut back to above a leaf node. If your pruning job was minor and this leaf node is an active one, so much the better. If you are trying to make a future silk purse out of a sow's ear and that top leaf node is now dormant and bare, that's okay too. You just have to know that it might not work: you might not get healthy new leaves surging out through the tough bark. In this case you will notice the stem dying back to the next lower healthy node. In older coleus plants, the stem often just turns black; in other cases, the stems soon feel hollow and woody and dead. That's the bad news. The good news is that you can simply cut back again; your chances will improve. Go to a spot just above the next healthy, likely looking node and cut.

## THE BRAVADO FACTOR

The most important element in successful pruning is bravado. Be radical. Go for the plant you really want. Don't leave branches that look only fair to middling. Bring the plant down to a point where you can envision future beauty without dilemmas. Even if this means going down to within an inch or two of the soil. In the first place, nearly everything you cut off can become a "cutting," to be rooted and potted for *more* plants. In the second place, life will spring forth from even the most preposterous-looking stumps. It may take some time, particularly if the original plant was in poor shape or if the fall and winter months are upon you. But to my way of thinking, it is easier to care for a plant that holds great future promise as a result of forthright action than to sulk and mutter each time you pass a reflection of your own unwillingness to be bold. You must be convinced.

## LEGGY PLANTS

It strikes me as a good time to come to the defense of the fast-growing, leggy wonders of the plant world. Coleus, wandering Jew, Swedish ivy, many begonias, aluminum plant, and some of the true ivies are famous for lower-leaf drop. They are fast growers; their needs for water and repotting and pinching and trimming are great and frequent; they need your attention during weeks when you're very busy as well as weeks when you're happy to be totally home. Consequently you are apt to miss a few ministrations and the plants will tend to have lots of bare lower stems. You must begin to look at basic shapes, understand more about the potential future of each plant, and come to terms with what you are allowed to expect. Much to the chagrin of many bargain hunters, the leggy wonders are difficult to maintain in their original bushy form. Of course they are less expensive; they grow more quickly for the greenhouse wholesalers as well. So enjoy their youthful bushiness, plan to pinch vigorously and then, when necessary, cut back.

Last year for my birthday I was overcome with an irresistible urge for a new Big One. I knew it was a dumb time to buy a plant since I was unbelievably busy and, to top it all, we were planning to move in another few months. That meant that as soon as the plant was perfectly settled and we were on best of terms with each other, I would throw it a loop. Even if you can accomplish the physical threats of moving day without overwhelming damage to the beast, the poor plant must then readjust to a whole new set of light, heat, and humidity conditions. Predictably, you will also be more inclined to find your toothbrush and coffeepot before your watering can or mister. However, nothing will deter a really serious plant buyer when the mood has set in. So I walked in and plunked down my eight dollars for a medium-big Swedish ivy. I entrusted it with my favorite white iron curlicue plant stand and, in the three month's time before we moved, it had grown down to the floor. In the week of packing, the summer sun began to burst through the front windows, with 6 A.M. blistering glee. I was too involved with my inventory of packing boxes to care much; I also knew that I would do a lot of cutting back as soon as we had moved. Moving day came; I made the last trip with the kids and the dog and the contents of the refrigerator. When a friend brought in the Swedish ivy, I could smell all the broken stems. Four hours later, after the appropriate beds had been set up, the blankets found and the floor picnic cleaned up, I unearthed my plant scissors and got to work. Most of the Swedish ivy plant was made into cuttings and three weeks later the plant looked none the worse for wear. You simply don't have that kind of flexibility with a five-foot palm.

# Root Trim

There is another specific pruning technique that is useful on occasion; it involves trimming the roots of a plant. Root trim is basically a stalling maneuver. You may choose to root trim periodically to keep plants from outgrowing their containers. There have certainly been weeks in my life when I couldn't afford the four new ten-inch clay pots and eight new six-inch pots that were suddenly indicated. Or, you might have a plant whose aesthetic balance is so pleasing in its present container and at its present size that you would simply like to enjoy it longer.

So you do a root trim. It is important that you do the job before the plant is drastically root bound. An opportune time is when you notice that growth has slowed down due to lack of fresh soil or when you notice a sudden need for more water or similar early signs. Do not wait for leaf drop or smaller size of new leaves; do not procrastinate until roots are begging for more room. Whereas these events are undesirable in themselves for normal repotting, they are even harder for the plant to correct with the added travail of some root growth whacked off. It is also of consequence that you are dealing with a plant which does not have strenuous objections to any disturbance to its roots. Impatiens (patience plant or dizzy lizzy) is the one which comes most promptly to mind; even simple repotting will bring on a deluge of lower leaves. Any such temperamental inclinations will be mentioned specifically in the illustrated index.

The process for trimming roots is quite simple. All you need to have at hand is some fresh wetted soil and a large, very sharp knife. You turn the plant out of its pot in the usual way. For the most likely candidate for root trim, you should see roots extended well into the outer surfaces of the soil and beginning to hold the soil mass together in a firm root ball. Hopefully you have not waited until the root ball is white with tangled, whorled root masses; but, even so, if you are determined, it is best to proceed. Set the plant on the counter, everything intact, but the old pot removed. Pick out any chips of drainage material entangled in the roots. Put new drainage material and an inch or two of fresh soil in the old pot, level it and firm it down gently with your fingers. You then pick up your knife and *slice*: an inch or so (perhaps more for particularly large plants) from the sides of the root mass all around and another inch clear off the bottom. It is essential that your knife is sharp and your slicing action is clean. Don't saw gently back and forth in an effort to be more sympathetic. Just remember that a sharp quick cut provides less damaged surface area and is thus easier for the plant to repair; when you go at a plant with hesitation you usually lacerate or abrade the tissue along with your cutting, and that will be more damaging. Pop the manicured root ball into its pot, level it on top of the fresh soil, dribble in soil at the sides, firm it down, add enough soil to fill in the sides and top to the proper level, and you are nearly finished. You want to water the plant as you do after any repotting —not for the sake of water, but to check the new drainage.

Then, in all but the most minimal of root-trim jobs, you will need to cut back the top of the plant. You cut back enough to approximate the amount you have trimmed from the roots. This returns the plant to a healthier, more normal proportion of foliage to root mass; it also serves to stimulate new root growth and top-leaf-node activity. Allow the plant up to a week in a quiet, undemanding location. That plant is now ready for months of fresh growth in its crummy old pot.

Upon rare occasions, you may choose to do a root trim as a way to improve growth. You have a plant that is doing poorly; when you turn it out of its pot you discover browning and weak growth at the edges of the roots. Particularly if this is a plant you suspect to be the victim of occasional overwatering, you may figure that you have caught a case of root rot in its earliest stages. Trim the roots back sharply to their healthiest place, return the plant to as small a pot as is necessary to fit its new size, add fresh soil all around, and check for proper drainage. Be particularly careful in the near future to water this plant only as needed and count yourself lucky that you have saved the plant from rotting away.

## Shaping and Training

I always start to laugh inside when I contemplate training plants. I imagine adding a leash and choke chain to my fertilizer shelf. Or I could try walking up to my kangaroo ivy with a firm step and my best no-nonsense voice; I could display a small leather crop in one hand and promptly, out of terror, the vine would begin to climb, stem over tendril, up its new trellis. How simple it all could be.

However, the ideas of general shaping for plants depend much more upon providing support when it is required. The other day, a nine-year-old friend told me he thought it was really terrific that we'd taught our twelve-month-old baby how to walk because it was a lot of fun for her to be able to get around so well. Plants are a good deal like babies in this regard. You try to anticipate what they will be wanting to hold on to as they grow, and try to have it there when it is needed. This all goes along with the basic notion that you keep your inner eye focused on the plant you want and then provide things as they are needed or just slightly before.

The most casual kind of shaping and training you can do involves the position of a plant in relation to the light. Plants which grow from a center crown or on a single stalk cannot be pinched or pruned. They rely solely on proper cultural practices to maintain their good looks. Your only manicuring job is to remove dead leaves. But you can affect their shape by choosing their relationship to the light. African violets grown with abundant light directly overhead display an open flat top; those grown reaching sideways to better light will have elongated stems on one side.

*The Daily Quarter-turn*. You can make excellent use of phototropism to guide your plants into desired shapes. The classic use made is to deny the plants their penchant for the light and practice the famous "Daily Quarter-turn." This also works well if instituted as the "Biweekly Quarter-turn," and simply means turning the plant a bit on a regular basis to keep growth even on all sides. The practice certainly has much to recommend it since your plants near the windows (as most plants seem to be) will invariably show you their less flamboyant side if left unturned. Hanging plants usually have only two options, frontward or backward; but this works out well enough.

Do practice the regular turning to maintain even growth, but feel free to vary the habit if you have a reason. A plant tucked up on a high shelf has neither the ability to produce nor display growth at its backside; so forget about it. Rooted tip cuttings may be replanted into the soil of the parent plant if you want a fuller look at some point. I have set myself up for great thrills at times by planning the shape of a plant. You want a big bushy branch moving out in one direction and all you have there now is a small, but eager stem. Place the plant so that its primary source of light is urging growth in the desired direction; pinch or prune consistently everywhere else on the plant.

*Slowing Down Growth*. You might also like to know that it is perfectly permissible to keep growth in check by supplying slightly less than abundant water, fertilizer, and light. We all do this by default; it is reassuring to have someone admit to it on paper, and you may at times want to keep a plant from exceeding its present size and bounds. In fact, the sole justification for going on at such length about watering and the like is that you will be confident to vary your chores as you see fit. You now know what to look for so that the lessened sunlight doesn't ultimately produce root rot or underwatering doesn't bring on lower-leaf drop.

## STAKES, SUPPORTS, AND TRELLIS WORK

Along with the notion of urging a plant in a desired direction through the influence of sunlight goes the practice of providing stakes, supports, or trellis work. From time to time you may elect to impose some form of self-improvement regimen on a straggly plant. There are many plants which depend on their environment for climbing supports, but even the least suspecting free-thinker may benefit from occasional help: a stalk top-heavy with flowers or a just-pruned plant that you intend to encourage in a special direction.

You may use stakes whenever you feel it necessary for the plant's improved growth or aesthetic appearance. The simplest temporary stake is a pencil or chopstick. The more professional choice is a length of green bamboo. If you do need to tie the plant stem to the stake use soft yarn (preferably green) or the pliable plastic tapes from nursery-supply houses or gardening shops. Should you occasionally resort to wire-enclosed Baggie ties, simply remember the two basic objectives in any tying maneuver. First, you are tying for an improved appearance; therefore your tying apparatus should be as unobtrusive as possible. Second, the binding must not harm the plant stem in any way. In short, since you are trying to go forward, take care that you don't go back. Tie loosely so that the plant is not injured. Tie square knots so that the string can't slip. Place your stakes deep into the soil so that they won't tip over, and plant them judiciously so that you aren't doing injury to the roots.

Next, we consider the plants with aerial roots which definitely need something upon which to climb. Climbing philodendrons, monsteras, nephthytis, syngonium, and pothos are among the plants that like to move on up. A variety of supports, sometimes listed in catalogues as "totem poles," have become popular for the climbing pleasure of these plants; a slab of rough bark, a wire-mesh cylinder filled with long-stranded sphagnum moss, or a pressed rectangle of osmunda fiber all fill the bill. It is obviously best to provide these at repotting time since they need to reach down to the bottom of the pot for greatest stability. But you can insert one later if you exercise great care or rig one up with wire to the outside of a pot if you are procrastinating on a repotting job. To be useful to the plant, the moss or bark must be moist at all times; you soak the totem pole thoroughly each time you water the plant, and

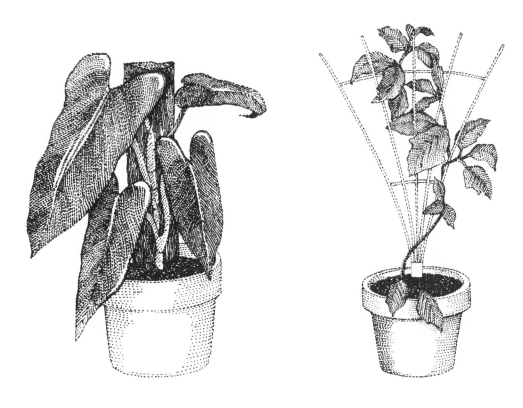

perhaps spray it as often as twice daily in between. You may need to encourage the aerial roots to make their first venture into the moss. You may do this with green tape ties or with pins, oversized hairpins or florist pins made for this purpose. Once the aerial roots have taken hold, you do not need to remind them of the goal; they will keep at it by themselves as long as the support is moist and inviting.

One of the most delightful of plant forms involves the tasteful use of trellis work to support climbing vines. English ivy, kangaroo vine, grape ivy, creeping fig, sweet potato, hoya, morning glory, and nasturtium are some of the more avid climbers. They will make do with whatever they can find. In a hanging or stationary pot, they will cascade or droop depending upon the size of the plant; given a structure, they will follow it. That might be a latticework fashioned of green string held by thumb-tacks at the sides of the window frame. It might be the cords of a macramé plant hanger. Or you might build or buy to suit your purpose. The disadvantages of the string latticework attached to the window are that the strings look silly until the vines have covered them and, should your plant develop aphids or the like and need to be sprayed, it is a highly unportable combination.

You might buy or put together a trellis support for these climbers and fool around with the possible pleasing results. It is easy to buy wood slats (1-inch-by-¼-inch or 1½-inch-by-½-inch) and cut them and nail them as you choose to make your own trellis. The most sensible ones I have seen are those made and then attached at right angles to a base of wood. The plant's pot stands on this platform, thus protecting the floor; at the same time it provides a neatly portable apparatus should you need to move the plant.

## TOPIARY

The furthest extension of our human habit to direct the form that plants may follow leads to the time-honored practice of topiary. As my *Webster's Unabridged* points out, topiary is the custom of training plants into "odd or ornamental shapes." Indeed, I have seen both as the result of this hobby. People have been involved with topiary design since medieval times. At the very least, it affords an opportunity to practice your supporting, training, and pruning skills, and is worth trying once in your life.

There are two basic techniques. The first is that of clipping small-leaved, bushy shrubs into chosen forms: cubes, spheres, birds, pyramids, lions, club sandwiches, Queen Victoria's bust, etc., or any combination of the above. The best plants to choose for your first effort would be boxwood (buxus) or winter creeper (euonymus) varieties; they are well suited in their compact, small-leafed habit and are readily available. And be assured that, despite the amused chitchat of the uninitiated, many who try their hand at topiary find it a lifelong avocation.

The second basic topiary-design technique depends upon creeping vines to follow the form of a wire frame. You buy or design and construct a frame from coat-hanger wire or from wire that is similarly weighted, but more flexible. Plant the wire frame firmly in a pot, and then add your chosen plant. Classic choices for this technique are needlepoint ivy or creeping fig. And for first ventures I would suggest combining several small plants in one pot; patience is requisite to topiary design, but no need to strain yourself the first time out. You tie the branches to the wire frame, maintain good even growth, and prune out any maverick side shoots as you go. Eventually the wire frame is hidden under lush, bushy growth and, in terms of topiary, you have arrived.

## Youth as an Attribute

It is impossible for me to leave this chapter without discussing youth as a primary attribute of good-looking plants. Pinching has the best results when done to a young plant; cutting back is also best before the main stem is hardened, tough, and old. Young plants are more adaptable to new conditions, to changes in humidity, light, water, or soil. A young plant is amenable to training of all kinds.

Your house plants will be in much better shape if more are new guys than old. Whereas it may mean a great deal to you to have a six-year-old coleus, an experienced indoor gardener would shrink at the thought. The more fast-growing is a plant's habit, the shorter is its good-looking indoor life. Palms, dieffenbachia, dracaena, and some ficus grow slowly indeed, and become as permanently fixed as the pictures in the dining room. But be realistic. When a plant has outlived its most beautiful years, prepare to take leave of it and go on. There are ways and ways; conveniently enough they are all discussed in chapter 3. Pinching and cutting back are clearly related to obtaining cuttings. Maintenance of proper shape and procuring cuttings for better-looking shapes are merely varying ways to achieve the same goal: lavishly healthy and therefore great-looking plants. The flame of eternal youth and boisterous good looks begins with cuttings.

# 3

# All Manner of Propagation

Taking cuttings is an easy, inexpensive, and rewarding way to increase your plant collection. An all-powerful, grass-roots movement of raising and sharing new plants claims your allegiance the moment you venture your first snip. Understanding the mechanics of the process is quite simple. There is no reason for a cutting not to "take" if you savvy the situation and give the plant half a chance.

## Reproduction without Sex

It is one of the wonders of the plant world that you need not wait for the next generation to achieve a fresh crop of your favorites. Plants are empowered to bypass sexual means of reproduction (flowers, fruits, seeds, germination) and use asexual or vegetative forms to ensure future growth. This phenomenon has great commercial significance for agricultural and ornamental practice. New plants derived by vegetative means, that is, cuttings, are sure to be like the parent plant; no new gene combination has been introduced.

To my mind, it is nothing short of miraculous: the inner or cambium layer of a plant stem is composed of specialized cells that are capable of dividing into new cells of a *different* form. These specialized dividing cells, called meristematic cells, boast thin cell walls, a large nucleus, and dense cytoplasm. Their mission in life—infinitely active cell division—is thus supported (or determined) by their basic form. Herein lies the proof of the pudding.

Meristematic cells are found in greatest concentration at the tips of the stems and the tips of the roots. V*oilà*, we have further explanation of the fact that a plant is capable of most active growth at its tips. These small, wondrous cells account for the phenomenon that a cutting taken from the tip of a stem can generate roots where once there was only plain green stuff.

The basic types of stem cuttings and their variations will be discussed specifically as we go along. Perhaps I won't mention every plant, but as you develop an increasing ability to recognize the similarities in basic patterns of growth and form, you will be able to generalize quite easily and glean a cutting from almost any plant you choose.

Your understanding of the power of dormant leaf nodes will serve you well. Pinching, cutting back, and taking cuttings to root are each a part of a big fat circle, and I trust you are now beginning to see how it rolls along. The goal is always the same; active growth wherever it is possible, encouraging new possibilities whenever you are not satisfied with the old. The more you know about the basic nature of a plant's life, the better you are able to understand the limits of your intent. Then simply go at the job with a whole heart. You will be able to buy an ugly old plant for fifty cents at a garage sale and bring it back to splendor or invest in a fifty-dollar giant and preserve its fabulous good looks.

## General Considerations

### THE PROPAGATION BOX

Cuttings are tender creatures and they need extra help—*a bright, warm, humid atmosphere and an even supply of moisture.* The classic greenhouse means of providing such an atmosphere is a "propagating box" or "propagating case." If you understand the various conditions the propagating box attempts to achieve you will be able to meet these conditions at home with a variety of more portable and less conspicuous set-ups. The propagating box is composed of a shallow bed of sterilized sandy soil enclosed on all sides by wood or glass framing. If the bottom of the box does not have drainage holes, drainage is provided by an inch or two of clean pebbles beneath the soil. Occasionally a soil-heating coil will be used. This is a waterproof electric heating cord that is set by thermostat to a desired temperature; it is coiled back and forth through the soil to maintain additional heat. I have never felt the need to use one but they are not expensive and you might indeed choose to add one to your propagating set-up should you take a fancy to exotic tropicals or midwinter rooting sprees. The classic propagating case is then completed by a sheet of glass over the top. This glass—an old wood-framed window would do well—is hinged at

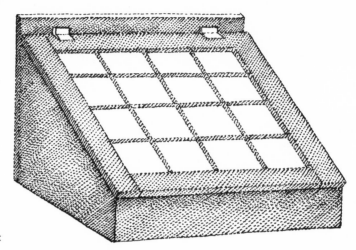

*Cold frame or
heavy duty box*

the back of the case. It can thus be kept closed for optimum humidity, propped open at the front for increased ventilation, or moved up out of your way when you are watering or otherwise working in the box.

The cuttings are set directly into the soil, they are lightly watered, and then checked at least daily during the rooting period. If the soil is less than delicately moist, a brief spray watering is given; if the atmosphere in the box is drippy, the hinged top is raised to provide added ventilation. The entire propagating case sits on a greenhouse bench that receives generous filtered light, but no direct sun.

## NECESSARY ROOTING CONDITIONS

Consider the four important factors here and the desirable limits of each. The elements are bright light, warm environment, humid air, and evenly moist soil. Basically each condition is understood to encourage optimum growth in a plant of any age. But with cuttings your goal is to provide conditions for optimum, effortless maintenance of top foliage while the new roots have a chance to form. Maintaining water in the existing plant tissues is the most stressful task during the rooting period, simply because new roots are not yet developed to draw the needed water up from the soil. Preventing the foliage from wilting is your primary challenge until the new roots have had time to form.

*Bright light* is obviously beneficial to photosynthetic food manufacture, but direct sunlight is taboo. There should be considerable humidity around the new cuttings, and therefore the leaves will be slightly wet; direct sun on wet leaves will burn holes in the foliage. The intense heat brought on by direct sun will also serve to encourage rapid fungus growth in a closed environment and you might lose your cuttings to mildew or rot. Even if you are rooting your cuttings in a glass of water and the leaves are dry, the direct sun merely accentuates the wilt problem and does no additional good. *Warmth* will encourage new growth at a faster clip than cold. This is why commercial growers and many private enthusiasts opt for soil-heating cables. As the temperatures of the soil and the air increase so do the rates of food manufacture (photosynthesis) and food use (respiration); faster results are seen. There are some tropical plants that can rarely be induced to root in our hemisphere without additional soil heat. Nevertheless I have found my life quite satisfactory without home-grown specimens of this tribe. The only problem with a soil-heating cable is that you need a large enough soil bed of cuttings to accommodate it and make it worthwhile. I have always been content with a few pots of soil and thousands of eager types thrust into jars of water. But, if you are not, move ahead.

The desired conditions of *humid air* and *even moisture available in the soil* are clearly twin requisites for maintaining water in the tissues of a plant that has not yet developed roots. As always, the more successfully you avoid stress, the fewer lower leaves will be dropped. The additional humidity in the air prevents water loss from the leaves. The constant level of moisture in the soil ensures that fragile new root hairs will not die of thirst soon after they strike out. Your mind is probably racing to the question of what container will best suit your cuttings. Indeed I have found nothing more adept at supplying even moisture than a plain glass of water. But you will need to know when to choose what. This is referred to in the trade as "the choice of rooting medium."

## ROOTING MEDIUMS

There are three possibilities: (1) water, (2) sand or sandy soil, and (3) a nonnutritive sterile medium such as vermiculite, perlite, or sphagnum moss. The choice is made on the basis of how eagerly the parent plant grows and therefore how readily the cutting will root. It is primarily a question of vulnerability.

Water has been my most frequent choice for an obvious reason; it is easy. There are many plants which root readily in water and they are among the most popular: ivy, coleus, Swedish ivy, wandering Jew, Chinese evergreen, piggyback, spider plant, and on and on. If you want to root one of these and all other factors are encouraging, you may simply pop the cutting in a glass of plain water and wait. The simple caution to observe is that the cuttings have good light, but no direct sun; the direct rays of the sun will heat the water to a sufficient degree that new roots may burn and you will be left with a jar of green scum. If at any time your water looks murky, empty the glass and fill it with fresh. You will need to know the optimum time for transferring the rooted cutting to soil, but for the moment let's complete the explanation of your first choices.

Sand or sandy soil or perlite or vermiculite or a half-and-half mixture of chopped peat moss and sand are all proper choices for a more fragile, more vulnerable cutting. There is a structural and functional difference between roots formed in water and roots formed in soil. Growth slows down when a water-rooted cutting is first set into soil; there is a period of adjustment during which time the roots must adapt to the new job before them, and consequently foliage growth is restrained. I have never found this adjustment period to be arduous or of a permanently discouraging nature and I still choose to root in water whenever I can. The difficulties of rooting in sandy soil are these: the soil must be kept evenly and lightly moist at all times and it can never contain excess water. These mediums—sand, sandy soil, perlite, vermiculite, or moss mixtures—are specifically chosen for the fact that they are composed of tiny particles. It is easier for new hair roots to wrap themselves around tiny particles and therefore these mediums encourage more rapid root growth. That's the good news. The bad news is that because they are of a very light texture you must be vigilant to see that the cuttings do not dry out.

## VULNERABILITY

Okay. How do you know when a cutting is more or less risky? If you have a plant with a strong, tough outer stem, it is probably an unassailably good choice for water. Healthy new tip growth from a healthy plant makes a likely candidate for prompt rooting. Any plant process is more powerful in the spring than in late autumn or winter. So if you are taking a healthy tip cutting from a plant with a strong outer stem and during a period of active growth, you can certainly root in water if you want to. On the other hand, a tender stem or a fleshy and/or hairy stem is more vulnerable to rot; the stem may absorb rather than resist the water in your glass and rot may develop before the new roots. A cutting taken from a diseased plant or a plant weakened for any reason is not a hardy specimen. A cutting taken as a last desperate measure during a resting period or a lousy, dull winter is similarly vulnerable.

Starting from the top, the tough ones, the unbeatably strong, the quick-growing, and the healthy cuttings will be likely choices for water. If a plant has had any trouble, go for the more conservative, sandy-soil choice. The decision process is basically a toss-up between inconvenience and fear; the inconvenience of keeping the soil or perlite or whatever constantly moist and well drained and the atmosphere humid versus the fear that the stem will rot or the foliage will wilt and leaves will drop before new roots can form. You can always opt for the safer, less carefree path. I believe there is a place in the world for the phase "a healthy risk"; some folks think risk never healthy at all. Choose whatever medium allows you enjoyment with your success.

You may take greater risks as you become more confident. For instance, African violet has a fleshy and a hairy stem. Ordinarily this would mean that you should root its cuttings in vermiculite or sand. However, if you have a supertough and aggressive

African violet, you may simply take a leaf cutting, pop it stem-down into a narrow-necked glass of water, and soon have new roots. Conversely, I might well choose to root even a coleus in sandy soil if it were a cutting taken to preserve an unusual favorite and the parent plant was too weak or ugly to try to save.

A friend once brought me a single cutting of velvet ivy from her own plant which was quickly dying from a sudden attack of red spider mites. Velvet ivy is an unusual and delicate plant, related to purple velvet plant but rarely available in the plant shops; and this was our last chance. So I set it in a tiny pot of sand, covered the planting with an overturned glass jar to keep the humidity up, and placed it atop the refrigerator so that the cutting could benefit from the heat of the motor. The refrigerator stood near windows with good general light. Four months and four-times-thirty daily inspections later, roots had formed. The cutting had become a new plant, and I felt rather remarkably expert.

Here are a few extra details. There are powders available that you might wish to use for your riskier cuttings. These contain both plant hormones and antifungus ingredients. You tap the stem end of a cutting onto the powder before you insert the cutting into the soil. It is quite a simple procedure even if you are setting out numerous cuttings but it is also a worthwhile and inexpensive precaution if you are extra-worried about a fragile favorite. The rooting powder is of no use for cuttings rooted in water since the powder would wash right off, but if you have opted for water you shouldn't be needing that extra help anyway.

Plants that store a great deal of water in fleshy, thickened tissue, i.e., succulents, may easily rot if they are popped directly into moist soil. The watery sap in the cutting must be allowed to dry out before it is planted. Obviously, cactus cuttings should not be attempted in water. So you take a cutting and let it sit out in the air with good light, but no direct sun, until the cut end has formed a lightweight scab or callus. The amount of time involved varies with the degree of succulence. Many growers recommend that African-violet leaf cuttings be left out to dry from a few hours to overnight. It may take a supersucculent cactus cutting several days to form a callus.

## CONTAINERS

The container used for any propagation operation should be whatever you have that works. Jelly glasses, crystal vases, or old crocks fill the bill for water rooting. Then, when you choose to root in sand or soil or vermiculite, you base your choice on the size of your project. For the most ambitious, you might buy or build a propagating case. You can also rig up smaller facsimiles. A plastic bread box would work; so would one of the clear plastic shoe boxes that were the rage in the housewares departments ten years ago. Special small plastic propagating boxes are now available through nursery-supply houses. For individual cuttings, you might use a clay or plastic pot of appropriate size. The little two-to-four-inch, dark green plastic seedling pots are quite useful for propagating; nearly every plant lover accumulates a stack of these as new plants are repotted into more attractive containers.

Whatever your choice, be sure there is drainage in the bottom—whether that is provided by drainage holes or an inch of pebbles underneath the sand. It is an easy matter to poke holes through plastic with a heated ice pick. Poke ventilation holes in the top as well if you have chosen a covered plastic box. This will be your insurance against rotting the foliage away with excessive humidity. Fungi and bacteria will be discouraged if the air circulation is good. You may also provide humidity to cuttings in individual pots with an inverted glass jar or plastic bag. Simply beware of wet, hot plastic or glass touching the leaves. You can set chopsticks or pencils into the soil to keep the plastic off the leaves and punch a few air holes to give you more latitude in your observation chores. If you are using an airtight humidity cover—an overturned glass or a virgin plastic bag—you must painstakingly watch for a drippy atmosphere and allow air circulation whenever necessary to clear the fog.

Put your cuttings wherever you will best remember to check on them. I have found the kitchen to be unbeatable in this regard. My mind tends to wander a great deal while my hands are doing the dishes and I usually conjure up at least ten other more interesting chores; at that point you're sure to check cuttings for water, humidity, or fresh air. It is also of note that the highest average humidity in your home will be found near the kitchen sink.

## WHEN IS A CUTTING "READY"?

Generally people forget to ask, but eventually everyone wants to know: when is a cutting "ready"? When may you call it a new plant?

*For the cuttings rooted in water*, you wait until the roots have branched and the branches have developed their own tiny hair roots. You might imagine the roots gathered up loosely, as if cupped gently in your hand; that cupped root mass should be the equivalent of a fourth to a third of the size of the foliage. It is particularly important not to wait too long before transferring such cuttings to soil. Roots that have formed in water are different in cellular structure than roots formed in soil. The potted cutting will adjust to the new function, but this will happen most quickly and easily if it is done before the roots have matured in their aquatic world.

To pot the water-rooted cutting, choose a pot of proportionate size. One good-size coleus cutting would be suitable for a four-inch clay pot; two rather small ones would also do well. If you have ready cuttings of any of the fast-growing and shallow-rooted plants, such as wandering Jew or Swedish ivy, you might put ten or fifteen into a six-inch pot. These plants are so eager to grow that you can pop cuttings—rooted or not—into the topsoil of the parent plant to ward off that old familiar leggy look; simply make a hole with your finger or a chopstick or whatever, insert the cutting, firm the soil up to it, water lightly, and you're through.

But the more common procedure is to pot a single well-rooted cutting into a single pot, and the process works like this: Place shards or pebbles in the bottom of the pot for drainage, then an inch or so of moist soil; hold the cutting with one hand and lower it into a proper position so that the roots are lying loosely but cozily in the center of the pot; with your other hand dribble in soil all around until the cutting is able to stand by itself. You then firm down the soil gently with your fingertips or by thumping the pot down against the table a few times. As with any potting, you want the soil packed firmly, but not tight: it must still have air in it and a springy feel. Fill in more soil to within an inch of the pot rim and press that down to the same degree; then water gently from the top to check for drainage problems, and you have a brand-new plant.

If your choice of cutting demands a more obliging environment, you will be *rooting in sand, sandy soil, perlite, vermiculite, or a moss mixture.* I have not yet detailed how to set up the cutting in the first place, so here goes: Imagine a two-to-four-inch plastic or clay pot; you can then extend your imagination as far as you wish up to a two-by-three-foot propagating case, even to a ten-by-forty-foot propagating case if you are feeling particularly grandiose. If your pot does not have a drainage hole, you should put some drainage material in the bottom. Then add wet soil or sand or whichever medium you've chosen and press or tap it down so that it is firm, but still spongy. Next make a hole with a pencil, finger, or chopstick that is sufficiently generous to accommodate the cutting; insert the cutting; firm the soil up to it for good contact with the stem, and water gently to check the drainage.

A cutting set in sand or other such medium is ready to pot when it begins to behave like a normal plant. This means that the water requirements become more frequent, new leaves may begin to show, and that the roots will resist if you tug gently, very gently, at the base of the main stem. Be timid about tugging. My first childhood garden failed abysmally because I would check the carrots every day by pulling them out of the ground and then I would sneak them back in; needless to say, the harvest was disappointing. When your pot of successfully handled cuttings shows itself to be cozy with roots, you pot-on to a larger container and quietly marvel at your propagating skill.

Be aware of the possibility that you may need to condition a freshly potted cutting to its new environment. As at any time that you are moving a plant from a pampered location to a more realistic new spot, you will have to give it a chance to adjust gradually to less humidity, more intense sunlight, and less watchful care. I have a small table in the kitchen devoted to cuttings that are rooting and plants that are struggling. But eventually some have to give up their luxury hotel and move out into the house. Just do not expect a plant to be able to jump from heaven to the hottest window sill; if the change will be extreme, follow the precautions for gradual conditioning discussed in the first chapter.

# The Varying Forms of Successful Propagation

I have a friend who submitted a brashly honest book report to his seventh-grade teacher; it read in full: "I have learned more from this book about penguins than I ever wanted to know." Penguins may have something in common with propagating cases and plastic bags and chopsticks, so let's get on with it. *Where* do you cut? The types of cuttings are determined by the form of the parent plant and how eagerly its cuttings are known to take root.

### TERMINAL STEM CUTTING

The easiest and most common form of propagation is a terminal stem cutting. This type of cutting may be taken from any plant that grows on a branching stem, upright or trailing. Coleus, ivy, nephthytis, branching philodendron, geranium, impatiens, wandering Jew, Swedish ivy, lipstick vine, aluminum plant, jade plant—the list of plants suitable for terminal stem cutting is nearly endless. It is obvious from the name that this is a powerful cutting and will be the most likely tissue to root. "Terminal," "end," or "tip" cuttings bring with them all of the meristematic cells and their urgency for active growth in any form.

Using a razor blade or superbly sharp, lightweight scissors, you cut off the newest leaves and three to four inches at the tip of a stem. Make the cut just below a leaf node so that the base of the cutting will be sure to contain the most potent ability to root. Dormant leaf nodes will probably spring forth to show roots elsewhere on the cutting stem, but you might as well begin with a sure start. The cut made must be clean, and the object is to avoid pinching or bruising the stem tissue in the process. A diagonal cut is preferred simply because it exposes more of the active cambium layer of the stem; I have always considered this a rather fine point, but far be it from me to refuse fine points. Simply be assured that if one of your cuts is made straight on, you aren't necessarily courting peril. You strip off any leaves that would find themselves below the water or soil of the rooting medium and therefore might rot. Many growers feel it important to remove any flowers or buds present so that no frivolous energy is deflected from the rooting process; coleus or impatiens or begonias would require this treatment.

Most plants suitable to terminal stem cutting may be rooted in water. But if you are in doubt, retreat to one of the safer mediums; or try some cuttings in water, some in sand, some in perlite, and see which medium gives you the best results. The illustrated index will mention each plant's propagation requirements; but often the easiest and yet proper choice of rooting medium depends heavily upon the condition of the plant.

As you become more experienced, you may confidently take cuttings of active healthy plants that are five to ten inches long. Swedish ivy, wandering Jew, pothos, and hanging coleus are particularly good prospects for this kind of treatment. To quote my favorite song writer, "You've got nothing to lose but the shine on your shoes," and you can gain a larger plant in shorter time.

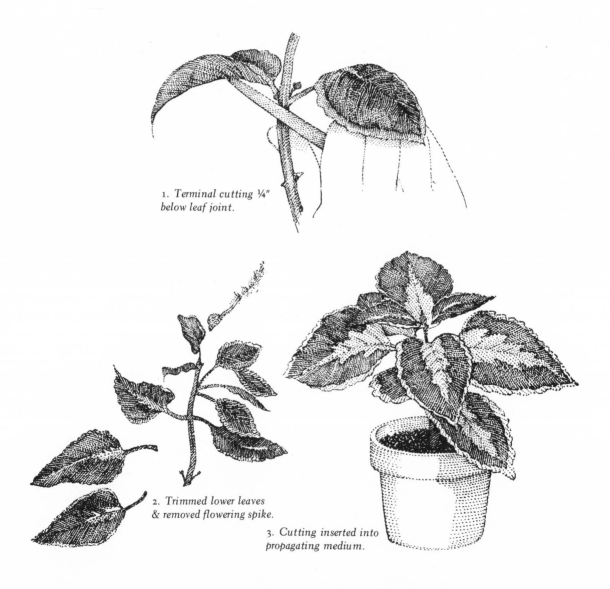

1. *Terminal cutting ¼"*
*below leaf joint.*

2. *Trimmed lower leaves*
*& removed flowering spike.*

3. *Cutting inserted into*
*propagating medium.*

You may often find yourself rich with terminal stem cuttings as the result of a pruning or cutting-back adventure. I have said that the last thing left at the top of a cut-back stem should be leaf node and that the base of each cutting must include a visible leaf node as well. What do you do? Play Solomon or toss a coin or try to talk either the cutting or the cut stem end into believing it does indeed have a leaf node? If the portion of stem pruned from the parent plant is larger than the cutting desired, the solution is simple. Cut the stem tip to the desired four inches, including a leaf node at the base of the cutting, and discard the rest. If what you have is about the size you want, just cut a bit higher to a spot with an obvious leaf node and throw away the extra half-inch of stem.

*LEAF SLIP*

There are many plants that do not show a branching pattern; or if they do, they do not require an entire stem tip to develop new roots. The form of cutting taken from such plants is known as a leaf slip. Plants that grow from a center crown are particularly suited to propagation from leaf slip; African violet is perhaps the best known of the center-crown pattern. You choose a healthy mature leaf and cut it off from the plant. It is essential that you cut all the way down to the base of the parent plant so that rot will not spread to the rest of the crown in the wake of your propagating enthusiasm. You want the leaf and at least one inch of its stem or petiole. The tip of the petiole is inserted in sandy soil or vermiculite or, for the most potent African violets or peperomias, you may use water. Narrow-necked bottles, such as those that contained cake-decorating sprinkles, or the lightly colored pseudo-antique pharmacy jars, are quite useful for this obscure purpose. Peperomias, African violets, sedums of all kinds, and kalanchoes are properly propagated from leaf slips.

### MALLET CUTTING

A variety of leaf slip that takes a bit more than a single leaf and its petiole is used for philodendron, ivy, and rubber plant. These three do not grow from a center crown, are branching in habit, yet they are impressively avid in producing new roots. Horticulturists have long since learned to make use of any peculiar enthusiasms. You need only what is called a mallet cutting; that is a leaf, its bud or node on the stem, and an extra inch of stem above and below that node. A shape something like that of a primitive mallet results. A mallet cutting is inserted into the rooting medium with the node and leaf pointing upward; roots will soon follow, although in a different direction. Any plant that can be used for a mallet cutting can also be used for a terminal stem cutting. You may always take more of the plant tissue for propagation; these special forms outlined here are merely the way to get the largest possible number of cuttings from a given four inches of the stem.

### STEMLESS LEAF SLIP

With prayer plant or maranta you may in fact take only a stemless leaf slip. You can take more, but all that you need is a single healthy leaf. Maranta is a plant that requires particularly high humidity and has thin, delicately structured leaves; for these reasons water would be an unsuitable rooting medium. In fact, a covered propagating box (or single pot with a plastic-bag tent) is required for reliable best results. Simply prop the leaf up in the rooting medium with the base of its prominent main vein buried in the moist rooting medium; maintain high humidity along with even moisture and ventilation, and you will have another prayer plant to boot.

### SLIT LEAF

Rex begonia and gloxinia have a remarkable ability to root anywhere along the prominent veins of their large leaves. Select a good-size, healthy, freshly mature leaf, and remove it from the plant. You will not need the petiole, but this must be cut

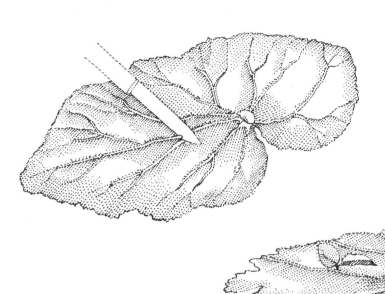

away cleanly from the main plant to prevent rotting at the crown. Take a razor blade and make several slits in the back of the leaf across each of the large veins just below the point where they divide. Lay the slit leaf on top of a moist rooting medium, most preferably sand, and make a hole to accommodate the leaf stalk as an anchor. Provide a pane of glass or plastic covering for heightened humidity. New plants will grow from each slit-vein location. As soon as they are large enough to be handled, separate the young plants with as many roots intact as you can manage and pot them individually. They will need a time of extra humidifying treatment until they gradually toughen up to the outside world.

## CUT LEAF

As long as we are in the profitable business of chopping up leaves, let us consider sansevieria or snake plant. It may be propagated quite astonishingly by a cut-leaf technique. You may take one of the upright leaves and cut it horizontally into three-to-four-inch sections; bury each section about halfway down into a moist rooting medium. Each section will form roots and a new plant. The striped varieties of this amiable plant may revert to a plain green; if you are content only with stripes, you will have to propagate by division of the root clump.

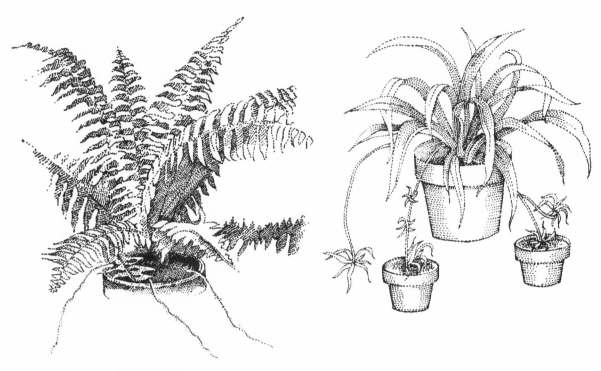

## RUNNERS

There are quite a few plants that come ready equipped with their own method of natural vegetative propagation. These are the plants which boast runners. Among them are Boston fern and its varieties, and spider plant, strawberry begonia, walking iris, and episcia. Many people are curious about the strange stringy bare fronds emerging from their ferns or the long shoots from a spider plant that culminate in miniature spider-plant clumps. These are runners; they are a back-up system for the plant's future growth. A runner will emerge from a mature, healthy plant, particularly when that plant is beginning to feel crowded in its original spot. The runner grows out aways; if it finds amenable air conditions, it grows on until its own weight brings it down to soil level and the tip of the runner is buried a bit and roots begin to form. If conditions are poor, the runner simply dries out and dies. Imagine the best: the runner has extended itself, found the right spot, and its new roots now anchor it firmly in place. Either a clumsy animal walks by and breaks the runner or the increasing weight of the new plant is sufficient to sever it; a new life has begun.

You may make use of these eager scouts to produce new plants. You can tuck a runner back into the soil of the parent plant, wait for the new roots to form, and then either cut it out and repot the new plant separately or leave it there to fill out the older plant. Or you can arrange a new pot filled with moist soil or sand so that the runner can arch down to its new home and form roots there; after the new roots are strong, you can cut the runner away. This latter method evinces possibilities of elaborate Rube Goldberg devices for holding extra pots of soil in midair around your Boston fern. Work out whatever set-up is pleasing and reliable.

New plants of Boston fern can be developed more dependably by division than by rooting runners so I have always either let the runners run or have tucked a few back into the soil for fuller growth. The other plants which grow by runners—or stolons as they are properly called—produce new tiny plants at the tip of the runner before they hit the soil. If this is the case, you can remove the plantlet when it becomes large enough to handle, when it looks nice and heavy and ready to head off on its own as it would in the forest. At this point, it is in fact likely that roots will have already begun to form at the base of the plantlet. Roots will emerge quickly either in soil, sand, or water, and the natural extension of the parent plant's runner system will have been achieved. And you will have a number of new plants.

I first became aware of the possibility of severing new plantlets before they are rooted thanks to my cats. I came home one day and found ten spider-plant runners on the rug. The cats had apparently become carried away in the midst of their game of catnip-ball hockey and had attacked everything in sight. I popped all ten into a single six-inch fern pot because I expected half of them to die from claw wounds. But within two months I had a fine, new, bushy plant and a new crop of runners on the victimized parent.

## OFFSETS

The ability of certain plants to produce offsets is similar to the production of runners; offsets are formed by runners which grow underground. Maranta, clivia, African violet and other gesneriads, fibrous-rooted begonia, and screw pine are among the plants that produce offsets or suckers at their base. It is difficult for me to decide whether the new plantlets produced by piggyback on top of the older leaves should be considered offsets or a variety of runner. Suffice it to say that you can recognize that some plants have the ability to pop up with progeny on or near the parent plant and that whenever this happens you can exploit the appearance of the new kid and have a new plant.

Piggyback forms a new leaf on top of an old at the junction of the leaf with the stem blade or petiole. As the new plantlet grows in size, its weight slowly forces the older leaf down to the soil, the new plant develops its own roots, and the old stem breaks or atrophies as the new plant becomes an independent. A mature plant of African violet will display numerous babies crowding up close to the base of the parent plant. Maranta will develop new plants off and away from the main plant as if by magic.

Here's how you can make use of such offset progeny to produce more independents. Remove the entire leaf of a piggyback plant; bury it in soil or drop it into a glass of water so that the base of the leaf and the base of the new plantlet are just touching the rooting medium. When roots have developed, you can repot it as a new plant. You can even remove the plantlet from the leaf base if the baby is particularly large and already well developed; it will root readily in soil or water without the older leaf to hold it.

For African violet, clivia, screw pine, or any plant with small miniatures clustered at the base, you take a sharp knife and cut the offset plant away from the parent. This offset or sucker is set to root in moist sand or other nonwater medium. It is important that the cut be clean rather than abraded, and I have found it helpful to think of the technique as cutting a small circular patch away from the parent.

When the offset occurs at some distance from the parent plant, as with maranta, you approach the process as if it were division of a root mass and make a clean vertical cut between the new and old plant and repot them separately.


*ROOT DIVISION*


Root division is the proper technique to follow if you wish to propagate new plants from Boston fern, pteris fern, sansevieria, various begonias, and many others that do not necessarily have a branching foliage pattern. All these plants keep getting wider at the base and present numerous stems growing directly from the soil.

Given such criteria, plants such as wandering Jew or Swedish ivy would be possible candidates. Indeed, they may be divided, although I think better results are achieved through pinching, replacing cuttings in the topsoil, and winding long stems around at the top so that they root at each leaf node available and induce a fuller shape.

To divide the root mass of an overcrowded plant you simply arm yourself with a large, sharp knife, plus pots and fresh moist soil to accommodate the results of the

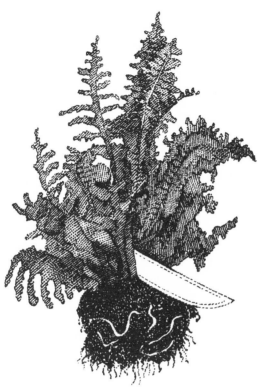

surgery. Turn the plant out of its pot and make clean, sharp cuts down through the root mass to obtain the number and size of new plants you wish. In the case of an enormously overgrown Boston fern, you might do well to slice off an inch or two from the very bottom of the root ball to bring the new plants into better proportion. Remember that a clean, sharp cut results in less root area to be repaired than does a timid, jagged tear. Occasionally, once a plant is unpotted it will simply fall away into its natural divisions. If this happens, fine and dandy; simply sever any hangers-on with a keen blow and repot your results. Protect the newly divided plants for a few days, sheltering them from direct sun and providing additional humidity while the new roots make repairs and begin established growth.

Root division is definitely best done in late winter or spring when the plant is most eager to cooperate. It is the time when most gardeners' fancy turns to improving the appearance of their favorites and the seasonal new growth will quickly correct any asymmetrical results.


## AIR LAYERING

We have now covered nearly every type of plant you might hope to spruce up and/or increase. There remains a singularly difficult but common situation and the ingenious method used to improve it. Rare is the observant plant lover or office worker in a large building who is not familiar with this sight: a sizable rubber plant or dieffenbachia or dracaena has developed a beautiful pompon at its top while all that remains below is a tough, bark-covered, barren stem. A lamentable situation, but what is to be done? If you were to cut it back, you would be left with a tree stump in a large pot of soil; moreover, it is impossible to imagine that the cut tip could be rooted without substantial or total leaf loss from wilt. Air layering, a technique developed on rubber plantations a couple of centuries ago, is the best way of handling this problem.

Air layering is an effective means to obtain a rooted cutting from a large plant without the shock and resultant leaf loss that a regular tip-cutting technique would bring. First, you select the spot on the stem where you would have new roots appear. Generally this would be a few inches below the lowest healthy leaf; in any case, limit the size of the air-layered new plant to two feet. Have at hand a sharp knife, moist sphagnum moss, cellophane or plastic wrap, and tape or plastic plant ties. You cut into the stem at the point you have selected. A variety of cutting styles are practiced, but the basic notion remains the same: you are exposing the inner cambium layer of the plant stem to induce root growth and you are taking care not to completely strip, sever, or girdle the outer bark. In this way new roots can grow while the top of the plant is still nourished and supplied with water from below. Style one: You cut a notch in the stem, a third to halfway in at the top of the notch triangle. Style two: You make a vertical cut into the stem, halfway in and about two inches long. Or, style three: You cut off a one- to two-inch–long, oval-shaped piece of the outer stem covering at one point and then directly opposite on the other side of the stem. You send the point of the knife through the stem from one bare spot to the other, remove the knife, and then hold the stem open with a toothpick or small pebble. Whatever the style of your cut, you then cover the surgery site with a double handful of wet sphagnum moss wrapped around the entire stem; the moss should be soaked in water and wrung out by the fistful. Cover the moss with plastic or cellophane or some other material that will retain moisture; gently tie or tape it top and bottom to seal. And you wait. If the seal on the plastic is good, you may not need to water the moss again. Each time you water the plant, check to see that the moss is moist and inviting to the new roots.

The air layering is finished when you can see a healthy tangle of roots through the plastic. You then cut the new plant away from the old just below the moss, remove the plastic, and pot up your well-proportioned result. It may take as long as six to eight weeks for the roots to develop well, and as with all such operations, you will have the greatest success in the spring. Best not to try your first air-layering operations in autumn or winter. The plants suitable for air layering are rubber plant, fiddle-leaf fig, dieffenbachia, dracaena, an extralarge Chinese evergreen, monstera, or strong philodendron.

After cutting off the air-layered tip, you have a bare tough stalk pretending to be a potted plant. Either discard this imposter or cut it back to a few inches above the

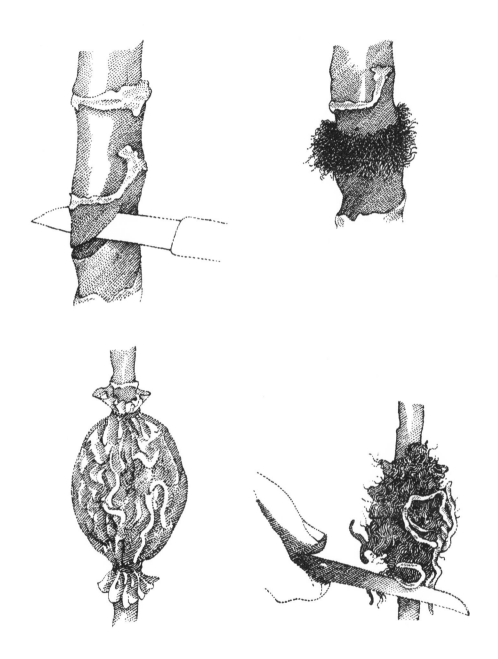

soil. If you have strong curiosity and a great deal of patience, you might try air layer-ing lower on the stem; if it doesn't work, you can still cut back. In the case of dracaena, dieffenbachia, a large philodendron, or Chinese evergreen, you can cut the original plant down to the size of a hopeful new beginning and make use of the middle stretch of stem for cane-section propagation.

*CANE SECTION*

The technique of cane section for propagation reveals yet another means to make miraculous use of dormant leaf nodes and their potential for active growth. You cut the stem into sections, each about four inches long. It is not strictly necessary, but you might dust the sections with sulfur, powdered charcoal, or an antirot rooting powder. Lay the sections down flat on a moist rooting medium and provide for added humidity by covering the dish or flat tray with plastic, glass, or the like, or plan to mist frequently. New roots will develop from the dormant buds on the cane stem and leafy shoots will rise from whichever end of the section was closer to the tip of the plant. You need not worry: the roots will know to go down into the soil, the leaves will know which way is up. When these leaves are well developed, you pot the new plants individually with the cane section buried; or plant several sections in a large pot. Cane sectioning may be used for dracaena, dieffenbachia, large philodendrons, or Chinese evergreens.

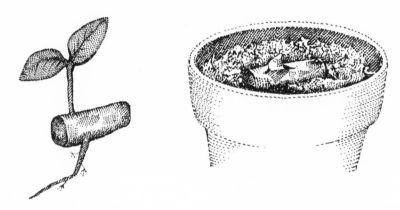

# Seeds

Planting seeds is a marvelous way to obtain large numbers of new plants; it is an inexpensive and easy adventure. Unlike cuttings, which involve the vegetative or asexual powers of the plants, seeds are the culmination of the plant's sexual development. One package of coleus seeds offers a choice of varieties from an enormous gene pool. You will undoubtedly find a color combination to satisfy your wildest fantasy;

you will also probably have a large number of all-green seedlings which you may either take to or discard.

The house plants that can easily be grown from seeds include: coleus, African violet, gloxinia and its dwarf variety, the pileas (aluminum plant, artillery plant, friendship plant), asparagus fern, numerous cacti, herbs, begonia, peperomia, impatiens, and more. You can plant the seeds of outdoor annuals such as marigold, alyssum, nasturtium, black-eyed susan, or morning glory, and either transfer the seedlings to an outdoor location or continue them indoors. I have found these outdoor standbys to be the most willing candidates for life on the extrahot and sunny window seat; they are beautiful and colorful and each eight-inch pot of dwarf marigolds represents about five cents' worth of seed. Many plant lovers whose households also boast plant-eating pussy cats have found great relief in germinating a flat of oat seedlings or wild grasses or catnip to divert the gourmet. (I might add that a heavy sprinkling of cayenne pepper on the leaves of a favored victim has similar good results. And many a hose-chewing dog has learned a great deal about life after finding the hose covered with tabasco or Louisiana hot sauce.)

My favorite container in which to plant seeds is the bottom half of a cardboard egg carton. It will be strong enough to last just about as long as you need it, and since excess water can seep out the bottom you don't have any worry about the drainage. The bottoms of shoe boxes or gift boxes also work well in this way. Or you can make use of any container on hand for propagating: small flowerpots, seed pans, bulb pans, plastic boxes. If what you've chosen has no holes, either make some or provide a thick layer of shards or pebbles under the soil. A wonderful seed pan for children to use is a clear plastic tub from the butcher shop such as is used for packaging liver. Drainage holes should be poked in the bottom of the tub with a heated ice pick. The children can plant it with pebbles, soil, and seeds and then can watch the roots develop through the clear plastic sides. So you choose your container. First, provide drainage material if you have any doubt about standing water. Freshly germinated seeds are highly vulnerable to rot. So proceed with caution. You don't need anything but soil in an egg carton if you are careful not to overwater.

Plant the seeds in sandy soil that has been wetted to the point that it is thoroughly moist, but no excess water will drip out if a handful is squeezed tightly in your fist. It is essential that you use sterilized soil. Many growers recommend screened sphagnum moss, perlite, or vermiculite, but use of these nonnutritive mediums requires that you water with a weak fertilizer solution at all times. I find it simplest to use soil. Firm the soil down gently. Then sow the seeds to the depth indicated on the package. As a rule of thumb for package-losers, seeds are sown approximately to their own depth. A lima bean goes down an inch, a marigold seed a quarter of an inch; tiny seeds such as sweet alyssum are simply sprinkled on the moist soil surface and barely tapped in.

Sow the seeds sparingly; beware of crowding them because they will probably all come up. If crowded, each plant will not grow as well as it might have for lack of elbowroom. I tend to sprinkle out seeds as if they were cinnamon-sugar on top of streudel but this only makes for poor results in the end. Go back and pick out any extra seeds if you feel you were overly generous.

You then give the gentlest watering from a bulb sprayer or extra-fine-rose can. As usual after a planting, this is not to provide water since you began with wet soil. It simply serves to settle the seeds in close contact with the soil. Next, you cover the top of the seed bed with plastic wrap or a sheet of glass. Do not enclose the bottom of the container in plastic since you are relying on your drainage holes to prevent standing water. To my mind, the egg-carton-and-plastic-wrap combination is unbeatable for economy and availability.

The most common failure of seeds is due to damping-off disease, a fungus attack that causes young seedlings to rot at soil level and topple over. I have encountered this in one out of a hundred plantings and feel it can be successfully avoided. Be sure that the seed container is clean and the soil sterilized, avoid crowding the seeds as you sow them, and maintain excellent drainage and high, but not drippy humidity. Use these guidelines and some common sense and you will avoid all the usual mistakes.

There is a Montessori seed-planting kit on the market for children's gardening adventures. The plastic seed pan has no drainage holes and the instructions would have you keep the seed pan covered with its plastic top. I feel the manufacturers struck a poor bargain between the universal truths that children tend to overwater and that mothers dislike water marks on table tops. My daughter Jessie wanted to plant it "her own self" and had a fabulous showing of damping-off disease within the week. It hardly seemed fair.

Lastly you must find a place to put your seeds while they germinate. The prime requirements of that place are that it provide warmth, dim light, and easy recall. Most house-plant seeds will germinate at temperatures between sixty and seventy degrees; some may require higher temperatures. If extra heat is necessary, you may wish to provide bottom heat with a soil cable. I have recommended dim light because it works well in most cases. The optimum light for germination varies significantly with each plant species. You may check each specifically, but I have found dim light to provide simple and reliable results. Bright direct sun is taboo because of the heightened humidity under the plastic and the fact that sunlight heats the soil surface to a point that is overly encouraging to fungus growth. The depth to which the seed is planted indeed determines to a great extent how much light it actually receives. The spot you choose to place your seed pans must be easy to remember; you will need to check the seeds at least daily. I have had best results with an upside-down crate placed under a small table between the kitchen sink and the stove. Since plastic-covered egg cartons are not fabulously good looking, their placement under the table provides both camouflage and dim light. The pilot light in the oven offers added warmth. And there is always some time during the dull spots of making a meal or washing the pots that I am sure to remember to check on the seeds.

In the interval between the time the seeds are planted and when they first pop up with green above the soil, you should check on them once or twice daily. If the plastic or glass covering is very foggy inside, lift it for an hour or more and let the atmosphere dry out. In the unlikely event that the soil is beginning to dry out, mist water onto the surface or add it gently with a spoon. A forceful spray could disturb tiny new roots. Most seeds will germinate in three or four days in the springtime and in up to two weeks, if at all, in winter. As always, you ought to follow the seed-package directions for best results in regard to planting times. But, on the other hand, who can do everything you're supposed to in early spring? You may try in fall or winter and get less exciting results; but during an unusually bleak December, the first few inches of visible charming young growth might just be worth the trouble.

When the first uncurling leaves or "cotyledons" appear, you can move the tray up to more light, yet still avoiding direct sun. For instance, at this point I bring them up on top of that kitchen table. The sunlight is needed to ensure greening of the leaves and you want to bring the seedlings to their natural growing conditions as soon as possible. Lift the plastic wrap or glass a bit so that the seedlings can begin to toughen up to the real world. In the next few weeks they must gradually accustom themselves to the greater light and lower humidity that suits grownups of their species. You do this by slowly sneaking the protective covering up and away by degrees and moving the seedlings closer to their proper light.

When the first true leaves appear, the seedlings are ready to be transplanted. You may transplant as soon as the new plants are strong and it is best to rush to transplant before any become crowded. With the egg-carton technique, you simply lift out each lump with a spoon and plop it into a small, crocked, and soil-prepared pot. If you need to thin a planting, remove all but the strongest young plants; do the thinning by removing any stragglers with your thumbnail or a scissors down to the soil level. Whenever handling seedlings, touch only their tops since the new roots are unbelievably fragile and a fine, promising seedling may have only one main root to support its entire life. After transplanting, you will probably need to provide another day or two of extra humidity and protection from sunlight. But the more promptly you condition the seedling to the environment that suits an older plant of its species, the better a future it will hold.

Fertilize the seedlings at one-third to one-half normal strength after the first two weeks; then gradually build up to normal strength at two-week intervals between applications. After this, no further special treatment will be needed.

There is an amazingly simple and successful seed-sprouting method that has been used in America since colonial times. Fine soil is sifted onto the top of an average ordinary red clay brick; the brick stands in a pail or puddle of water, seeds are scattered atop the soil. The only thing missing is increased humidity, but that is really frosting on the cake for outdoor seeds. When the first true leaves have appeared and the seedling is hardy, the entire soil mass or a particularly good chunk is sliced off the brick and deposited in some deserving spot of the garden. Imagine a shaded patio encircled by seed-sprouting bricks.

## Garbage Gardens

There are numerous attractive, useful, or silly plantings you can enjoy from kitchen leftovers. Most are temporary plantings, some come close to being permanent, a few are edible later. Your inner child or your real child in tennis shoes will thrill to their simple pleasures; it seems to me that most involve the element of surprise.

### ROOT VEGETABLES

Root vegetables—carrots, beets, parsnips, rutabagas, and turnips—can become miniature forests. Cut off all but the top and an inch or two of vegetable. Cut the top foliage down if it has not already been barbered at the market. Prop up your stubs in a shallow dish of water into which pebbles have been placed for supports. In a week or so, new foliage will appear; carrots display finely cut, delicate green fronds, beets have tough leathery leaves. Your forest will last for a month or more.

### SWEET-POTATO VINES

Sweet potatoes, yams, and other starchy tubers will take about two weeks before they stretch up and begin to vine. If you choose your sweet potato or yam at the supermarket, look for one whose buds are trying to activate and grow; many large stores buy tubers that have been treated to prevent further growth and that won't work very well for you. Most health-food stores can be relied upon for untreated produce. Or you just take your chances.

You cut off one end of the yam and suspend the cut end into a jar of water; use three or four toothpicks if necessary to hold it up in place. The ideal spot for a yam to grow would be very bright, but without direct sun to heat the water and encourage scummy muck. It may take two weeks or more for roots to begin in spring and summer, longer in autumn and winter. Each yam has a determination all its own, so you simply have to wait. At all times you must be sure the roots have an adequate supply of clean, warm water; change the water if it becomes cloudy and add more as it is used by the plant. After the roots form, tiny shoots will emerge from the top of the potato and then your plant is on the way. If you provide a trellis or string-lattice support, the vines will climb; if they can't find supports they will cascade and droop.

As the roots become crowded in their original jar, you may transfer the plant to soil or simply to a larger water container. If you do plant them in soil, be gentle with the root mass and be sure to leave an inch or so of yam above the soil level. However, the plants do seem to last longer if they remain in water.

The life of your vine is limited by the supply of nourishment in the tuber. Some plants remain beautiful for four months, some six, some ten. Enjoy them while you have them. Perhaps you might like to start three or four at once and experiment with any tuberous relatives you find at the Mexican or Japanese vegetable markets. Each variety will have its own distinctive leaf shape and flower.

## FRUIT SEEDS

While making fruit salad, reserve the seeds of oranges, apples, lemons, or grapefruits. You can sprout these by placing them between moist paper towels in a soup bowl or wide-mouthed quart jar. Be sure that the towels are kept constantly moist and in one to three weeks the seeds will have sprouted. Pot them in dirt, either collectively for a pygmy forest or individually for separate tiny trees. It is most unlikely that plants obtained in this way will ever bear fruit, but they are wonderful additions for a child's garden or your own experimental collection. These are fast-growing outdoor plants, so their need for nitrogen far exceeds what is available in indoor potting soil. An application of a dilute high-nitrogen fertilizer every two or three weeks will serve them well; if you forget, the leaves of the seedlings will begin to yellow and thus remind you.

## AVOCADOS

The world has gone mad in recent years over home-grown avocado trees. This recreational activity has never quite caught my fancy, but if you are inclined to try your hand at an inexpensive indoor tree, remember to start the avocado pit with the point end up and the fatter blossom end down. Also be sure to cut back and pinch with violence if you want your young plant to be anything other than a stick with a froufrou of leaves on top. Those are the basics; here come the fine points.

Choose a ripe avocado or wait until your rock ripens at home. Extract the pit with care not to damage it. If your pit permits, gently remove the thin dark skin that covers it—it may well be necessary to leave the pit out to dry overnight before you can rub or peel off that outer coating without scarring the pit inside.

There are those who say to plant the thing in a four-inch pot, leave it in a sunny place, wait three months, and see what happens. There are also those who don't. I

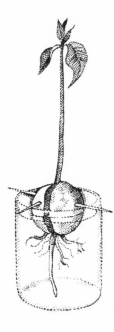

feel that sprouting avocado pits without toothpicks is practically un-American. Ah but we seem to debunk ageless traditions daily without hesitation or regret. Avocados need toothpicks.

Use three or four toothpicks to suspend the avocado pit in a wide-mouthed glass of water; be sure the fatter end is in the water and that the water is kept fresh and covers the bottom of the pit. Place the glass in a dark cupboard and wait several weeks for roots to sprout. Check the pit every day or two to see if you need to add water. If scum, fuzz, and rot sets in to the pit, discard it and start a new one. Eventually a shoot will rise up from between the two halves of the pit. When that shoot is about eight inches tall, arm yourself with a sharp knife and cut it back to three or four inches with a clean diagonal cut. If you are not drastic now, you will never have a bushy, well-branched, lush plant. Pop the jar back into its cupboard and wait another few weeks. This period of suppressing upper growth will force additionally strong growth in the root system and you will have a fighting chance for an admirable young tree.

Finally you remove the avocado from its cupboard home and plant it in soil. Take an eight- or ten-inch pot, supply drainage material and a thick layer of moist soil. Continue as you would for potting any well-rooted cutting, holding the pit in one hand at its proper level while you dribble in soil with the other hand. The toothpicks may come out or stay in if stubborn. Your finished planting should allow the top third of the pit to be exposed to the air. Water gently but thoroughly to settle the soil in good contact with the roots, and add more soil after the watering if the soil level has fallen too low.

After a few hours of shelter from wind or bright sun, move the potted avocado to its permanent spot. The avocado needs abundant bright light with as much sun as possible. It also needs lots of water and more than average humidity. For best results you should mist it daily at a time when the window is not flooded with bright sun; nonmisters might set the pot on a dry well. The avocado is a tropical plant, and the warmer and more humid its indoor environment the more naturally lush the growth will be.

Pinch the avocado constantly. Any new buds may be pinched, the more the better. It is only by pinching that you will have a bushy, well-branched result. When the main stem is nearly a foot in height, you will probably find it beneficial to stake and tie the plant for support.

It is improbable that an indoor avocado will ever bear fruit, but as the plant becomes a tree and the tree becomes a threat to your ceiling you might choose to move your prize to the outdoor garden. It is also unlikely that the avocado will grow to full tree size in Northern areas. However, I know of a fruit-bearing avocado started by a small boy many years ago; his mother banished it from the house; he planted it outside and had avocados in cold foggy San Francisco; when he went to college his mother had the tree surgeon come by since the avocado had overgrown every window in the house and it was either it or they who had to move.

## PINEAPPLE CROWNS

Another tropical bit of greenery to rescue from the kitchen is the top of a pineapple. You may take the top leaf crown and an inch of the flesh in one clean slice before you begin to peel and gobble up the rest of the fruit. Set the crown rosette into moist sand to root as you would any cutting. When roots have formed, pot the plant in soil. You may even bypass the rooting procedure and pot directly into soil. The soil for a pineapple plant must have extra moss and rough stick material or leaf mold and perhaps extra charcoal mixed in; the drainage layer in the bottom of the pot should be increased to perhaps two inches. The pineapple is a bromeliad, and bromeliads require a rich and particularly porous growing medium.

Find a spot for your pineapple that is sunny, humid, and warm. It will not thrive at a temperature lower than sixty degrees. The pineapple is more insistent on its tropical environment than the avocado. If you are able to meet these requirements, the pineapple plant will grow into a striking bit of foliage. After two years or more, you may indeed find edible rewards growing out of the center of the rosette of leaves.

## SPROUTS

Following the basic principles for sprouting seeds, you may have your own home-grown alfalfa, mung-bean, lentil, or whatever sprouts for salad. There are two popular set-ups, the cheesecloth method and the glass-jar method. These techniques differ from the basic seed-sprouting methods described before since you have no concern about the future development of the root systems and you will be harvesting the edible sprouts while they are still quite small.

*The Cheesecloth Method:* Wash the seeds or beans, soak them in plain water for four to six hours, and drain them. Spread a clean, damp piece of cheesecloth on a tray, spread the beans or seeds over it, and cover with another clean, damp cheesecloth. Pour cool water over the tray about four times a day. The cheesecloth *must* be damp at all times. You pour the water over and then tip the tray sink-ward to drain out the excess. After three or four days the sprouts will be at least as long as the seed and ready to eat. So eat them! Thoroughly wash the pieces of cheesecloth and you are ready to begin another tray.

*The Jar Method:* You begin with a sterilized glass jar. Soak the seeds or beans in it for four to six hours, even overnight. Cover the top of the jar with a piece of cheesecloth held by a rubber band or use the original jar top punched full of tiny holes. Our local market even has special plastic jar tops for sprouting purposes. They sell three tops with successively larger holes so that as the sprouts sprout you can gradually rinse out the empty hulls; it's a wonderfully efficient system. So you drain the soaking water out through the cloth or jar top and the sprouting period begins. Rinse the sprouts three or four times a day by adding cool water and draining well.

The sprouts are ready to eat in another three or four days. The jar is best left on the counter on its side to accommodate a greater number of seeds. I like this method the best because the sprouts are so much easier to harvest; you don't end up mindlessly pulling sprouts from behind cheesecloth threads. It's also nice to watch the sprouting happen.

## HANGING CARROTS

The inclusion of this next item is a testament to the fact that any gardener may loose his or her perspective at any moment and flip over the edge into obsessive plant hobbyism.

Choose an extralarge carrot and cut off the top. Working from the top, hollow out the center of the carrot so that you have a sizable bore, but leave the outer walls intact. Make two tiny holes in the walls so that you can thread a string through and hang the carrot. Fill the center cavity with water, hang the entire contraption in a sunny window, and make sure that you supply more water as it is needed. The center of the carrot must stay full of water. Beautiful, fanlike, finely cut foliage will emerge from all sides of the carrot until the vegetable itself is completely hidden.

As is usually the case with vegetable endeavors, the results are not permanent. After several weeks, the nourishment stored in the carrot will be depleted and the foliage will begin to go downhill. Nevertheless this is a silly and quick bit of fun; children love to hang them but, if you can't pawn off the motivation on young ones, try it anyway.

## FLOWERING EGGS AND RUTABAGAS

Another old-fashioned touch of spring and nonsense may be had by planting flower seeds in neatly halved eggshells. The traditional approach is to begin eight to ten weeks before Easter and have the results as your centerpiece at the table. If you choose this time of year, you might, of course, wish to dye the eggshells before you plant. Sow seeds of dwarf sweet alyssum or other miniature flowers in moist, sandy soil. Provide humidity and keep the soil evenly moist while the seeds sprout; then wait your eight weeks for the charming flowers.

Another version of this activity is to sow morning-glory seed in the scooped-out lower half of a turnip or rutabaga. When the seeds have sprouted, you hang your flowering vegetable in a sunny window by means of small macramé or string baskets. Keep the planting well watered and you certainly have a surprise for anyone who walks by.

# 4

# Alternatives to the Standard Pot

## Drainage Without a Hole

The essence of this chapter is nothing more than variations on a simple theme: drainage. If you understand that plants must not be forced to deal with accumulated or standing water, then you understand the whole thing. Excess water drives oxygen from soil and invites root rot. The risks are too great. If a pot does not have a drainage hole, you make one up; you provide some other way for unneeded water to drain away from the root system. With that requirement to the fore, you can devise any attractive planting you wish and be assured of its healthy success. Jardinieres or decorative sleeves, planters or dish gardens—all require the same conditions and care for good health discussed in regard to plants in standard clay or plastic pots. Everything else being equal, watering is the main variable. A bit of common sense is the key.

## Jardinieres and Decorative Sleeves

You may use just about anything to camouflage a standard pot. The classic Italian and French ceramic jardinieres are the favorites for a more formal appearance. Old pitchers, brass buckets, straw baskets, cracked teapots, or anything else of adequate size can also be perfect choices, according to your tastes. You may have the added advantage of floor or table protection if your outer container is waterproof. A good way to waterproof permeable sleeves such as straw baskets is to line the inside with strips of newspaper, muslin, or cheesecloth; use a paintbrush and clear shellac or liquid plastic to lay the strips in place and then add another coat on top. Having a waterproof outer container will also allow you to bypass the saucer under your plant.

If you do not choose to use the decorative container as a sleeve, but want to plant directly into it, it really becomes a planter or dish garden and this kind of planting will be dealt with anon. The more likely approach with a jardiniere is double potting, one inside the other. The simplest form of double potting is to put the planted clay or plastic pot inside the decorative one and be done with it. This works well if you can conveniently remove the plant for watering and are sure that it is drained thoroughly before you cart it back to its beautiful home. A clay pot is preferable to plastic when double potting because of its ability to absorb air and to leach out excess moisture through its sides. Poor air circulation and the possibility of accumulated excess water are the main threats of double potting; but if you are careful to loosen the topsoil regularly and permit thorough drainage after each watering the danger can be kept to a minimum.

It is sometimes difficult, however, to remove the inner pot each time you water. If you choose to water the plant where it sits, you will need a dry well. Put a thick, level layer of clean pebbles, vermiculite, perlite, or broken bits of pot in the bottom of the jardiniere. Extra water will drain into this space and thus be kept safely away from the roots. This water in the dry well will also be available for the roots to draw up whenever water is needed. Therefore, although your watering chores are lessened, you must be very careful and sparing with water; when the capacity of the dry well is exceeded, you will have a plant sitting with wet feet. Taboo.

If the height of the jardiniere far exceeds that of the planted pot, place some sort of block or support under the pot to bring it up to an attractive height. Check periodically to see that you don't have old mucky water down below and scrub out the jardiniere if necessary.

An excellent method for ensuring against overwatering is to use moss as a filler in the gap between pot and jardiniere. This is an essential safeguard for slow-growing plants: the less demanding the need of a plant for water, the greater the risk of rot when double potted. So you set up the same dry well, pop your plant into place—a clay pot only this time—and fill in the spaces with moist sphagnum or peat moss. From then on, whenever the topsoil of the plant is dry, you water the moss only. The plant's roots and soil will draw in the needed moisture via osmosis and only at the rate that the water is needed. This set-up is ideal for preserving good health in plants grown under dim light conditions. However, if at any time growth appears unreasonably slow, take the plant out of its pot and check the roots for signs of impending doom; the soil may need aeration and a chance for a thorough drying out.

# Dish Gardens or Planters

A dish-garden or planter arrangement implies that there is no drainage hole. Plants and soil are set directly into a decorative bowl or ceramic pot or found object that may serve as a container. An abandoned bathtub, the old coffeepot, a ceramic jardiniere, or a specifically intended planter dish all fill the bill. Occasionally, planter dishes come supplied with drainage holes; usually, however, they are not adequate for a guaranteed rot-proof job, so add more drainage material if you have any doubts.

Simply make a drainage layer at the bottom. Suitable materials for drainage remain the same: clean pebbles, perlite, or shards. The drainage layer should be one to three inches deep, depending on the general proportion of the planting. Then add a fine scattering of charcoal; the charcoal acts as a cleansing and filtering agent for water on its way to the dry well. Some gardeners like to put in a layer of peat moss before they add the soil. The peat enriches the soil mixture and its texture discourages fine soil particles from falling into the dry well. But the peat moss is optional and if, as often happens, the planter seems a bit shallow for the eventual size of the plants, you may omit it. Finally, a suitable soil is added for the plants intended and the actual planting is done.

Design is an important factor in a successful planter. Traditional and formal designs feature scenes to suggest a story, complete with figurines and a contoured landscape; informal schemes present the plants in a natural and simple relationship to each other. If you are combining several plants in an arrangement be certain that they all thrive in similar circumstances—soil, water, light, humidity—and that their future proportions are not incongruous. Obviously, cactus plants and ferns would be poor companions. A creeping fig would look ridiculously dwarfed next to a dieffenbachia; perhaps they would seem to go together as three-inch seedlings, but in another six months an entirely different proportion would occur. Use common sense, but don't be cowed by your inability to predict an absolute future. Choose one general group or another—tropical, temperate, or arid. Select plants that you think would do well together. If one doesn't, you can always replace it. And learn a little. The successful gardeners of my acquaintance share a basic attitude of "Okay, let's try it and see what works out." It's the seeing what works out that makes the project interesting.

Water extremely sparingly until you become acquainted with the planter's water needs. Wait until the topsoil feels dry to the touch and then add a small amount of water. If a dish garden is small enough you may ensure proper drainage by watering, waiting fifteen minutes, then picking it up, tipping it over in your hand, and letting any excess water run out. If the planter is too large for drainage by hand, give just enough water to prevent wilt until trial and error lets you know how much it can take.

# Window Boxes

Window boxes may be hung indoors or out. They either have no drainage holes and are treated as planters or they have provision for clear passage of water and you can pour with abandon . . . and due regard for your downstairs neighbors. Whatever the arrangement, there are few things more cheering to the spirit than a well-planted box at the window.

Hot sunny windows may accommodate a variety of cascading and upright succulents. A window with good sun may also boast a planting of colorful flowering annuals, coleus, or bloodleaf surrounded by Swedish ivy or boxwood or asparagus fern. A cool patio window box receiving average light might include small ferns, begonias, wandering Jew, ivies, or impatiens. Geraniums and petunias have long been a favorite choice for outdoor boxes. There is a special aspect of public generosity in planting colorful flowers for all to enjoy. The private sector holds other promises. A friend of mine built an indoor box across the enormously long, sun-drenched windows in her studio; she planted cherry tomatoes, lettuce, and scallions and had the makings for salad from April to September.

You begin to experiment and see what you like best. A window box may be arranged by planting directly into soil or by popping in the potted plants and using soil or filler around them. The primary advantage of the second tack is that you can easily rearrange or replace plants if necessary. It is preferable to use perlite or peat or sphagnum moss rather than soil as the filler between the pots since the weight of a planted window box is considerable; therefore, use plastic pots whenever possible. If you plant directly into the soil, the plants will need to be watered less frequently and the entire arrangement will be lighter in weight. You can also have more plants and a more natural spacing arrangement.

Do be sure that your window box is attached firmly before you begin all of this. Wet soil is heavy; it would be enormously disappointing as well as dangerous to have your finished planting land on the sidewalk.

If the window box has no drainage holes, begin with several inches of perlite to make a dry well. Pebbles would be unnecessarily heavy. Then add a sprinkling of charcoal, then soil to suit your plants—or the plants in plastic pots with moist moss as the filler in between. A light mulch of sheet moss or sphagnum moss or a ground-creeping plant is most beneficial for holding moisture in the box. When you have a window box equipped with good drainage outlets, just plant ahead. You may mix normal soil, half and half, with sphagnum moss for any box planting; this mixture will provide less weight and less nourishment, but you can make up for the latter with more frequent fertilizing.

An ideal window box may be easily constructed by the willing and able. Choose whatever dimensions work for your window; the box ought to be at least six to eight inches deep so that it can accommodate plants of good size. Instead of wood at the bottom, nail on only chicken wire, an old window screen, or hardware cloth. A light layer of sphagnum or sheet moss will serve to keep soil from washing out the bottom. Then add the soil and plant away. You have a lightweight, easy-to-care-for rig.

## Hanging Wire Baskets

Plants in hanging wire baskets lined with moss provide some of the most exciting visual effects in indoor gardening. It seems to me that the preplanted baskets are priced way beyond the expertise involved; it's a simple task to make your own.

Choose any cascading plant or vine, or plant a single basket with several varieties if they share common tastes for warmth, light, humidity, and water. Just remember that any hanging plant will require more water than a table sitter; the passage of air on all sides and under the root ball has a marked drying effect. When that hanging plant is in a wire basket, evaporation is even more pronounced. So you should have a strong aesthetic reason to house a specific plant in a basket as well as a great deal of time to water.

My favorite wire-basket planting is of the footed ferns—squirrel's-foot fern, bear's claw fern, or rabbit's-foot fern; their "feet" are furry, cinnamon-colored rhizomes that creep out of the basket and soon cover the bottom moss for a most unusual effect. Beautiful hanging arrangements are made with cacti and succulents using the small rosette types to pop out on the lower edges of the basket. Episcia or strawberry begonia would make good sense for a moss-filled basket because their stolons will root in the moss wherever they find it. Fuchsias surrounded by cascading lobelia present a stunning picture for a sheltered porch or under the eaves at the front door. Outdoor baskets may be filled with petunias, tuberous begonias, dwarf marigolds, sweet alyssum, or numerous other annuals. You may use shallow-rooted creeping vines for a professional finish at the basket's edge; choose Swedish ivy, pothos, creeping fig, vining types of peperomia, or grape ivy. Check the specific plant's range of growing conditions and begin to experiment and combine different ideas. Flowering baskets are exceptionally good looking and there are many plants that will flower indoors and are suitable for basket planting: flowering maple, lantana, star of Bethlehem, hoya, sweet alyssum, marigolds, begonias, columneas, fuchsias, oxalis, and monkey plant are among them.

Wire baskets are available from nurseries and garden-supply shops in a range of sizes and shapes. Florist's sheet moss is very handy for this kind of planting; if you can't find it, use sphagnum moss that has been soaked in water and wrung out by the handful. Line the inside of the wire basket with moss, making the layer no less than two inches thick. It will pack down considerably so make it thicker if you like. If you doubt that the moss pack is dense enough to keep soil from dribbling through, put in a piece of sheet plastic or aluminum foil or coarse muslin. You punch tiny holes in the aluminum foil or plastic to permit the water to drain through and lay this down on top of the moss. I have always preferred to add enough tight moss to hold the soil in place, but it's your basket. Then add a layer of moist soil appropriate to the plants you will use, place the plants for best aesthetic appearance, fill in with soil, water lightly to settle the planting, spread some more moss on top, and you're through. The footed ferns and outdoor annuals will require a rich, loose soil of added humus, moss, or leaf mold; succulents will need extra sand or tiny gravel. You can check on these specifics as you choose your plants.

As with a window box, it is possible simply to place potted plants in a moss-filled basket and then fill in around them with soil or sphagnum. Your basket would then be heavier by the weight of the pot, but it is an admirable technique if you are feeling cautious. Weight is a prime consideration when hanging the basket, so use stout hooks and thump around in your ceiling to find a lath board if you can. I have not yet had a hanging planter or basket that defies the strength of a sturdy screw hook into wood or a butterfly bolt or toggle bolt into plaster. If you are renting you can always make use of a can of spackle when you move.

Water a hanging basket by submerging it for a thorough soaking in the sink, a bucket, or giant pot. Spray the leaves and make sure that the moss is wet all around. Drain the basket well enough to save your floors and take it back to its hook. There are saucers available to attach to the baskets, but I feel they spoil the whole look of that great clump of eye-level moss. If you drain the basket well, a saucer or folded bath towel on the floor will be sufficient to catch last minute drips. An outdoor basket may certainly be watered in place if you are sure to soak it completely and clean the foliage with a strong water spray.

Basket plantings benefit from more frequent fertilizing than do sitting potted plants. Generally the plants chosen are flowering or fast-growing annuals and their planting contains more moss than nutritive soil. Fertilize once a month during their active growing season. It is further essential that you pinch and cut back with vengeance if you want a compact, thick, well-rooted showing. The more you pinch creepers the more vigorously they will seek new possibilities in the moss. If you shear off petunias after the first burst of flowering, they will come back with a late-season blooming. You may find it necessary from time to time to stuff more moss in from the bottom. You can also add small new plants at the sides by poking through the moss and setting them in. I prefer planting schemes that allow the arrangement to develop and progress. The more crowded the planting at first, the shorter its attractive life span will be. Be conservative; your plants will grow and you can always add more later.

# Planks

A plant has to be shallow-rooted to make do with life on a wood plank. A most popular and dramatic plank arrangement is of a multitude of cacti and succulent plants. The staghorn fern also does stupendously well. Staghorns are expensive plants; they grow slowly and any impressively large plant that you see has been nurtured in a greenhouse for years. But they are not difficult to maintain in good health.

Go to the public library and consult the phone books of nearby, less densely, populated counties. You may very likely find a private greenhouse specializing in ferns (or succulents, or whatever); a leisurely Sunday drive may bring you home with a carful of unusual ferns at a fraction of the city price. I make an annual pilgrimage to a fern lady in St. Helena, Napa County; she offers staghorn ferns on planks that are priced around eight dollars and would demand twenty-five at a city shop. If you buy young plants in four-inch pots you may plank your own.

*A well-established staghorn fern on a plank planting.*

## STAGHORN FERN

Begin with a piece of wood at least one inch thick and a foot square, the larger the better if your ambitions are soaring. It is most helpful if you add a lip on the bottom, attaching a piece of wood at right angles that is as long as your plank, about one inch thick and two to three inches wide. Make some provision for hanging the finished product; bore a hole through the plank since it will often be water-soaked and a screwhook could easily pull loose. Put the plank flat on its back and begin loading it with moist sphagnum moss. Pack the moss down firmly so that it is dense and spongy. You should have two to three inches of moss at the bottom and sides and about an inch in the middle. Some growers prefer to lay in osmunda fiber at the center to accommodate the roots, but the staghorn naturally grows tucked into an irregular crevice of a tropical tree and the roots will soon move through the moss layer and grip firmly into the wood. I know of one staghorn that dropped off from its aged, rotting plank, and an inch of wood came down with the roots.

After the moss is settled into place, cover the entire front of the plank with chicken wire and bring the wire around to the back. Secure it there with heavy metal staples or bent nails at the side and bottom edges. The top is left open for adding new moss and for better aeration of the roots. The base frond of the staghorn will clamp down everywhere but at the top; in the tropical forest gravity would thus supply it with dripping moisture and falling decayed matter to sustain growth.

Insert the small plants through the holes of the chicken wire. Cut a few wires if necessary and bend them back so that sharp edges do not injure the base of the plant. Generally you want only one fern to a plank, but if your dimensions are grandiose you may opt for more. Leave each staghorn with plenty of room to grow as it moves out from the center. Each spring a new base frond develops and anchors in place over the smaller one of last year. It is green in the spring and brown by winter. You may count the base fronds and know the age of your beast. A twenty-year-old staghorn can measure two feet across.

When the fern is in place, you are basically finished. You can pull out small bits of moss to camouflage the chicken wire or add more tucked in from the front. Give the planting a thorough soaking and opportunity to drain and keep it somewhere out of the way and on its back until the roots have taken hold. This will take a week or more and then the plank can be hung. It requires moderate-to-good indirect light, and should be misted or otherwise provided with added humidity. Water the planting whenever the moss begins to dry; this epiphytic plant does not need to be constantly moist. Any ragged fronds should be cut off at their base. Even if you fail enormously and need to shear off the foliage, the fern will recover its good looks if the rooted base is still healthy.

If you want to avoid chicken wire and perhaps plant on something more charming than a slab of lumberyard wood, proceed to experiment. You might use a large, interesting piece of driftwood or a chunk of barn siding. You can use clear fishing line or even thread to secure the fern; the moss is only necessary as an assist in watering and humidifying chores. If you have enough time to devote to your bizarre beauty, skip the moss, hold the fern in place by other means until it is well rooted and then cut away the lines. The fern will hold itself.

*SUCCULENTS*

Follow a procedure similar to the above for planting succulents. First, set up the plank with a bottom lip and a thick moss layer at the bottom and sides. Then the planting area is filled with a moistened soil mixture; for those plants which retain their own water, sand and tiny bits of gravel or broken clay pot should predominate in the soil. Attach the chicken wire, insert the plants, and pull out extra moss for an attractive finished look. Small rosette succulents such as echeverias and semper-vivums make an exceedingly attractive center. Trailing and creeping sedums may be inserted toward the top of the planting. Remember to allow room for future growth as the plants will spread, multiply, and creep for the finished look. Be sure that any cut chicken wire is bent back carefully to prevent bruising plant tissue. A damaged fleshy wet leaf will invite rot.

*Do not water* the finished planting. Leave it on its back for the roots to take hold and do not add water until the soil mixture feels hard, gritty, and thoroughly dry. This may take from four to eight days. Then water the plank, drain it well, and leave it on its back until the plants are firmly rooted, another week or more. Hang the planting on a wall where it will receive excellent light; you only need to avoid the burning intense sunlight in summer. Water only when the soil mixture is thoroughly dry.

*A plank newly planted with succulents.*

## WATERING, FERTILIZING, ETC.

You may water a plank planting at its wall if drips are no problem. Misting a stag-horn in place is of course tremendously convenient. I know of one immense beauty who lives above a bathtub. A staghorn near the kitchen sink would also make for easy watering. At any rate, you may water a plank in its upright position, or, if you take it down and water it on its back, then be sure to prop it up for a thorough draining. But when you are fertilizing, you must lay the plank down and drain it as much as pos-sible in the same way. The point here is to avoid a collection of fertilizer salts in the moss or soil near the bottom.

The extent of your plank endeavors is limited only by time, imagination, and bravado. I know a crazy marvel of a gardener who used old wooden doors for a plank-style arrangement of rosette succulents. They hang on the outside walls of her house just by the back door. Delivery men wind their way through the wild English garden and stand speechless on the porch; one doesn't usually come upon a wall of living plants. Then in a plant shop one day I saw an incredible planting that I've yet to try. It was going for two hundred dollars, but I think it could be reproduced for thirty-five dollars' worth of materials. It was a five-by-six-foot plank, terraced with pieces of wood at right angles in different spots. A rich soil and moss covering and then the entire thirty square feet was planted as a miniature cascading woodland: small ferns, baby tears, creeping fig, miniature begonias, wild grasses, selaginella. It was absolutely stupendous.

# Terrariums/Terraria/Gardens in Glass

Dr. Nathaniel B. Ward is the fellow generally credited with starting us all on the terrarium craze. The inventor of the "Wardian Case," this English botanist of the early nineteenth century found he could have success with tropical specimens if he enclosed them in glass. This act of enclosing the environment provides a greenhouse effect. Water evaporates from the soil and saturates the terrarium's atmosphere with lush humidity; eventually water droplets condense on the sides of the glass, roll back down to the soil, and bring fresh mositure to the roots. Older leaves that drop and decay return their nitrogen to the soil to nourish new growth. And carbon dioxide and oxygen fulfill their own cycle as the paired by-products of respiration and photosynthesis. Indeed, plants so enclosed will flourish for years without interference from a human hand.

Any clear glass or plastic container makes a fine terrarium. The only element you cannot contain is the sunlight, so the walls of the terrarium must be transparent. An admirable arrangement for dim-light locations is a planted five-gallon water jar, corked and equipped with a light-bulb fixture pushed into the cork. With the addition of a lampshade, you will have a new lamp and a terrarium assisted by the artificial light. Or, large terrariums can occupy a retired aquarium. Smaller ones can be planted in plastic canisters, glass apothecary bottles, or cookie jars. Terrariums make most appreciated presents for overly busy and generally plant-killing friends.

To my mind a brandy snifter or otherwise open vessel is not a true terrarium. It is a planter with the added advantage of increased humidity to the degree that its sides almost reach up and close. I find the real fun to be in watching the development of the closed environment. The higher the walls of the open case, bottle, or jar the higher the humidity will be, and accordingly it will benefit your moisture-loving plants. As you can see, a terrarium is not much different in theory from a propagating case. The high humidity encourages lavish plant growth.

Most containers you will choose will not have drainage holes. If yours does, follow the same directions, but bear in mind that while you will not need such elaborate precautions for internal drainage you will need something to protect the table top. It is only fair to advise that planting a terrarium in a narrow-necked bottle is a lengthy process and you might prefer to lavish your first efforts on a jar that permits entry of at least one hand.

If you are using a narrow-necked bottle you will be planting by remote control and will need three primitive tools. A digging or scooping tool can be a narrow piece of lath board or a small spoon attached to the end of a stick; indeed, you can bend a wire coat hanger so that it offers one clumpy spoonlike end. You will also need long-handled tongs or a grasping tool for holding the plants and setting them into place. Many plant stores sell a mechanic's grasping tool initially intended to lift dropped bolts out of the bottoms of engines. I have found the prongs much too sharp (but you can wrap them with heavy tape) and the spring mechanism too strong; the risk of injuring the plants must be weighed against the appeal to convenience. You can find bamboo tongs in many Japanese stores. Or you can make a pretty good pair with two long, flat sticks held apart at one end with a large pebble and then wrapped with tape or string. Or you can simply drop the plants down in the hole and shove them into place with your pushing tool. You will benefit from the use of a funnel for adding the drainage material and soil, but a rolled cone of aluminum foil or newspaper easily fills the bill.

The first order of business is to choose your plants and decide upon an arrangement. You can be as informal or formal as suits your fancy. There are those who favor built-up or terraced miniature landscapes complete with ceramic wishing wells and statues of deer and birds. Others prefer a loose design, simply placing a few plants in a pleasing relationship to each other, perhaps adding a stone or sea shell or bit of moss-covered bark. Just be sure that everything that goes into the terrarium is as clean as possible and preferably sterilized. If bacteria or fungus growths are introduced they, too, will thrive in the enclosed environment.

Choose plants that will all flourish under the same conditions. A tropical group for warmth, high humidity, and good light might include any of the following: croton, prayer plant, nerve plant, small ferns, dracaena, palms, Chinese evergreen, begonias, wandering Jew, selaginella, peperomia, pileas, African violet, or sinningia. A terrarium for a cool spot would do well with camellias, strawberry begonias, ferns, ivy, boxwood, creeping fig, daphne, or winter creeper. Be assured that you can always replace a plant that is obviously failing. One of the most exciting possibilities of a terrarium is that you can grow the plants which require high humidity and would otherwise perish in your home. Maidenhair ferns, exotic begonias, and delicate sinningia suddenly come to the fore. You might also consider preparing a terrarium and dropping in a few African-violet seeds; pull out the weaker seedlings and eventually leave one massive, omniblooming, spectacular plant.

## PLANTING PROCEDURE

Here is the planting procedure. Begin with a perfectly clean container. It is important that you use lots of hot water and soap and possibly a dilute chlorine-bleach solution to destroy any fungus organisms in a found object. Rinse the container several times and let it dry exposed to the air. That's the night before.

Then: (1) Add clean pebbles, gravel, or shards for a layer of drainage. This dry well ensures against overwatering and will guard against root rot, the most common form of terrarium disaster. The smaller the pebbles, the easier they will be to get through a narrow opening. The drainage layer should be from one to three inches deep, depending on the general proportion of the container. You may have an outer ring of sphagnum or sheet moss against the glass if the sight of pebbles disturbs your notion of finished charm. (2) Scatter a thin layer of charcoal on top of the pebbles. Charcoal acts as a filtering agent and will keep any water in the dry well fresh. A quarter- to a half-cup of charcoal is ample. (3) Then add moist potting soil. The regular packaged sandy soil is just fine although you might wish to mix it with extra humus or leaf mold if you've chosen mostly ferns or flowering tropicals. It is essential that the soil be sterilized. Landscape the environment as you wish—build up the soil at one side, form gentle hills, terrace it, or leave it flat. Thump the bottle down on the table a few times to settle the soil. (4) Next the plants go into place. If you are using your own rooted cuttings, they just come out of the water glass and slide down the hole. If you are using store-bought plants in two- to four-inch pots, turn them out of their pots and rub off any loose extra soil. Check to see that the roots are healthy and the soil is free from bugs or evidence of fungus growth. (I only mention this latter dire possibility because it seems that since the house-plant boom has hit you are able to buy plants from many sources more interested in their cash-register receipts than their reputation.) Dig a hole in the soil, insert the plant, get it into place, and bring the soil up to cover the roots. Press down all around to make firm contact and continue until all the plants are in place. (5) Finally take a bulb sprayer or other extremely gentle water source and wash off any soil splashed about. Using a gentle mist, clean the side walls of the terrarium and the leaves of the plants and give a few shots at the soil surface to settle it slightly. Beware never to add more water than the drainage well can hold. If you have been a very tidy planter, so much the better. The soil was moist when you began; this watering is only for clean-up and to settle the topsoil in good contact with the plants. Any plants that are slightly off kilter will right themselves to the light of the sun; they know which way is up. Any damage or asymmetry will quickly heal or correct itself in the encouraging and humid terrarium environment. So quit early. (6) Cork or cover the terrarium. Take it to a dim-light resting location for the next day or two. During this first period watch it carefully. You want to see evidence of humidity in the jar. But if the glass gets so foggy that you cannot see the plants, there is too much water inside. Take off the top and let it air out for a few hours or overnight or longer until evaporation can counterbalance your zeal. Then cover it again and watch once more. After the first day you place the terrarium in its permanent location; it should have a home that offers average or good indirect light, but no direct sun. The leaves will often have tiny droplets of water around or on them and the sunlight will burn. The heat of the sun will also encourage unwanted mold and rotting in the jar.

The essential rules of terrarium care are simple, and you should convey them to any friend along with your terrarium present. Particularly for the first several weeks, but true forever, you must guard the water balance in this contained ecosystem. Tiny droplets of condensed water and other evidence of misty heightened humidity indicate that things are functioning as they should. But, if at any time, the internal atmosphere is so humid that the glass is foggy and you can't see the plants, you must open the top and let the terrarium dry out a bit. It may take several openings and closings before you have an established water balance. From then on add water only when the humidity level falls way down and the topsoil begins to dry; it will be lighter in color and less dense in texture. It is a cautious hit-or-miss affair until a terrarium sets its own pattern. The one we had planted as a lamp went unopened and untouched for five years. Finally the ivy had taken over to such an extent that I decided to dump it all and "renew" the glass bottle. An uncorked, narrow-necked bottle might need a light mist of water every two-to-four weeks. A brandy snifter or otherwise-open container should be treated like a planter and would probably need a light water spray as often as once a week.

Turn the terrarium regularly to maintain even growth in relation to its light source; that is, if you want even growth. Remove any large dead leaves or dying plants should any such demise occur. Remember that you can always reenter the ecosystem to prune, remove, or replace plants. If everything is going well, I like to leave single fading leaves alone; you can watch their fossillike decay and finally have a silvery outline pressed to the glass. But each terrarium is made to suit its keeper; weed out, add, or subtract, however you choose.

# 5

# Doctoring

## The General Idea

Any plant that is looking less than lovely is due for a careful inspection. Consider light, water, humidity, and pot problems; a yellowing or loss of green color in the leaves means *something* is happening to this plant that is unfavorable to peak chlorophyll production and food manufacture. Ponder a few variables: has the plant recently been exposed to an unseasonable cold spell? to drafts? does it need fertilizer or a new pot? has it been fertilized too often or with a solution that was too strong? are you watering in response to the plant's need for water? is it getting enough light and the right humidity? It seems that most plants are far more subject to insect invaders when the humidity is low. If you cannot determine a cause for the plant's poor health related to its growing conditions, turn the plant out of its pot and examine the health situation of the roots. Hard-packed soil or uneven clumps may have impaired the drainage. Check for early signs of root rot. Then return the plant to its pot and carefully examine the undersides of the leaves for minute insect invaders.

### AN OUNCE OF PREVENTION

A well-cared-for plant collection holds little truck with bugs and disease. It would be unfair to say that you will never have to deal with an invasion of mealybugs or an attack of scale. But if you are prepared to meet the invaders head-on, as well as to sustain your plants in general fine health, the bouts with the enemy will be infrequent and short-lived.

## PREVENTIVE MEDICINE

The prime prevention activity is a forceful water spraying of the foliage each time you water a plant. This spray washes off dust and other bug camouflages, insects too small to be seen *yet*, and keeps the plant's pores free to absorb oxygen necessary for normal good health. If you cannot spray a plant, dust it occasionally with a dry, soft, watercolor brush (for fuzzy-leaved plants or cacti) or wash the leaves with a damp, soft cloth (for heavy plants in the middle of a white rug). When spraying, cleaning leaves, or inspecting for foreign creatures, pay particular attention to the undersides of the leaves and the tiny crevices at stem junctures. The little fellows will congregate there first; they collect on the underside of stems and main veins to suck the plant juices and multiply in privacy.

If you thus keep the leaves clean and quickly inspect for any difficulties at every watering, your plant collection is assured of a continuing top-grade bill of good health. Subject any new plant to intense scrutiny and, if necessary, isolate it before you let its leaves touch other plants. Give heed to the general rules of good care for your plants: use sterilized soil, keep the pots clean, remove any dying leaves from the plant or soil surface, aerate the topsoil to keep it loose and friable, and maintain proper growing conditions for each species.

## IMMEDIATE TREATMENT

On-the-spot attention is the cardinal rule for dealing with a plant caught with bugs or disease. *Isolate the plant immediately.* Hand pick the visible bugs or promptly dislodge them with a firm spray of water. The insects that bother house plants multiply and spread with alarming ease. These fellows at the lower end of the phylogenetic scale work quickly; wait three days and the great-grandchildren have just been hatched. Take the plant to a recovery room where it will have absolutely no contact with the rest of your collection. Wash your hands before you touch other plants and carefully inspect any plants that were near the fellow who just took sick. Do *not* wait to see what develops.

If from the descriptions that follow you cannot determine which bug you now confront, ask someone: call up a local nursery or pop an infected leaf into a plastic bag and take it to someone who can identify the problem. Decide upon your plan of attack.

## THE PLAN OF ATTACK

Here are some things to consider. All treatments, poisonous or nonpoisonous, must be repeated three or four times. You treat an ailing plant right away and then two or three more times at weekly intervals. The final treatment is given after you can see no new bugs, but you want to be doubly sure to knock off the invisible babies. I will describe both organic treatments and poisons. I have had success for years resorting but once to poison, and unless a stricken plant is of irreplaceable value in your collection and the infestation is severe, I would say that poison is an unfortunate choice. But you nevertheless have three choices and you should formulate your plan on the basis of the value of the plant, the time you have available, and how willing you are to use a poison.

The three choices are to throw out the plant and possibly take clean cuttings, to use a nonpoisonous treatment, or to walk out the door and buy a poison. The organic methods are more time consuming. Most pests lodge in tiny crevices and you must get into each one to do a worthwhile job. You must repeat treatments at regular intervals; if you treat the plant now, again next week, and then get too busy and forget for a fortnight, you may have only slowed down the attack and the bugs will reappear full force a month later. The plant, however, will be in a weaker condition than it was when you began; perhaps you should take strong healthy cuttings now and toss out the rest (pot, soil, and all). Certainly, if I had a leggy coleus that was suddenly invaded by mealybugs, a trash-can destination would be my first thought; a few cuttings can be treated quite quickly.

This is one of the luxuries of a small collection. A store owner or a greenhouse supplier may not be able to afford such decisions. But at home you can choose the path of greatest convenience or emotional appeal. The use of nonpoisonous methods is possible and in fact preferable when your home includes small children or pets or when outdoor spraying is impossible or if your own physical sensitivity or ecological distaste for poisons is high.

Bugs will come to everyone. The insects that bother house plants are small enough to be carried in with the wind, on your clothes, unseen on new plants. I met a fellow who cared for the plants on the thirtieth-floor patio of the Bank of America building in downtown San Francisco; one day he had put in new bedding begonias and a week later he returned to find them swarming with mealybugs. It happens. It is encouraging to know that calamities on this scale are so rare that this experienced gardener was complaining about his to everyone he met. But it does happen and you must know what to do.


*POISONS*

If you are using a poison, do so with great care. Follow the directions on the label to the letter. Never make a stronger solution than is indicated or the plant may succumb along with the bugs. Do not store diluted poison. Keep any container used to hold poison well out of reach of children or pets; lock it up; a neighbor's dog or a visiting child might find it in the most unlikely place. When I proudly announced to our family doctor that one-year-old Jessie had begun to climb, his experienced reply was, "Of course, how else will she find out what's in the cupboard above the refrigerator." If a child swallows poison, the outcome can be fatal. Protect yourself as well, particularly if you are sensitive to irritants; wear gloves, glasses, and a face mask or washcloth over your mouth and nose. Wash thoroughly afterward. Do any spraying in a well-ventilated room; if you are using the bathtub, scrub it thoroughly when you have finished. If you have an outdoor area to use, be sure that you do not spray into the wind.

Discuss the possible poisons and the specific problems involved with a nursery-man or trusted shop owner. There are poisons you can spray, others to dip the plants into, and some to add to the water for systemic treatment. There are also poison sprays specifically diluted for plants with a particularly porous leaf surface. I once killed a four-foot-high coleus planting by applying malathion to abate a mealybug invasion. I learned two things from this experience. One is that there is a preparation called Tender-Leaf for coleus and other open-pored plants. And, two, that malathion makes me quite sick to my stomach. I lost that round completely.

Water and drain a plant well before you treat it, particularly with a poison. It is also better to choose a cool day or cooler part of the day to spray, when the plant's pores will not be opened to the fullest. But, if the days are particularly hot, begin treatment rather than wait for the weather report; the insect-multiplication problem increases with the heat as well.

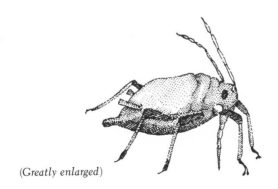

*(Greatly enlarged)*

## The Big Four

*APHIDS*

Every plant lover will eventually encounter one of the four major pests: aphids, mealybugs, red spider mites, or scale. Aphids are perhaps better known for their love of outdoor roses, but they hit the indoor garden too. There are hundreds of varieties of aphids: they may be green, pink, red, or black; their bodies are soft and either round or pear shaped; they have long legs and antennae; they may be winged or wingless. Despite your inability to identify your own home-grown variety, you will notice them as a giant energy buzz, particularly clustered on new growth. Any plant is subject to an aphid invasion; they play no favorites as some other bugs do.

Aphids suck the plant juices. Their other destructive act is to secrete a substance known in the trade as "honeydew"; honeydew secretions attract ants and encourage the growth of a black sootlike mold. Plants infested with aphids may appear stunted; their leaves may be curled or distorted; their healthy green color begins to yellow or fade.

These symptoms are similar to those you will notice on any plant under attack, from aphids or other pests. Since most insects that bother house plants are sucking parasites, the invaded plants will manifest the fact that they are losing their nutritive sap. It is also important to point out that you will have bigger trouble if you have not noticed the pest before the symptoms. Any house plant lost to bugs could probably have been saved if the trouble was noticed when there was only a small colony. If you wash foliage and give your plants a visual once-over on a regular basis, you will take care of any invaders before they can multiply and weaken the plant to the "infestation" stage.

So what do you do? Here are the treatments for aphids in their upwardly lethal progression: (1) Use repeated forceful water spray to dislodge the insects and send them down the drain. If convenient, you can turn the plant upside down and dip it in a tub or sink full of water to drown the little fellows. Then continue spraying at regular intervals. (2) Use a soapy water solution as a dip or spray. Do not use detergent on plants, only soap. It has long been a custom in rural communities to walk out the back door after you've done the dishes and throw the soapy water on the rose bushes. It works. Whenever you use soap or any other agent that will block the plant's pores, wash it off with clear water several hours later. Repeat as each new crop of aphids emerges, at least weekly, and then a few times after the most stubborn individuals have disappeared. (3) Make a spray of garlic and onions in the blender. Chop and blend two or three onions and several large cloves of garlic with water. Dilute the result with more water to a passably strong brew and spray your plants. There are many insects repelled by members of the onion family and much success has been found in the outdoor garden with use of such natural repellants. One example of companionate planting used victoriously outdoors is to plant clumps of chives in between the roses. Indoors you might just move your chive plant over next to the victim of the aphids and see what results you get. That, plus forceful spraying, might just do the job against a limited attack. (4) Poison: malathion or pyrethrum preparations will eradicate a severe infestation. These poisons may be used as sprays although, if feasible for the plant, a dip method is preferred. Aphids love the minute crevices and folds of new leaves; a dip is more assured of reaching the sly ones.

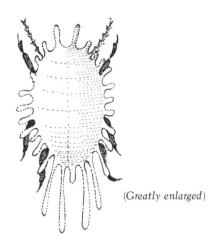

*(Greatly enlarged)*

## MEALYBUGS

Mealybugs are easily visible, like little specks of white cotton candy. These soft-bodied, oval, pinkish insects are covered with a powdery white fuzz. You will often find larger clusters of white fuzz at the leaf axils; these are the mealybug egg cases. Mealybugs congregate along the undersides of leaves, particularly on the main veins, at the stem-and-leaf junctures. Then, given their rapid reproduction habits, favorite feeding spots become overpopulated and they move to the tops of the leaves and coat all stems.

Like aphids, mealybugs suck the plant juices. Their secretions, also called honeydew, attract ants and are favorable to the growth of sooty fungus. A severe infestation will cause undersized and stunted foliage on flowers. However, mealybugs are quickly apparent to the naked eye and you will probably have done something about them before the damage is severe.

These destructive fuzzy creatures have an overwhelming fondness for coleus, African violet, jade plant, cactus, piggyback, dieffenbachia, croton, and wax plant. If their first-choice dinner selection is not available, they will nevertheless not go hungry.

Here are the ways to attack. Isolate the plant, hand pick or spray the greatest collections and then: (**1**) You may simply pick off the bugs if they are few in number. A toothpick is helpful for this job. (**2**) Dip a cotton swab in rubbing alcohol (70 percent isopropyl alcohol) and touch the top of each bug. They will succumb. You may have a few skeletons remaining attached to the plant, but you can poke them the next day and find them to be hollow. The alcohol treatment will cure even a heavy attack if you can be diligent and see that no small crevice is overlooked. (**3**) Use equal parts rubbing alcohol and water as a spray. Pay heed to all leaf axils and minute hiding places. You may use this same mixture as a dip. Wash the plant with clear water after the treatment. Remember that all the above treatments must be repeated at weekly intervals until after no new adults appear. (**4**) Poison: malathion in standard or gentle dilutions is the universal choice. You may also treat a light attack by touching the insects with a cotton swab dipped in nicotine sulfate solution (Black Leaf 40).

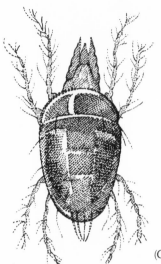

*(Greatly enlarged)*

## RED SPIDER MITES

This vicious, infinitesimal beast is a dark red, flat mite, invisible to the unpracticed naked eye and sometimes to the practiced. With a hand magnifying glass you can observe the mites scurrying about on the underside of the leaves. They gain the word *spider* via their habit of spinning a spiderlike web first enclosing the tip of a leaf; if left to their own devices, the mites will continue to spin until the entire plant is consumed under their web. The web is protection, under which they can work undisturbed. You will most often have your first suspicion of their presence when you notice a delicate bit of web and a mild decline in the general appearance of the plant. They are sneaky devils.

Leaves begin to lose color. The green appears mottled or flecked with grayish yellow dots. Leaves drop en masse. Growth may be stunted and leaf edges damaged. The proliferation of red spider mites is encouraged by hot dry air and poor circulation of the air. Dust left on leaves allows them places to hide and take hold. These fellows are the most dangerous of the common plant pests because they are well established before you have a hint that they are there.

There is one bit of preventive medicine that is essential in the control of red spider mites: a regular forceful spraying of the foliage with water. This is most effective since the plants the red spider seems to prefer are those with smooth, shiny leaves—plants most amenable to safe and frequent spraying. Ivy, fuchsia, piggyback, and asparagus fern are its chief victims. As mealybugs are to coleus so are red spider mites to ivy. Yet, if the humidity is high and the water-spray cleansing frequent, red spider mites find other dens.

If you do have them occupying a favored plant, attack diligently since they are difficult to destroy. Here are your options: (1) Repeated and forceful spraying of water will sometimes be sufficient to break the webs and send the mites down the drain. Pay particular attention to the undersides of the leaves and the stem tips and junctures. Spray the plant daily until you can find no more evidence of the occupation and then watch it carefully for the rest of its life. Any plant that once hosted a red-spider-mite convention must always be suspect and sprayed regularly. Increase the general humidity if you fear that was a contributing problem. (2) You can use a soapy water solution as a spray or preferably as a dip. Rinse the plant with clean water after a few hours and repeat the treatment at frequent intervals (every three days, then once a week for several sessions). (3) Poison: Kelthane, malathion, or other miticide is applied as a spray or dip. Be sure that the label indicates effectiveness against red spider mites and that your plant is not one specifically listed as an unsuitable candidate for the preparation you intend to buy. Even poisonous treatments must be repeated at weekly intervals for three or four applications.

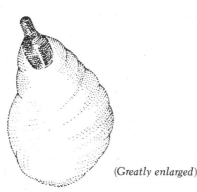

(*Greatly enlarged*)

## SCALE

Scale insects are related to mealybugs, but instead of white fuzzy stuff they carry a bit of armorlike scale on their backs. Underneath it all they are soft bodied. They may vary in color from white to black, although most you will see will be gray or brown. There are several species with a variety of culinary tastes, but they all suck the plant juices. They may attack the stems and/or the leaves; they secrete honeydew and therefore bring forth ants and sooty mold. Mature adults are the ones you will notice. They are round or oval and about as broad as an oversized pencil lead. When treating scale remember that the infants are the enemy. The tiniest immature and invisible scale insect attaches for life and begins to suck and grow at the expense of the plant. Repeated treatments and steady surveillance are therefore essential.

Foliage yellows promptly under attack from scale. If stems are affected, they may dry and split open. Leaves drop and the plant's growth is generally stunted.

More than anything in the world scale loves English ivy. The insects then show a fondness for palms, aralias, rubber plants, cacti, and ferns. Like red spider mites, scale prefers the smooth-leaved varieties although not to the exclusion of a tasty cactus or fine bumpy fern. Be careful that you do not confuse fern scale with fern spores. Ferns reproduce by tiny round or oval spores which appear on the undersides of the fronds. The defining characteristic is that spores will appear in symmetrical pattern along the midvein of the frond while scale insects choose their feeding sites at random.

As you might have suspected, the best preventive measure is regular spraying with plain water and keeping the leaves free from dust. Any treatment must break through the outer scale armor to kill the little fellow beneath. The best specialized tool for this endeavor is a soft-bristled toothbrush. (1) Wash the plant thoroughly with a soapy water solution. Use a toothbrush to scrub at the scale clusters, taking care not to damage the already weakened plant. Use elbow grease, but no vengeance. Rinse the plant with clear water after the treatment and repeat quite frequently. (2) Add a teaspoon of kerosene to a quart of soapy water. Apply this with a toothbrush and cover every bit of surface on the plant. For a large plant, you might scrub the larger scale collections and then dip the entire plant in a solution-filled bucket or sink. At any rate, rinse the plant well after the treatment and repeat at regular intervals. The big problem with using organic methods to combat scale is the time involved in application. You must scrub out every niche and crevice along the stems and under and on top of the leaves. A methodical and thorough treatment of a bushy ivy plant in a six-inch pot might take an hour or more. If you do not have the time to be painstaking, better take cuttings and treat them well. Misplaced partial efforts have most unsatisfying results. (3) Poison: Apply a properly diluted solution of malathion or Black Leaf 40 (nicotine sulfate) or Sevin insecticide. You will be most effective if you still apply it by hand, using a damp sponge for foliage and a toothbrush for crevices. Take care that you do not scar the plant by heavy scrubbing. Rinse the plant well after the treatment. Empty bits of armor may be left the next day; poke them with a toothpick or your thumbnail to see that the insect inside is dead. (4) Attacking fern scale is a special problem. It is too difficult to scrub all the crevices without permanently damaging the delicate fronds. If you catch the invasion early enough, you may be able to control it without poisons. Remove any mature scales; cut off all yellowed or weakened fronds at the soil level. Then wash the entire fern with a hard spray of water to dislodge the young. Repeat this washing every three or four days for several weeks and keep your eye out for any stowaway who dares to mature. I have had excellent results from this sensible although time-consuming approach.

You can use a systemic poison if it is safe for your particular fern. Or you can cut off all the damaged fronds, wash the plant thoroughly with plain water and then dip it into a suitable poison mixed to its weakest dilution. Even if you have had to shear off every bit of top growth, a healthy root mass will bring forth new fronds. Rinse the fern well after you have treated it with poison.

# Less Common or Less Threatening Pests and Diseases

## *THRIPS*

Thrips are little yellow, black, or brown scurrying insects. Their flat, thin bodies are pointed at either end; although they are barely visible to the naked eye you may easily notice their frantic rushing about. They suck the plant juices and leave tiny scar marks where they have rasped away at the plant tissue; they also leave behind the minute black dots of their excrement.

Thrips favor palms, ferns, fuchsia, aralia, begonias, dracaenas, orchids, crotons, or gloxinias. The leaves of an affected plant are silvery or bleached in appearance and often wilt or drop off. If you cannot find red spider mites, suspect thrips. The treatments are similar: (1) Repeated hard sprays of plain water. (2) A soapy water solution used as a forceful spray or as a dip. Be sure to rinse the plant well afterward and repeat the treatment regularly. (3) Poison: Kelthane is the one to use. Prepare it as a spray or dip, and rinse the foliage thoroughly when the operation is complete.

## *WHITEFLIES*

These tiny mothlike creatures are most obvious. They will fly up in soft clouds whenever the plant is touched or moved. The insects that so behave are the adults. However, when a plant is infested with whiteflies, the nymphs will be present as well. Their flat, oval bodies are less visible, ranging in color from white to pale green. Both nymphs and adults suck the nutrients from the plant sap and secrete honeydew which brings on other problems.

Whiteflies show a distinct taste for coleus, fuchsia, geraniums, begonias, ferns, flowering maple, and chrysanthemums. It has been my experience that they generally cluster around a plant weakened from other causes, often old age or lack of humidity. Severely infested plants will display yellowed or drooping leaves.

Treatment is difficult because the enemy can take flight whenever you approach. Water sprays at the sink are of little help as the flies will not follow you. Consequently, many invasions of whiteflies soon become severe; the gardener doesn't really know how to get rid of these tiny creatures and the affected plant soon worsens. Here are the possible plans of attack: (1) Throw out the plant. Do this at night or on a particularly gray day when the winged adults are more sluggish. This is an especially appropriate solution if the plant victim was in poor condition before the whiteflies arrived. Remove all neighboring plants and spray them with a firm stream of water. While they are away from their spots, dust the table or sill thoroughly and air out the room. A vacuum-cleaner hose does a fine job of picking up stragglers from the drapes and moldings. (2) Poison: Remove any damaged leaves and burn them;

then choose your poison. Malathion or the less toxic rotenone may be used as a spray or dip. I have also been told by a reliable nurseryman that good results can be achieved with a household bug spray formulated for general indoor use. Hold the aerosol can at least a foot away from the infested plant and aim the spray so that the mist will fall to the soil in a gentle arch. You should first check the can for its ingredients to be sure that plant spraying is not expressly forbidden.

## CYCLAMEN MITES

These invisibly small brutes are anathema to the African-violet fancier, capable of wiping out an entire collection. The mites are pale brown, oval creatures, difficult to view even under a microscope. But the damage they can do is enormous. They feed in the crevices of opening buds and new leaves. An affected plant will show the damage at its center, in the youngest growth.

The leaves will be pale in color, distorted, brittle, or wrinkled along their edge. Growth is stunted and the petioles may be shortened to the point that the leaf blade appears to come right from the soil. Cyclamen mites spread from one plant to another with nothing more than a whisper; wash your hands thoroughly after touching an affected or suspected plant.

Here are the treatments: (1) Throw out the plant. Take healthy leaves as cutings and dose them before they are rooted. Watch the new growth carefully to be sure that you have thoroughly eradicated the mite. (2) Cut out any affected center growth and then submerge the entire plant in hot water for fifteen minutes. The water temperature must be kept at 110 degrees Fahrenheit for the entire time. This treatment will kill the mites without harming the plant. (3) Poison: Cut out the infested center growth and spray the plant with a miticide effective against cyclamen mites. Growers with large collections of African violets often use sodium selenate diluted with water as a systemic preventive measure. They water with the miticide solution and the poison is absorbed through the root system and carried to all parts of the plant. Any foolish mite who chews on the poisonous tissue is quickly undone.

## SOIL MEALYBUGS

Soil mealybugs are slow-moving creatures that cluster on the roots of plants. They are gray; they resemble the foliage variety of mealybug; and, in addition to sucking the plant juices from the roots, they secrete masses of fibrous gunk into the soil thus impairing the drainage and inviting simple rot.

If a plant is failing and no cultural explanation can be found and no foreign creatures have appeared on the foliage, check the soil system. You may find subterranean mealybugs.

Here are the treatments: (1) Dump the plant, pot, soil, and saucer. Take cuttings with gay abandon because they have not been affected. (2) Remove the plant from its pot and wash away every bit of soil from the roots. Be sure to throw away the infested pot and saucer. Cut off any damaged or infested parts of the root system. Then repot the plant in sterilized fresh soil and in a well-scrubbed, dry pot. A plant treated in this way will need a week or two of extra care, higher humidity, and less demanding light—as would suit any plant subject to a severe root trim. After the roots have had a chance to repair themselves, the plant is on its own again. (3) Poison: Again, you unpot the plant and wash all soil away from the roots. You then dip the roots in a malathion solution before repotting. Send any infested pot or saucer to the garbage can and scrub the plant's former location before you trot it home.

## BLACK FLIES, FRUIT FLIES, GNATS

You may occasionally notice a crowd of tiny black flies hovering in the air as if scouting about for ripe bananas. These gnats or fruit flies are harmless to your plants. They live on the organic matter in the soil and don't suck sap. I have found that they exit of their own accord after you have eaten all the ripe bananas in the house or after you have a session with your plants that includes aeration of the topsoil, spraying the foliage with water, and general cleanup. If you are paranoid about them, the weakest possible dilution of malathion will leave them dead in their tracks.

## SPRINGTAILS

Springtails are similarly harmless, but less easily observed. They are tiny and white and jump about madly on the surface of the soil after a hard watering. You might also see them scurrying about in a saucer that has just been deluged with water. Like the gnats, they live on the organic matter contained in the soil and succumb promptly upon one shot of a weak malathion solution.

## ANTS

Ants may be found on the march to a potted plant, but they are camp followers rather than the true enemy. They are attracted to the honeydew secretions of aphids, scale, mealybugs, or whiteflies. Occasionally, however, the general health of the plant has nothing whatsoever to do with the ant problem: I have found half-eaten cookies tucked into the soil of large plants as well as more disturbing contributions from small feline creatures. Locate and deal with the source of the trouble and the ants will be washed off and further discouraged in the process.

### NIGHTFEEDERS: EARTHWORMS, CENTIPEDES, SOW BUGS OR PILL BUGS, SNAILS OR SLUGS

These creeping, crawling, night-feeding fellows present a minimal threat to the indoor garden. They are usually discovered as lone individuals who strayed into the pot in an open-lath house or at the sidewalk door of the plant shop. They can indeed do damage but their numbers are usually few. Centipedes are voracious feeders, earthworms impair the drainage in a closed pot, and slugs will eat their weight in young leaves.

Most of these pests become active and starving at night. I once walked into the kitchen at 3 A.M., snapped on the light, and found a centipede picnic taking place at the expense of a new potful of caladiums. In an attempt to survey the damage, I tugged on a stem; when it came off in my hand I realized that the centipedes had been intimate with the caladiums long before I. Yet usually the results are not so catastrophic. My husband and I were sitting having breakfast one day when a well-fed millipede popped up out of a large pteris fern for a breath of air. He crawled right up and out of the pot and found his eternal reward. I checked the plant's soil, found nothing, and the plant has been thriving ever since.

Here are some treatments: (1) Pick off the one or two bugs that you've seen; you have probably taken care of the whole problem. To be sure, place the plant in a completely dark closet or leave it in a dark room at night; wait several hours and then turn on the light to see if any new individuals have surfaced. (2) To be on the safe side, you might choose to wash off all soil from the roots and repot the plant in sterilized soil. Throw out the old soil and give the pot a good scrub. (3) Submerge the entire pot and root system in very hot water for fifteen minutes or more. This is an admirable technique for eliminating a variety of soft-bodied intruders. The plant can take temperatures far higher than can the bugs. After finding tiny holes and then sow bugs in the base frond of my staghorn fern, I was enraged enough even to contemplate a poison; but a thorough soaking in hot water took care of the whole problem. Earthworms, centipedes, and sow, potato, or pill bugs will also find an unpleasant destiny if you soak the entire plant (foliage excluded) in a lime water solution; then soak the root ball in several successive plain water baths to remove the lime and restore the acid balance of the soil. (4) Poison: If handpicking of snails or slugs doesn't work, you may have to throw out the plants or resort to a commercial snail bait (metaldehyde preparation). Worms, centipedes, or little soil bugs are eradicated by soaking the plant in a chlordane solution.

### FUNGUS DISEASE AND LEAF SPOT

When you have a plant that displays irregular brown or black spots on its leaves, you usually begin to contemplate causes. It is reasonable to attribute perfectly round leaf spots to the sun shining through water droplets left on the leaves. Irregular leaf spots are sometimes caused by sunlight magnified by an imperfection in the window glass. They may also have been caused by excessively cold water chilling the roots, by drafts, or by very hot or cold water splashing on the leaves. In all of these cases, the spots are limited to the current physical damage and you can root successful cuttings from unaffected tips. However, in some cases fungus diseases may be the culprits. Fungus growths manifest themselves in leaf spots, mildew, powdery mold on the leaves and stems, or peculiar rotting areas about the plant.

Diagnosis is indeed the most difficult part of the treatment. Fungus diseases will respond to fungicides. Limited problems of any nature may respond to removing diseased leaves to prevent spreading of the blight. In any case, with proper general care fungus diseases are rare indeed.

Here are some of the preventive measures and useful treatments: (1) Observe these cautions both to prevent fungus invasion and to clear up any mild disease: Pick off and burn any rotting or infected leaves. Keep the soil well aerated through proper potting and regular sessions with a fork. Do not crowd plants or allow moist leaves to touch each other. See that the growing area has good circulation of fresh air and keep pots and saucers scrubbed clean. If a mild fungus disease is present, it may disappear with the simple treatment of *under*watering the plant for a few weeks or more. You can use a mild chlorine-bleach solution to disinfect any pots or saucers that you fear might harbor fungus organisms. (2) Throw out the plant. Although it sounds drastic and harsh, this is a supremely sensible approach for the rare instances when disease strikes. Better to witness one untimely demise than to risk spreading the disease to other plants. (3) Poison: If the problem is in fact a fungus disease, application of a fungicide by the name of Bordeaux mixture will be the remedy. If what your plant has is not a fungus, but a bacterial or viral disease, there is no remedy on the market. If the disease does not respond to Bordeaux mixture and is spreading, throw out the plant (pot, soil, and all).

# 6

# Bulbs for Winter & Spring (& Then a Few for Summer)

A bulbous plant is one which grows from and dies back to a bulb—an underground stem overlaid by fleshy, scalelike, food-storing leaves; the bulb is basically a dormant, concentrated source of energy, next year's bud.

## Forcing Spring-Flowering Bulbs

There need be no great mystery about "forcing bulbs." Nor are there any specific instruments of force required. Forcing bulbs merely means that you take bulbous plants that would normally bloom in spring and dupe them into performing a few weeks or even months earlier to pop some pizazz into the middle of a dull winter. This duping is done by providing indoor warmth and ample water a bit earlier than nature intended.

Spring-flowering bulbs are classified into tender or hardy types. The hardiness refers to winter fortitude. In other words, the hardy bulbs have adapted to and depend upon cold winter temperatures for proper spring growth; they can withstand freezing while the tender bulbs cannot. If you can provide hardy bulbs with the cold conditions they require in autumn and early winter for the proper development of vigorous roots, you may bring them indoors and trick them into an unnaturally early springtime growth. So the hardy bulbs are the ones most suitable for forcing.

# Hardy Spring-Flowering Bulbs

These include daffodil and other narcissus, tulip, hyacinth, crocus, grape hyacinth, scilla, and several less common, but lovely others. Dormant bulbs are offered for sale in September and October. They may be planted anytime until December, but best results seem to come from October and early-November plantings. Buy the best quality bulbs available from a reputable source. Choose "Jumbo," "Top-line," "Grade A," or whatever other superlative indicates a superior beginning. Each bulb already contains all of next year's flower buds; nothing that you will do can affect the number of flowers, only that they reach their full quality and size. It is always best to begin with unhampered potential. Choose firm, plump, unbruised bulbs without any sign of darkened, spongy, or moist areas; you probably are most experienced with bulb shopping in regard to onions, so apply similar criteria. The bulbs are thrown out each year when the burst of flowering has ended or they may be planted outdoors in a perennial border; there they will bloom the next season or surely in two, but they will never again be useful for forcing. Even so, bulbs are a relatively inexpensive source of indoor winter delight.

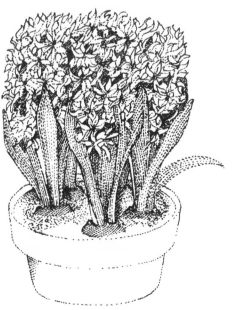

*PLANTING*

(1) *Pots:* Use an ordinary clay pot or the shallower fern pot or a squat bulb pan. Adapt the pot to the bulb in mind, using the deep standard size for taller plants, such as tulips or daffodils. You may plant several bulbs to a pot for a fuller look. For instance: *a six-inch standard pot* could accommodate three daffodils or five to six tulips; *a four- or five-inch standard pot* would do well with two daffodils, two to three tulips, one hyacinth, or four to eight of the smaller bulbs (crocus, scilla, miniature daffodil, or grape hyacinth); *a six-inch fern or three-quarter pot* would accommodate three hyacinths, three to four daffodils, four to six tulips, or from four to twelve small bulbs; *a six- or eight-inch bulb pan* could be planted with four to twelve small bulbs with no jeopardy to their development. A general rule for planning is to allow one-half to one inch between each bulb.

You may also try a *double-decker planting* that is wonderful for double-nose daffodils or tulips. Prepare a standard pot with drainage material and about a third of a potful of soil, put in three bulbs, bring up the soil level, and put in four more bulbs. Stagger the second set of bulbs so that they will not interfere with the growth of their downstairs neighbors. You may simply remember where you've placed the first set of bulbs or you can use chopsticks or whatever to mark the safe places for the upper-row planting. The growth from smaller bulbs is much denser if handled in this way, and the results are quite dramatic and flowery.

At any rate, remember to use clean, dry pots and to soak new clay pots before they are used. Varieties of bulbs may be mixed; simply make sure that you are combining bulbs with similar rooting and forcing times.

(2) *Soil:* Bulbs will flower if they are provided only with water or other inert ingredients (fibers, moss, peat, and charcoal). But they will produce larger and higher quality flowers with a good soil. This is well within your power. Use the standard indoor mixture with additional humus and perhaps a bit more sand (3:1½ or 6:2:1). Add a heaping teaspoon of bone meal to each six-inch pot, scattering it on the surface and scratching it in; this slow-release, high-phosphorus nutrient is most helpful for lovelier flowers. (If you are a bulk planter, use a half-cup of bone meal for each peck of dry soil.)

(3) *Potting:* Choose your clean, dry pots, prepare moistened soil, and remember that the best time to plant bulbs is October through early November. Lay down a generous layer of shards or other drainage material, then enough soil so that the bulb noses (the pointed ends) will be planted about an inch below the pot rim and protrude slightly above the soil. Press this first layer of soil down lightly. Then press the bulbs in, using very gentle motions and avoiding all screwing, shoving, or thumping motions which might rub off tiny developing rootlets. Some growers like to lay a small pad of moist sphagnum moss at the base of the bulb to protect the surface and encourage the new roots; try it if you like. Once the bulbs are in place, apply firm

pressure to the topsoil. The idea of light texture below and firm packing above is to make it easy for the roots to move downward and a bit more difficult for the bulbs to thrust themselves up once the roots have begun to exert some force. Finally, water the planting thoroughly; bottom watering seems the easiest method for a thorough but gentle soak although you may water from the top if you have the patience for numerous gentle sprinklings. Drain the pots very well, even for hours, and then they are ready to be packed up for the rooting period.

## ROOTING

The hardy spring-flowering bulbs require a period of cold and darkness to develop their robust roots. The rooting period is from six to ten weeks long and the important conditions to satisfy are (1) darkness, (2) constant moisture available to the roots, (3) a temperature between thirty-two and fifty degrees, and (4) protection from hungry mice. The bulbs store a considerable amount of food energy and young roots are quite delicious (to a mouse). The required temperature is perhaps the most difficult part of the adventure. Thirty-two to fifty degrees is the total permissible range, thirty-five to forty-five degrees is best and an old rule (The Standard) demands forty degrees for rooting, fifty degrees for growth of stems and leaves, sixty degrees for longest enjoyment of the flowers. Come as close as you can. Here are some possible set-ups:

(1) *The Classic Plunge Pit:* Choose a spot in the outside garden that is well drained and shaded. Dig a trench one foot deep. Lay in a few inches of cinders, gravel, or clinkers (the professional name for large shards); this is to discourage hungry worms. Place the planted bulb pots in the trench. If you are going to be filling it up with the dirt you now have at the side of that trench, lay a thin coating of sand and/or peat moss or straw on the surface of the soil of each pot so that you will know where to stop digging when you come to retrieve your pots. If you have more than one type of bulb, insert tall stakes with wax-crayoned labels into the edge of each pot to identify varieties and rooting times. It will be disconcerting to have to dig them all out if you can't remember the floor plan or your inked label disappears in the first rain. Then fill in the trench with the soil liberated by your shovel or use a mixture of sand and peat moss that is more porous and easier to distinguish when dig-up time comes along. If a hard freeze is likely in your area, add a thick straw or hay mulch on top of the filled trench so that you will be able to budge the pots when the time comes.

(2) *The More Portable Apple-box Method:* Get some sturdy bushel boxes. Put a two-inch layer of cinders or shards in the bottom of each and then place the planted pots into the boxes so that they are two inches apart from each other and two inches away from the sides of the boxes. Label each planting with a stake or write on the

outside of each box if you have separated the varieties. Fill in around all sides and over the top of the pots with moist peat moss. Then, place the boxes outside in a cool, shaded, and well-drained part of the garden; you may even stack several on top of each other. It is an excellent idea here as with the plunge pit to use common sense and arrange the bulbs so that the earliest rooted ones will be the most easily available. If freezing temperatures are expected or even as extra coolness insurance, mulch the top and sides with a thick layer of straw, dirt, or sand. Fool the mice by blocking all possible entrances with small-mesh screen or hardware cloth; many fine people who have never seen a mouse have seen a mouse-eaten nonblooming bulb, so a bit of protection is wise.

(3) *For those without a garden:* Try the apple-box method in a root cellar, basement, garage, closet, or back porch. If the boxes will be exposed to rain, stand them on a few bricks so that the bulbs will not become waterlogged. If they are in a roofed spot, check once or twice to see that the soil is still moist and water lightly if you need to. The roots will not grow properly should the soil dry out and you will have no blossoms for all your trouble. Label the pots or boxes as you ordinarily would and protect the bulbs from mice even under the most unlikely circumstances. If you've found a spot where the temperature is close to forty degrees, the results should be excellent.

(4) *For bulb lovers in Miami* and other warm fall and winter spots, try a pan or two of bulbs in two heavy brown paper bags at the back of the refrigerator. You might even find an inexpensive used refrigerator to buy when your bulb ambitions develop.


*FORCING*

When the bulb pots are filled with roots, they are ready to come indoors. Proper rooting will take between six and ten weeks, depending on the variety and how cold it has been where they were. There is no harm done in leaving them to root beyond the minimum period; in fact, the closer to their natural outdoor blooming period, the more assured is the success. But you can check early varieties in late November and mid-December if you are lusting for blooms. When roots are poking out the drainage hole, the development is just right. If need be, you can turn the soil ball out of its pot; a massive tangle of white root growth lets you know the bulbs are ready. Properly rooted bulbs may even begin to show a bit of top growth. Indeed, you can leave the bulbs in their rooting spot until these first shoots are a few inches tall.

When you have rooted a great number of bulbs, the idea is to bring them in for forcing a batch at a time, every few weeks from December or early January until March. In that way you will have a constant parade of flowers. The ones brought in later will develop flowers more quickly as it is closer to their natural season, so toward spring you can speed up your harvesting expeditions.

## CONDITIONING

The bulbs are brought in, placed in a light but not sunny location for a week or two or three. The purpose of this part of the forcing period is to gradually accustom the plants to house conditions and to allow the first shoots to become green without undue strain from the direct sun. The indoor temperatures encourage the flowers and growth is soon under way. The closer the temperature is to forty-five or fifty degrees the taller will be the flower stalks and the more exuberant the flowers; near sixty degrees or even higher, the blossoms will develop more quickly but they will not be as hardy and fine.

The plants are ready to leave this cool, light, but sunless location when they boast a few inches of good green growth. (Hyacinths are the exception: keep them in the dark until they are quite tall and the flowers are about to open; the shoots will green quite quickly for an exceptional display.) As the shoots appear, and especially as the buds develop, take care that you are watering to keep the planting evenly moist but not soggy; from the first potting until the flowers are permitted to wither naturally, the soil must never be allowed to dry.

## DISPLAY

From their sunless spot, you move the plantings to a sunny window with a temperature near sixty degrees. Again, because cooler temperatures bring finer blooms, avoid a window where the sun is quite strong or hot. Keep the soil moist and turn the pots regularly to maintain even growth. You may find taller plants beginning to lean over; if so, prop them up with green stakes as unobtrusively as you can.

When the flower buds are ready to open, cart the plants off to wherever you are most pleased by their display. The flowers will last from several days to a few weeks depending on the variety, how well the bulbs were rooted, and the temperature of the living room. Sixty-five to seventy degrees is ideal. The flowers will last longer if you take them to a cool (forty to fifty degrees) spot each night before you go to bed. That's it.

## WHEN THE BLOOMS FADE

You may continue to water and enjoy the foliage while it lasts. Then either discard everything but the pots or prepare to plant the bulbs in the outside garden. If you are planning the latter, cut off only the flower heads when they fade. Leave the flower stalks alone and keep the plant in a cool, sunny spot and continue to water amply to allow the foliage to wither at its own speed. This process of food production in the leaves and the subsequent collapse of those leaves enables the bulb to store food energy for next year's growth. You may remove the bulbs from their pots and plant them out when the ground is diggable, or store them (in a cool, dark, dry place) for outdoor bulb planting in the fall. A seemingly less fastidious, but more assured method is to avoid disturbing the bulbs at all. Dig a single hole nearly a foot deep for each potful, place some bone meal at the bottom, gently knock out the entire bulb-ous root ball, and put it in the hole. Cover any remaining stems with an inch of soil, water thoroughly, and forget about the bulbs until next spring's flowers appear. Even if you had stakes in that planting, do not remove them until the bulb is quite dormant at the end of summer. This approach offers extra insurance against bruising the deli-cate bulbs as you free them from the soil.

## Tender Spring-Flowering Bulbs

These are not so demanding, but the list is shorter. It is really only the tender daffo-dils called paperwhites and their yellow variety, soleil d'or, that are most commonly thought of in this group. Other tender spring-flowering bulbs are freesia, amaryllis, Easter lily, lily of the valley, oxalis, and calla lily, but each demands a different treat-ment. Here they are in brief form.

**Narcissus/Daffodil**—Paperwhite and Soleil d'Or Types: These admirably satisfy-ing bulbs are the easiest of any to root and enjoy. They are blooming in their natural season; they do not need remarkable cold for proper rooting and, indeed, they re-quire only pebbles and water as a growing medium. Buy bulbs in September or Octo-ber; you may begin planting them in mid-October. They are so lovely and amenable that most growers choose to plant dozens, a fresh batch every few weeks. Again, buy the largest, plumpest, highest quality bulbs available; you should check each bulb to see that there are no signs of impending rot (moist, spongy, or black-flecked areas), that the fine outer skin is undamaged, and that the base of the bulb is smooth and without bruise. Store the bulbs in a cool, dark, dry, and well-ventilated spot until you are ready to plant them; lacking more conventional locations, you might try the crisper bin of the refrigerator, but take care that the bulbs are kept separately from any moist foods.

Paperwhites and soleil d'or narcissus are planted in any container that is at least three inches deep, about twice the depth of the bulbs. The classic fancy choice would be a good china bowl or shallow tureen, but any watertight container will do. These daffodils look best when planted communally so try for something large enough to hold from four to twelve bulbs.

Fill the bottom of the bowl with a one-inch layer of clean pebbles, special bulb fiber, or a mixture of damp peat moss and aquarium charcoal (1:1). The purpose of the rooting medium is really to provide support rather than nutrition to the bulbs and most people opt for the ready availability of pebbles; however, if you are planting extratall varieties you may need to stake them later and will need the bulk of fibrous mixtures to hold the stakes. The fibrous mixtures are laid in moist; the pebbles go in dry and you water later. Next, plant the bulbs by simply setting them in, half an inch apart from each other, and placed down gently to avoid any damage to the rounded end or basal plate of the bulb. Fill in with more pebbles so that the final planting finds the pointed ends or bulb noses sticking up with about two-thirds of each bulb above the rooting medium. Add water to a pebble planting so that the water is just touching the base of all bulbs.

Find a dark, cool (fifty- to sixty-degree) place where the bulbs can root and leave them there for two or three weeks until the top growth begins. Then bring your soon-to-be beauties to a sunny window with a temperature near sixty to sixty-five degrees and enjoy the flowers. As might be expected, the fibrous plantings must be kept evenly moist at all times from potting until after the flowers fade, and the success of tender narcissus bulbs planted in pebbles depends upon your ability to maintain the water level just at the base of each bulb for the same period.

The bulbs are discarded after the blossoms fade. They can be rested and used again, but really this is rather foolishly difficult unless you are working in a greenhouse. The only possibilities for failure with new bulbs of this kind result from temperatures that are above sixty degrees during rooting, a drying out of the planting particularly during rooting, or not enough light or humidity when the flowers are ready to unfold.

**Freesia** is a lovely spring-flowering plant of the iris family that comes from South Africa. It boasts tall erect leaves and tubular flowers with a wonderful spicy scent; the colors may be white, yellow, pink, violet, or other pastels. Unfortunately, however, its requirement for abundant winter and spring sunshine coupled with temperatures between forty and sixty degrees, and even fifty degrees as the ideal, remove it from the realm of possibility for most homes. If you are willing to try it, here's what to do. Plant the bulbs, or more properly, corms, in the fall; use a standard indoor soil mixture, plant perhaps six corms to a five-inch pot, and set them two inches apart from each other and one inch deep in the soil. If you really are planning a freesia carnival, prepare new plantings every few weeks throughout the fall. The plants require their cool sunshine from the very beginning and do very well in a sunny cold frame if there is no danger of frost.

Until the first growth gets under way, water lightly and fertilize frequently with a dilute solution. Once top growth is active, the plants need no more food, but must be thoroughly soaked whenever the topsoil has become dry. You may well need to stake these tall plants just before their top-heavy blooms are ready to appear. In about March, the foliage will begin to die down naturally. Gradually reduce the watering until the soil is quite dry. Store the corms in or out of soil until next fall's repotting.

**Amaryllis** (*Hippeastrum*) is perhaps the showiest of the winter and spring bulbs; the flowers are enormous and are held on a tall stalk at the center of the plant. The most common color is a fiery red, but plants with white, pink, rose, lavender, and variegated flowers are also available. The bulbs are sold between October and April and, since the care the bulb has received in the previous year determines its ability to bloom for you, it is important that you buy the largest and finest bulbs possible and ones specifically offered for indoor planting. The individual bulbs are expensive but, if cared for properly, they will last your lifetime. Many are sold already potted and you may find these a more secure approach the first year of your two- to five-dollar investment.

The amaryllis bulbs are planted one per pot from October until January. Choose a pot only one to three inches larger in diameter than the bulb; use a standard indoor soil mixture with additional humus (3:1) and bone meal (1 teaspoon per pot), provide an excellent deep layer of drainage material, and set the bulb so that finally one-half to two-thirds of the bulb is above the soil surface. It the bulbs have roots already beginning to emerge, handle them with great care and spread them gently into the soil; if the bulb is still dormant, you might wish to add a moist pad of sphagnum moss under the base to encourage root activity. Water the planting to settle the soil and drain it very well. You will have flowers within a month or two.

Take your amaryllis to a dark, cool (sixty- to seventy-degree) place and give no more water until the flower bud is visible. The amaryllis flowers appear before the foliage. Once you can see the flower bud, bring the plant to good indirect light, rotate it regularly to keep the tall flower stalk moving in an even upward direction, and water it sparingly until the long straplike leaves begin to show. Once the leaves are growing actively, the plant will need a good bit more water and should be fertilized every two or three weeks with weak manure tea. If you do not have a cow available, you will find "instant" liquid or powdered cow manure available at garden-supply shops. This rich feeding is important for proper blossoming next year so do not forego it if you wish to carry the bulb over; however, if you cannot find or manage cow manure from any source, use a complete well-balanced chemical fertilizer as you would for other flowering house plants. When the flowers fade, you should remove the heads, but not the stalks, to allow for fullest ripening of the bulb.

Amaryllis can be grown through the summer indoors or out; outside you may sink them in their pots or plant them directly in the soil. In the fall, they must be brought in for protection against the cold. Some plants will lose all their leaves in summer and others will not. The bare plants may stay in their pots and spend the rest of the summer in the basement or cellar and need not be watered. Those with leaves should be given light watering and good sun (indoors or out).

If your amaryllis has been growing along as a foliage plant through the end of summer, gradually reduce the watering in the fall. Keep it only moist enough to prevent wilt of the heavy leaves. Provide average to dim light and wait until you see the new bud and the plant begins all over again. For the plants that lost their leaves in summer, leave them alone and begin checking for signs of life in late September or October. If no flower bud has emerged by mid-November, you decide that it's high time and begin watering again to encourage the growth.

Then once the new buds have shown themselves, top dress the planting with fresh rich soil and bone meal and follow the same pattern as the year before. The only difference is that you might begin fertilizing earlier. Amaryllis needs a thorough repotting only every three or four years, and this should be done just after the bulbs begin new activity. You may then remove any offsets from the bulb and pot them separately. Seeds are also available, obviously much less expensive, but they take several years before they yield flowering plants.

**Oxalis** is a lovely blooming bulbous plant with cloverlike foliage. Because there are everblooming varieties and varieties which bloom profusely in seasons other than spring, oxalis and its cultural requirements are discussed in the index section on flowering plants.

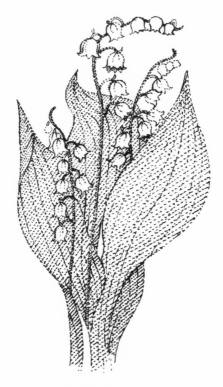

**Lily of the Valley** (*Convallaria majalis*) grows from underground rootstocks peculiarly known as "pips." Since these lovely white, bell-like, and fragrant flowers are popular for the outdoor garden, be sure to purchase specially prepared rootstocks for indoor use; they are available in some stores and by catalogue during the fall. Many are prepared with a fibrous root packing that needs only to be watered for assured good growth. Or you may plant the pips in standard indoor soil—first trimming the roots slightly with a sharp knife, then setting the pips (or buds) so that they are an inch or two apart and barely peeking out of the soil. Water well and keep the planting near seventy degrees, moist, and dark for ten days; lily of the valley needs to be kept near seventy degrees and evenly moist at all times. After the dark period, bring the plants to average light and gradually move them to full autumn sun. The plants are easy to grow and beautiful. After they fade, discard everything but your pot or plant the soil ball out in a shady part of the garden. They cannot be used indoors again.

**Calla Lily** (*Zantedeschia*) and **Easter Lily** (*Lilum longiflorum*) are other bulbous plants which may be planted indoors in fall for late-winter or spring bloom.

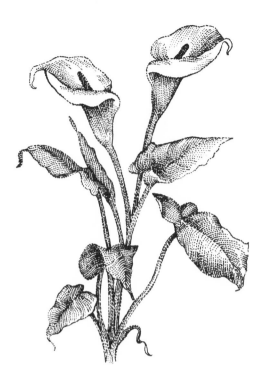

They really do best in a greenhouse or with the help of a cold frame or outdoor garden. If you have these at your disposal, buy your bulbs and inquire about their specific care from your supplier. Nearly all purchased bulbs come with hints or instructions; never be afraid to ask and ask. Of these two, the tubers of calla lily are more reliable for year-after-year performance.

## Summer-Flowering Bulbs

There are many beautiful summer-flowering bulbs which have taken a firm place as house plants.

**Caladium** will be discussed in the index section on foliage plants, and **achimines** in the section on flowering plants. Other likely beauties include tuberous begonia, the gloriosa lily, spider lily, and zephyr lily.

**Tuberous Begonia** is the showiest of these summer-flowering plants; it is perhaps best suited to growth as a basket plant for the outdoor porch or as a bedding plant in a semisunny flower border. It is difficult to grow indoors, but it can be done.

This begonia is native to the Andes and thrives where summer nights are cool. Start the tubers in March or April, planting them in peat moss and sand (1:1) or leaf mold and sand (1:1). Choose fat, strong tubers (one and a half inches or more in diameter), plant them five inches apart, hollow side up, and level. Keep the planting uncovered, moist, at sixty-five to seventy degrees, and in moderate light until growth has begun and the new shoots are three or four inches tall. Then lift and separate the plants carefully and place each in a four-inch pot for potting on or directly into a six- to eight-inch bulb pan; you must have excellent drainage; use a rich, loose soil (standard indoor mixture with additional leaf mold or humus, 3:1), and set the young plants so that the top of each tuber is just below soil level.

Tuberous begonias then require abundant light without strong direct sun, relatively high humidity (50 percent or more) and a constantly moist but not soggy soil. Stake and tie them as necessary or allow them to cascade. Once the roots have filled their pot, fertilize regularly with a dilute, well-balanced solution. Debud for largest blossoms, removing all tiny side buds to concentrate energy in just a few flowers; or enjoy the fullest number of the colorful, delicate blossoms that are available in a variety of forms.

When the plants have finished flowering and flowers begin to fade, gradually reduce the water; when the foliage has thoroughly withered, the soil should be quite dry. Remove any dead foliage, lift out the bulbs, and store them cool (fifty degrees) and dry, in sand or peat moss, until next spring's repotting.

**Gloriosa Lily** (*Gloriosa rothschildiana*) is a marvelously handsome flowering vine. The strong tubers are planted in the spring. Use a six- or seven-inch bulb pan for each tuber, rich loose soil (standard indoor mixture with additional leaf mold or humus, 3:1), and lay the tuber horizontally three inches below the soil surface. Water well to settle the soil and provide a bright location, high humidity, and moderate temperature (sixty to seventy degrees). The gloriosa lily should be watered lightly until full growth gets under way and then it is an abundantly thirsty plant. This lily is an avid climber, so provide some lattice, trellis, or string support it can use. Fertilize with a dilute, well-balanced solution throughout the period of active growth. Once established, it will do quite well in full sun, but will make do with a bit less intense light if the humidity remains high and the temperature close to seventy degrees.

In the fall when the vine tips begin to die back, gradually reduce the watering until the soil is quite dry. Store the tubers in their pots until the following spring.

**Spider Lily** (*Hymenocallis*) and **Zephyr Lily** (*Zephyranthes*) are also attractive large plants for summer bloom. The requirements are very similar to those for the gloriosa vine and you might try them whenever they are available.

Needless to say, there are dozens of other nonmysterious bulbous fellows you may wish to plant once you've had your first successes; the catalogues are full of tempting new choices.

# Greenhouses

Having a greenhouse of one's own is a recurrent element in the fantasy life of many a confirmed gardener. My own dream-state construction plans include an aviary, wild English garden, and fireplace-lined study, all adjoining the massive plant room. But the greenhouse itself reigns supreme; it is surely the most likely of these plans to become reality.

## Building Your Own

I am including this discussion of greenhouses so that other dreamers may be able to flesh out their reveries; I will describe the basic elements involved in greenhouse construction and the roughest idea of cost. You may be encouraged; a greenhouse is closer within your grasp than you would ordinarily dare to think. You can certainly begin with a homemade indoor version and I will offer a general design so that you can toy with as many indoor greenery boxes as your present floorplan will allow.

The act of enclosure of a space with transparent or translucent material provides the essential makings of a greenhouse. The plants are offered an exclusive growing area in which the limitations of normal indoor gardening are removed. They can receive the full measure of sunlight available from nature or can be shaded to whatever degree they require. You can easily keep this growing area far more humid than your living room, and indeed you can control temperature, ventilation, and growing space as you see fit.

Obviously greenhouses originated as supplements to the outdoor garden in order to provide shelter from snow, rain, wind, and freezing temperatures; but come upon from the other direction, as indoor gardeners would view them, they offer an unlimited source of what is most scarce indoors, namely abundant sunlight. That—plus the opportunity to provide high humidity—makes for ideal growing conditions. For the gardener there is an opportunity to escape from the trappings of normal life and be surrounded as if magically by unlimited green foliage and luxuriant flowers.

I am assuming that most readers are not ready to rush out and buy a greenhouse tomorrow. So I merely want to list the basic components of a greenhouse's internal workings. The appendix listings include a number of reputable greenhouse manufacturers to whom you may wish to write for catalogues and further information, and of course, there is always the Yellow Pages.

## Elements of the Outdoor Greenhouse

### THE COMPONENTS

*Foundation:* A foundation of some kind is required and this is your responsibility rather than the manufacturer's. The purpose of the foundation is to provide a level surface upon which to build; local codes will tell you how deep it must be laid to protect the structure from damage due to freezing ground temperatures. It may be poured concrete or laid-in cinder blocks. In any event, local requirements and size and cost will determine your choice for you.

*Lights:* The rectangular sections of material through which the sun casts its beams are known professionally as "lights." Classically the lights are made of glass, although modern prefabricated greenhouses often rely upon fiberglass and smooth or corrugated plastic to serve the same purpose. Glass does break and most traditional styles of glass-greenhouse construction require that the putty around the lights be touched up each year; however, glass also admits as much light as you could hope for and frankly its aesthetic appeal alone would allow me no other choice.

The range of plastic lights available increases and improves every year. Plastic may be initially less expensive or more expensive than glass, due to be replaced every few years or permanent, inclined to darken with age or guaranteed to remain as clear as it began. The corrugated plastics are nearly essential in areas of possible heavy hail damage and consequent glass breakage, and many orchid growers prefer them because they offer subdued light and thus eliminate the need to put up special shades.

*Flooring:* The floor of the greenhouse must of course be level. After that you may do whatever you like. The simplest, most convenient, and classic approach is to lay down gravel over the primordial dirt; aisles between the benches may be finished with brick or tile or slatted wooden walkways. You want to be standing on a comfortable surface while you work—but one that will not inhibit you from splashing water all over the place and working out with the hose for cleanup and humidifying purposes. Wood chips can also be used or well-drained brickwork or whatever else suits the way you choose to use the greenhouse.

*Heating:* Greenhouse heaters may be electric or gas powered; most are controlled by thermostat. Older professional greenhouses are often heated with spreading fin-shaped pipes through which hot water flows; the fins may pass under benches, up the walls, or near the floor. This form of heating system is more expensive to install but assures that the heat will be exactly where it is wanted. Your choice is naturally influenced by the availability and expense of power sources, the size of the greenhouse, your local weather, and whether you plan to grow plants that demand consistent tropical warmth or those that prefer cool temperatures. Unknown to many greenhouse beginners, you cannot grow lavish specimens of both inclinations in the same greenhouse. There are ways to strike something close to a happy bargain and arrange plants close to or away from the heat source but the very best results come from a decided move toward warm- or cold-temperature plants throughout.

*Humidity and Cooling:* Warm- or cool-air humidifiers, cooling evaporators, or water splashed from the hose onto the floor will all humidify the air. The possible choices range from the simplest and least expensive—the hose—to more significant investments for automatic and large-capacity humidifying units.

*Ventilation:* Every greenhouse must have vents. Most growers make use of fans to ensure adequate air circulation and maximum efficiency of those vents. The vents are automatically operated or the grower opens them by hand. In any case, all plants require ample fresh air and the amount of work necessary to provide that varies with the size of the greenhouse, how full of plants it is, the season, and the kind of heater used.

*Shade:* Even the grower raising plants that require full sun will occasionally want to shade an area for propagation or recovery-room purposes. Most greenhouse operators want more shade than that. Some of your plants may require less than full sun or some months of the year may prove entirely too bright. Wooden-slat shades, fiberglass shades, or sheets of vinyl are installed to protect the plants from overly abundant sun. There are also several mixtures of shading compound which are widely used to coat the inside of the glass to diminish light intensity. Growers of plants that require average or low light may even begin with corrugated plastic to bypass shading each summer and provide permanently diffused soft light.

*Benches:* The plants themselves are grown on benches to bring them up to back-saving height. Standard benches may be purchased with your greenhouse and are available in redwood or cyprus, aluminum, or asbestos. The wood benches are the older of the styles; they are attractive, rot-resistant, long-lived, and heavy. Aluminum and asbestos benches have recently gained enormous popularity since they combine durability with lighter weight. Clearly the benches would be among the more easily undertaken home-construction projects for outfitting your own greenhouse. They are useful either in a slatted or solid-bottom form. Plants stand directly on the slatted benches and drainage problems do not exist, although you must take care that whatever is under the benches will not be harmed by water. Solid benches are filled with sand or pebbles; the plants stand atop this layer and thus receive the advantages of a dry well, while the underbench areas have even greater usefulness for dry storage of dormant bulbous plants, soil, and potting materials. The solid benches can also be filled with sand or another medium and be used directly for propagation.

*Water:* Need I say it, a greenhouse consumes a lot of water. It is an important element in the planning because you will be wanting water available and convenient to you throughout most of your greenhouse working hours. Plan on a sufficient number of faucets or outlets and see that you have a mixing faucet for the ready availability of warm water.

*Other Stuff:* Plan for electrical outlets in reasonable numbers for the size of the greenhouse so that you will not be threading extension cords through it later on. You may want to use extra lights for working at night or extra outlets for an artificial-light growing area, soil cable, or emergency portable heater during an unusual cold spell. It is also a boon if you can devise a plan that includes a convenient out-space or annex to the greenhouse; you would want a sink, a potting area, and storage space for supplies. Greenhouse manufacturers and agents are eager to help you with this kind of planning but, obviously, the more forethought you bring to the project the better will be your final design. I also happen to enjoy this kind of mental exercise; it allows my dreams to be in architectural Technicolor.

Understandably enough, the first large-scale home greenhouses fell only within the province of the very wealthy. One had to be able to support a greenhouse staff to keep constant vigil over the plants. Vents were opened manually; coal furnaces had to be constantly fed, each plant was watered and misted in turn. Today, however, you can tease your sense of budgetary discretion, weigh your freedom against possible plant collapse during heat waves, cold spells, and weekend vacations, and then perhaps opt for one of the many automatic systems that are available. Automatic control of ventilation and humidity, thermostatically controlled heat, constant water-level maintenance systems, and an alarm bell on the heating system to signal temperatures out of a fixed range—these are all gloriously described in the catalogues and serve to lighten your sense of nonstop responsibility. However, these are extras, and you may add them as time and the bank account progress.

*FRAMING, EXPOSURES, STYLES, AND COST*

What goes into your greenhouse is actually the small picture, however central all the equipment may be to your gardening hours. The big picture is which greenhouse to buy: redwood or aluminum, built-up or all-glass, lean-to or freestanding, within the budget or, as we say in my family, absolutely, totally, out-of-the-question final. In my experience, the big picture usually takes care of itself so I will just sketch out the basic points.

Redwood greenhouses provide excellent insulation for your plants. They are less expensive than aluminum to heat during winter and easier to cool during summer; in fact, if you live in an area of extreme winter cold, you must consider whether you would be able to afford to heat an aluminum greenhouse and also light it to work at night should winter fuel shortages recur. To my eye, the redwood greenhouses are more attractive and blend more graciously with general home design, but there again I'm only displaying a bit of traditional preference. Most redwood houses do need periodic painting to protect them from the elements whereas aluminum green-houses, although generally initially more expensive, have gained widespread popularity for their maintenance-free life.

Lean-to greenhouses are those that make use of an outside wall of an existing structure—such as your house or garage—for one of the greenhouse's long sides. A freestanding structure is simply that, off by itself. Lean-tos are generally more limited in size but may be far more enjoyable for their convenience. You may find yourself more inclined to check on your plants in a spare moment if you do not have to find your umbrella and raincoat first. Do take care, however, to see that a greenhouse of the lean-to style has a door opening onto the outside; carting supplies in and muddy feet out will prove less anxious tasks if you do not have to go through the living room.

Another consideration of style is whether the greenhouse is built-up, as most are, or all-glass. The built-up greenhouse is simply one with a solid wall below the level of the first bench. An all-glass (or all-plastic or all-vinyl) model will greatly increase the available growing area and the difference in cost is not striking. How-ever, you will perhaps be giving up the use of underbench space for storage, shady growing areas, and artificial-light set-ups and you may be tempted to grow plants on the ground at the expense of your sore back. Consult the catalogues to see which of the standard models best suits your fancy, budget, and needs. Well-camouflaged underbench space is obviously less important if you have another planned area for storing pots, soils, and plants in awkward stages of development.

A southeastern exposure for the long side of the greenhouse is considered A-1 ideal. The point here clearly is to begin with the optimum amount of sunlight since it is not within your ken to increase it, only to install shades. However, if the only spot I had for a greenhouse was less than ideal, I would surely plunge ahead anyway; which-ever way you face, you will have more sunlight than you do under the house roof and behind solid walls.

Forgive me if I've saved discussion of cost for last. Money doesn't seem to have much relationship to reality anymore but, on the other hand, you cannot buy greenhouses with jellybeans, bead necklaces, or love. The expense of laying the necessary foundation is usually not included in the manufacturer's price. Then you can count on something in the neighborhood of a thousand dollars for a prefabricated greenhouse and another three hundred to eight hundred dollars for benches, equipment, and supplies, depending on the size of the greenhouse and how fully automated and equipped you plan to be on Day One. Where money is no object—or less of an obstacle than it is to the rest of us—a custom greenhouse can be built as an architecturally fabulous extension of a home; the price would be as many thousands of dollars as the gardener cared to spend.

So the price of a greenhouse really falls into the same range as buying a small car—or half of a small car at recent prices. Many companies are able to arrange for long-term bank financing if the buyer requests it and an aggressive greenhouse-hungry person might find a way to arrange it himself. Perhaps a home-improvement loan. Some manufacturers will also sell you a set of plans and you can save perhaps 20 percent of the cost by assembling the materials yourself. And a less than professional greenhouse could be attempted by anyone with sufficient know-how or nerve. However, bear in mind that a quality greenhouse can provide you with challenging pleasure throughout your lifetime; cutting corners without sufficient expertise is probably bad business.

## Building a Small Greenhouse Indoors

There is an intriguing possibility for indoor gardeners who want to urge the greenhouse idea a bit beyond the reverie stage, but are not yet able to afford or find a place for the full-blown outdoor style.

You can build an indoor greenhouse box and outfit it with fluorescent lights. Indeed there are manufacturers who now sell small ready-made greenhouses to attach to the outside of a window but this seems to me to be the kind of project that most folks could manage more economically themselves.

The box can be of any size you choose, tailored to where you want to put it or determined by the materials you can locate at a good price. One approach is to hang this indoor growing box at a window; the window is one large side of the box and sliding glass doors are the other. Or you may suspend the box on any indoor flat wall, lay in a sheet of plastic, glass, or plexiglass at the back to deter mildew, and again use sliding glass doors for entry. Or convert an old, cast-off, glass-doored china cabinet by the simple addition of artificial lights, back-wall glass, and plants. Or enclose a set of shelves with glass doors, again adding light, wall protection, and plants.

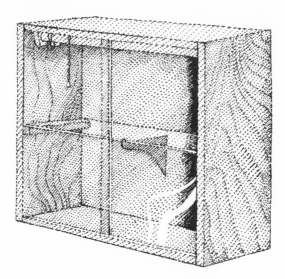

So you begin with a wooden box let's say three or four feet long, four feet high, and about fifteen inches deep (although the dimensions can certainly be as grand as you like). Install a glass shelf halfway up for a second level of plants. For front access you use glass windows of the sliding-door kind. If the height of your box exceeds three feet, you will probably find it easier with two sets of windows, one for each shelf. The window frames should be painted with white enamel to discourage mold and reflect maximum light; if you are using aluminum windows, buy them already enameled to save yourself a difficult job.

The top of the box then gets outfitted with two fluorescent light tubes. If your box is hung flush with a window receiving good natural light, you do not need to use the special plant-growing lights, but indeed you might as well. If your box is on an interior wall, you must use the fluorescent tubes specifically balanced for plants to ensure proper growth. Automatic timers are inexpensive, easy to install, and will bring reliable periods of day-length brightness to your plants.

A tray of some sort goes into the bottom of the box. The tray is filled with an inch or two of pebbles, the potted plants stand on the pebbles, and water is kept up to a level just below the pots to humidify the growing area. This tray may be made of galvanized metal, fiberglass, or plastic. Metal shops will make galvanized trays of custom sizes for you or you may find a useful size at a plant-supply store or through a seed-and-plant catalogue.

You then have everything you need but the plants and perhaps a temperature-humidity gauge. You can buy an instrument to measure temperature and relative humidity through greenhouse or seed catalogues or at a well-stocked hardware store; the price of the gauge may range from five to thirty-five dollars and the five-dollar variety is the one you want now. Why go overboard for a box? Hang it in the center of your growing area and watch it for a while until you discover how much to leave the sliding glass doors open to maintain a relative-humidity reading of near 50 percent.

That's it. You have a greenhouse, albeit one which makes primary use of artificial light. You control humidity by the dry well in the bottom tray and the degree to which the doors are left open. The entire inside of the box should be painted with enamel so that you can clean away any mildew; using white paint assures maximum light reflection to the plants. Use a piece of glass, plexiglass, or plastic at the back of the box flush with a plain wall for the same antimold cleanup purposes.

If a box at a window gets too hot and bright during the summer months, cover the inside of the window with rice paper, a gauze diaper, or other material that will cut the intensity of the sun's rays. It is unlikely that the box will get too cold during winter, but frost at the window might blacken leaves; if the night temperatures threaten to be a problem, cover the outside glass with newspapers or fabric. If you wish, they may be left in place for the duration of the cold spell, since the plants will receive ample growing light from the balanced fluorescent tubes.

You water as you would ordinarily and you will find that a great deal of your plant-tending responsibilities are given over to pinching, pruning, and cutting back; the plants grow at an exuberant, healthy clip.

It is difficult to give a reliable estimate of cost for this kind of indoor box. You need the lumber for the outside frame, glass for the shelf halfway up, sliding doors for front access, a tray and pebbles for the bottom, perhaps a piece of glass or plexiglass for the back wall, fluorescent tubes and a fixture in which to install them, an automatic timer for the lights, some white enamel paint, and the optional humidity gauge. The doors and the light fixture are the most expensive items on your shopping list. Fluorescent tubes for plants come in two-foot or four-foot lengths; two-foot tubes would be fine for a box three feet in length and you would then place the sun-loving plants in the center and the more shade-tolerant plants out at the ends.

If you were planning to buy new materials for everything you need at current prices, you could build a box three feet long and four feet high for under eighty dollars. However, I would certainly frequent garage sales, flea markets, and wrecking-company yards to see about buying used sliding windows and fluorescent fixtures. I would in fact be tempted to find whatever windows I could that slid open easily and were within a reasonable size range and then build the box to match them.

Need I say it, you can extrapolate from a simple design like this and turn a whole corner of a dull bathroom or dining area or any room into a fabulously beautiful sight.

# 8

# Some Extra Bits of Information

This chapter includes some basic points which simply refused to fit comfortably or sensibly any place else. Like the extra catchall drawer in the kitchen, it may not be the most tidy, but you may find here what you were looking for some place else.

## Odds and Ends

### ACID-LOVING PLANTS

Many people have fallen prey to the notion that great mystery and difficulty accompany the culture of acid-loving plants. Really this is not so. There are simply some plants—most notably azalea, camellia, and gardenia—that because of the acid condition of their native habitat prefer to continue with a distinctly acid soil. Maintaining proper acidity in their potting soil is a relatively easy task. Failures with these acid lovers stem more from the fact that they require consistently cool air temperatures than that their roots are hard to please.

Where rainfall is plentiful and decomposition of organic matter in the soil is rapid, the soil will tend to be more acid. Azaleas or rhododendrons thrive in Northern California, Oregon, and on up the Pacific Coast; the same acid soil that nurtures the redwood trees holds great promise for these flowering shrubs. In regions of infrequent rainfall and sandy soil, the soil condition is more alkaline. The measurement of acidity or alkalinity is made in terms of pH; the scale runs from 0–14 and 7 is neutral. Most house plants as well as outdoor ornamentals and food crops thrive in a slightly acid soil. A pH range of 4.5–5.5 suits the acid lovers; most plants prefer their soil between 5.5 and a bit above 7.0; 7.0–8.0 would be an alkaline reading. As you can see, the extent of the pH variations is not tremendous and this is what you might expect. Whether you put the cart before the horse or the horse before the cart, the plants of the earth and the soil of the earth have had a long time to develop a satisfying, mutually nurturing relationship.

The standard indoor soil mixture is slightly acid as suits most plants. Leaf mold, humus, and peat moss are common soil ingredients and since they are in fact decaying organic matter they tend to be acid. If you are trying to please an acid-loving plant, you can simply add more peat moss—the most acid of the three—to increase acidity. Plants, such as cacti, that are accustomed to dry alkaline soils simply require that you add mortar (or clay-pot) rubble or pulverized limestone or some other base material to increase the alkalinity of the soil mixture. These are all easy ways to change the soil.

If you like, you can buy chemically treated papers and perform the pH tests on your own. This is by no means a necessary part of plant care, but it is an enjoyable experiment and worthwhile if you are concerned that your soil might not suit your plants. Indeed, the pH of soil ingredients will vary according to their sources. Leaf mold made from oak leaves will be more acid than that from maple. Pine needles also yield a strong acid reaction when they decompose. A high content of peat moss in the soil will offer a marked acid reading. You can, however, trust that the packaged soils will be suitable to the normal range; indeed most package labels state the pH reading of the soil therein and you can easily vary it for the three main acid lovers or for cacti that require alkaline soil.

For azalea, camellia, and gardenia, here are the specific suggestions. (Their general growth requirements are discussed in the flowering plant section of the illustrated index.) You may assume that plants bought from reputable nurseries or florists are potted in the proper soil. Do not water them with tap water if you live in an area with very hard or alkaline water; this is one special case where you might resort to bottled or purified water for your plants. Use one of the fertilizers specifically formulated for acid-soil plants. These fertilizers make use of sulfate of ammonia rather than nitrate of soda for the nitrogen and muriate of potash rather than sulfate of potash for the potassium to achieve an acid rather than alkaline reaction in the soil. While the ready availability of these special foods provides great convenience, you will also achieve fine results with the more classic approach of alternating between a well-balanced general house-plant fertilizer one time and a solution of one ounce of ammonium sulfate in two gallons of water the next.

Chlorosis is the name of the condition you are trying to avoid. These plants which require a distinctly acid soil will exhibit a yellowing of the foliage if the soil is too alkaline; you will recognize chlorosis by a yellowing in contrast to distinctly green veins. Treat chlorosis by watering with a solution of one ounce of iron sulfate in two gallons of water and prevent it in the future by making sure to incorporate plenty of peat moss in repotting soil.

A good homemade recipe for the rich, acid soil these plants prefer would be standard indoor soil mixture (three parts) with additional leaf mold (one part) and peat moss (two parts). When repotting, be sure to provide an excellent deep layer of drainage material.

## Bonsai

The art of bonsai is a Japanese form which has attracted people for centuries. Specific horticultural techniques are employed to grow purposefully dwarfed plants. A well-grown bonsai is meant to present the appearance of great age in a miniature outline. The bonsai is intended to evoke traditional images of a stylized landscape, aesthetically well-balanced and pleasing to the eye.

While bonsai is not typically a mode of gardening that can be carried on indoors, it does seem to bear a kinship to house-plant enthusiasm. Perhaps what is common to them both is a sense of scarcity and of limit in the physical world. You do not need to plow an entire field of barley to participate in the rhythms of seasonal growth. A single plant presents its entire physical being or anima to your care. Through proper cultivation, nurturing, and reshaping, you can transform a group of seedlings into a microcosm of the larger landscape.

Bonsai plants are primarily grown outdoors in a place where they will receive filtered or dappled sunlight and where they will be sheltered from strong winds; they can, however, be brought inside for short periods if you can provide them with a cool, light, and airy spot. Many apartment dwellers find they can have success with bonsai on a patio, deck, or even a shelf hung from a window. So if you have a suitable growing area and your heart finds itself greatly attracted to the form, you might try working with bonsai plants.

Suitable and classic choices for bonsai culture include evergreens such as camellia, cedar, larch, cypress, cryptomeria, and pine; and deciduous trees such as Japanese maple, Chinese quince, flowering cherry, and hornbeam.

The plan of care bears a great similarity to that for any plant but, for bonsai, each element of nourishment is provided in as small a quantity as possible and just in the nick of time, in order to dwarf the plant. The challenge is to sustain health while limiting size, a notion quite contrary to the normal view of things; and therein lies the potential satisfaction. If a plant is growing new branches and robust foliage each week, it is easy to know that you're doing things right; a bonsai may be ten years old and your measure of success is the appearance that it is hardly growing at all.

The plants are watered only when they are dry; a small amount of water is given and allowed to soak in thoroughly. Most plants are misted at least daily to minimize surface evaporation from the leaves and thereby allow the roots to maintain a healthy stance in relation to the internal water-supply system despite their limited water-finding role. In hot weather, a plant might therefore even need to be misted four or five times a day; its dwarfed roots are simply not equal to a vigorous water-finding job. Moreover, no fertilizer is given for an entire year after repotting and then a well-balanced house-plant food is supplied at half-strength every week during the spring and summer period of growth. This serves further to condition the plants to their limited growing space and merely sustains health while curtailing extravagant size.

Bonsai plants are repotted as infrequently as every three years: the deciduous specimens every two to three years; the slower-growing evergreens can get by with the same pot for three to five. Repotting is undertaken in early spring, just before new growth appears; it is important that you work in a sheltered spot because you will be exposing some very delicate roots. A glazed pot of small size and distinctly personal appeal is chosen. Wire mesh is placed over the drainage holes to discourage outbound wayward roots and inbound unwelcome soil beasts; then a layer of pebbles is added to ensure drainage. If the plant is large enough, its roots are pruned at each repotting. You remove about two-thirds of the old soil and cut back the roots of deciduous plants to nearly half and those of the less exuberant evergreens to a remaining three-fourths. You then work new moist soil into the root ball, working gently but assuring good contact with the roots. A suitable soil mixture would include rich sandy soil with additional humus (3:1) or two parts loam, one part sand, and one part either leaf mold or peat moss.

Well-conditioned, established plants are then set higher in the new pot than they were in the old to encourage a disproportionately large and gnarled trunk as a valued sign of age; an off-center placement is also attempted to provide graceful balance to the open, asymmetrical outline of the plant. The bonsai planting is then bottom watered, the topsoil and foliage misted, and the soil finally allowed to drain. It is essential that you then provide frequent misting and shelter from drafts and high temperatures, thus allowing a complete recovery period to protect the investment of your time over the last several years.

A well-tended bonsai is also pruned and pinched periodically to direct growth into desired shapes. An open, broad, asymmetrical outline satisfies the classical mode. A clean open top is encouraged to allow great visibility of the miniature's stylized outline. Copper wires are used to support spreading horizontal branches and to mold supple growth into less upright forms. Support wires are passed through the drainage holes during repotting and are brought up through the soil, to be wrapped around the trunk and perhaps a pendulous heavy branch. New growth is similarly whipped into shape. Moderately stiff copper wire, perhaps heated slightly to improve bending ability, is wrapped spirally around a likely branch; if the bark is tender, the wire is first enclosed in rice paper to prevent scarring. The wrapping begins at the top of the branch and the wire is pegged into the soil near the base of the trunk. Then the branch is bent gently but firmly in the chosen direction, the wire is made firmer, and training has begun. Such wires are left in place for six months to a year and they may then be replaced for another stint of enforced cooperation and progress.

Obviously, one can begin to appreciate the devotion with which growers view their well-established bonsai plants, for many years of careful attention and artful craft are seen in each older specimen. Plants are passed from generation to generation as a loving heritage. However, you can go away for a vacation, and indeed the plants pass the winter outdoors with only basic sensible protection from severe freeze. So you need not treat bonsai with kid gloves; try it if you choose.

# Choosing a Plant Store and the Plant

Although I am delighted by the house-plant "boom" of recent years, I find it enormously depressing that the average eager buyer finds it hard to distinguish between those shops with quality plants and those without. How can you choose a reliable plant store? How can you best tell which plant among the twenty on a table is the one to buy? I am not saying that you cannot find a wonderful plant at the discount drugstore or that you will never go wrong at a shop you have decided to trust. But a bit more discernment and insistence on quality will raise the standards for all.

Understandably, most shops will not refund your money if you have had enough time alone with a plant to kill it yourself; but if you have suffered several failures with plants from a single store and find them definitely not of your own doing, I encourage you to let the owner know that he has permanently lost a customer. Hopefully things might improve.

### THE PLANT STORE

The primary quality to look for in a plant shop is accountability. Can you rely on these folks for healthy plants and friendly advice? When you return with a question will you be talking to the same person and is that person knowledgeable about plants? I must say I am a bit leery of stores that do not really depend upon your return, but have geared their business to the walk-in customer and many extravagant reduction sales to guarantee volume.

One point in question is whether the store is dealing in numbers that it can manage and still retain control over quality. Plant shops receive their plants in one of two ways. Someone from the shop makes a trip to the wholesale grower and personally selects each plant or group of plants, taking advantage of varying special prices; or the wholesale distributor fills and delivers a standing order. Obviously the larger or more casual stores accept whatever their delivered order includes and may not be well equipped, in terms of a trained staff, to provide excellent care for the plants once they've arrived. So unless the prices are unbelievably low, it does not really seem worth your time and anguish to try to discover the one healthy raging beauty on a table full of trouble.

Feel free to ask a shop owner how he buys his plants. You may also be interested to find out where his suppliers are located. There is much to be said for buying plants grown as close to your own area as possible. They have adjusted themselves naturally to the climate and will prove healthier in your home as a result. Of course, plant lovers have been shopping crosscountry by catalogue for years, and reputable catalogue dealers provide fine plants; but the plants are usually shipped in two-inch pots, with bulbs delivered in a semidormant state since it is planned that they will do most of their growing in the climate to which they are expected to adapt.

I think it is also encouraging to find a plant store with basic supplies available in bulk. It demonstrates a bit of interest on the part of the owner in providing service and convenience as well as potted plants. In large quantities, perlite, vermiculite, sphagnum moss, peat moss, and the like are quite inexpensive; if the store buys a bale of peat moss and breaks it down into fifty-cent plastic bags, I would say you have found a friend and a needed supplier. Look to the prices on the plants and on pots and other supplies, comparing them to those at other stores. The markup on plants is generally 100 percent over the wholesale price, a bit less as the plants get more expensive. If the quality and selection of clay or plastic pots is the same in two stores or if you are choosing between two equally beautiful begonias, I see no reason to pay an inflated price.

Also be sure to ask for information, advice, or growing information whenever you buy a new plant and haven't grown it successfully before. I know of one store in San Francisco that provides Xeroxed care instructions with each plant. Even if you have all the information about cultural requirements at hand in a general form, it is always interesting to hear another view. New varieties and hybrids appear each year; their habits and care may vary from the more common plants of the same type. Climatic factors may influence regional habits. Moreover, you will want to see what works best for you when two roaring opinions appear to conflict.

One of the best ways I know of to accumulate expertise in regard to plants is to visit the botanical gardens or conservatories in your city and voyage to nearby green-houses and rural growing areas. Ask as many questions as you can. The trained staff members at nurseries and gardens can help you enormously with your troubles. I am much in the habit of calling the Conservatory at the Hall of Flowers in San Francisco's Golden Gate Park; a man answers the phone and I say, "I've got a question," then he says, "Shoot." You can count on friendly, fast, and accurate advice. A phone call or letter to a nearby university horticulture department is another basic resource available to the home gardener.

## THE PLANT

When it comes to choosing the particular plant you will buy, look for vibrant, healthy green color. On a branching plant check to see that the space between active leaf nodes is short, that the plant is bushy and full, and that it has a well-branched, leaf-laden lower stem. When a plant grows from a central stalk, choose the individual that has not had many lower leaves cut away. There seems to be no good reason to begin with a plant that has already seen hard times. Check palms (as well as dracaenas and other similar narrow-leaf-tipped plants) to see that dry brown tips have not been cut away; it is a common practice to manicure brown leaf tips with a scissors, and indeed you may do this at home, but when buying I would prefer to start with the entire frond. Choose flowering plants with a profusion of closed or nearly closed buds; you will enjoy their blossoms for a longer period of time.

Of primary importance when choosing a new plant is that it brings with it a pleasing shape. When you buy a new plant, you are paying for the expertise of the greenhouse grower; that expertise should certainly include the ability to provide optimum growing conditions and suitable pruning, pinching, and training to result in a beautiful form. Any plant tender knows how difficult it is to keep constant watch and maintain a beautiful shape once it has been achieved. So unless you are feeling very much the reformer, the bargain hunter, or the missionary, begin with a plant whose present aesthetic lightens your heart.

Check the undersides of leaves and along the stems of any plant you intend to buy. It would be foolhardy to bring home an insect-ridden or diseased plant. I also tend to poke my finger into the soil. Occasionally I disturb little interloping soil creatures, but generally I find out if the soil texture is loose enough and the roots are not crowding up into the topsoil of the pot. You may indeed choose to buy a pot-bound plant if it has not yet shown any signs of stress. I prefer to buy a robust fast-growing plant when it has a few roots poking out of the drainage hole; I know I can take it home, repot it into the next-size pot and be that much further along.

The main idea is to use your common sense and find the plant that suits you best. Buy a plant in a tin can if the attractive price of that plant more than makes up for the clay pot you must then buy. When buying small plants for a terrarium planting, choose well-rooted ones for a deep planting, but barely-rooted ones for a container you worry may already be too small.

Be conservative in your leaps of faith in the midst of internal controversy. One often finds oneself caught between love of a certain plant and definite lurking suspicion that one's own home conditions will probably not satisfy the plant's needs. Although I have gone on a bit in the first chapter about the adaptability of plants and the procedure for acclimating them from one situation to another, there is no way you can pretend that a hot sunny window is a cool humid greenhouse. First buy plants that you know will do well with what you happen to have; move away from that conservative midline only after your own level of confidence is such that it will not be shattered by disappointment or an occasional defeat. Remember, too, that the younger the plant the more readily it can adapt to new conditions. If you have a difficult spot at home you wish to fill, decide upon a plant that is likely to be happy there and buy a small one—or several small ones and pot them together. The larger the plant the more extensive the consequences if a sudden case of impetuous leaf drop follows its arrival in your less-than-greenhouse home.

One last word of caution and protective advice. The plant is yours the minute you walk out of the store; so get it home carefully. While offering a romantic, robust vision for the passer-by, the fellow striding through town with his five-foot *Ficus benjamina* waving in the wind may arrive home with a decidedly less vigorous plant than he has purchased. Most plant stores will wrap your plants or cover them with paper sleeves if you need such protection from rain, cold, wind, or strong sun to cart them home in an undiminished form. If you are driving your plants home, place them on the floor inside the car; arrange and support them so that they do not topple, get stepped on by the dog, or lose branches as you close the door. In any event, do not put them in the trunk on hot days. It is unbelievably hot inside a closed trunk, and you do not wish to arrive home with a steam-cooked philodendron on your hands.

All exhortations aside, it is really not so difficult to find a fabulously handsome and desirable plant, bring it home safely, and enjoy it for years.

## Where Do You Live? Where Do You Go From Here?

It is important to take into account that plant care varies with locale. I found it most frustrating when I began to read plant books that most of them presumed that all gardeners live east of Chicago. Geography and climate make a big difference. Whereas summering plants out of doors is an extremely convenient habit in the East and Midwest, it doesn't really accomplish much in California. California's summer coastal fog, cool nights, and house conditions that are not unbearably hot and dry encourage the house plants to remain in place with remarkable aplomb. Coastal regions offer different conditions than landlocked states: a more temperate situation prevails, freezing is rare, and the growing season is longer. How long and how cold your winter is will determine how devoted you are to your home-heating devices; it is the effect of artificial heat in lowering indoor humidity that will greatly influence the condition of your plants. So where you live has a great bearing on how hard you have to work to maintain encouraging levels of humidity. Or how great may be your need for some color by late January and your subsequent enthusiasm for forcing winter-blooming bulbs. Everyone knows, for example, that California is bizarre. What grows well grows mammoth and what doesn't organizes a society. Rubber plants cast outside will grow to tree size; the tuberous-begonia nurseries and annual-flower fields here supply the entire country; bits of succulents can be thrown into a pot and will soon take possession of a back porch.

Take this book or any other as your starting place and remember its limitations. No two growers follow exactly the same plans. So see what grows well in your area, and then for you. Visit local nurseries, conservatories, and greenhouses. And check to see if your state department of agriculture or a nearby university can supply you with any bulletins about local growing details. They will probably have a great deal of advice to offer about food crops and little if anything about begonias. Therefore, your next step is to buy a small notebook, begin compiling observations on your own, and write that unavailable bulletin yourself.

What can I say? A book takes you a distance along a certain path and then you choose your own favorite roads. Most of your choices will be grounded in common sense. The more informed you are, so much the better. But the only eyes, heart and hands you can manage are your own. So you walk around and ask questions, gathering food for the eyes and for the notebook. To paraphrase the late Jacob Bronowski, it is the impertinent questions that tempt the mind toward pertinent answers.

# ILLUSTRATED INDEX OF HOUSE PLANTS

# 1
# Foliage Plants

This first section of the illustrated index includes the most time-tested and readily available of house plants. While many of the so-called foliage plants do flower indoors, they have long been cherished for the lush grace and vigor of their leaves. Nearly all plant collections begin with these leafy stand-bys. Indeed house-plant lovers soon find that, no matter how grand and varied the plant population may become, the bulk of it remains green.

Foliage plants thrive—or can at least survive—in a broad range of house conditions. Their requirements have become the norm of plant care and everything you've read in earlier chapters will find fewest exceptions in this list. Any individual peculiarities will be noted in the discussion of each plant. Obviously, the closer you come to providing a plant with its optimum growing conditions, the more luxuriant will be its response and the more famous your green thumb will be. Still, it is encouraging to know that you have dozens of choices here and that all of these plants have managed to bring beauty and pleasure to thousands of homes before you had ever thought of trying your luck with a house plant.

*Note:* The "standard indoor soil mixture" referred to throughout the plant index is detailed in chapter 1. Either of the following mixtures satisfies this basic soil requirement:

1) Half a lightweight African-violet mix and half a dark, dense, sandy potting soil.
2) One part dense, sandy soil; one part vermiculite; and one part perlite.

Light, water, humidity, and the effects of temperature in an "average" house are discussed fully in chapter 1. Specific propagation techniques are covered in chapter 3.

*Adiantum*, see **Maidenhair Fern**

*Aglaonema*, see **Chinese Evergreen**

Airplane plant, see **Spider Plant**

*Allium schoenoprasum*, see **HERBS, Chives**

**Aluminum Plant**   *Pilea cadierei* and
                        var. *minima*
Aluminum plant is a *Pilea*, native to Vietnam, whose green leaves are marked with silver and have a remarkable quilted texture. The leaves are actually puffy with air pockets between the plant tissue and the epidermis of each leaf. The plant grows in an upright form. Some aluminum plants are naturally bushy; others seem bent on legginess and must be pinched with a vengeance.

LIGHT: Bright indirect to almost dim light. Growth will be weak and spindly if the light is too poor.

TEMPERATURE: Average house.

HUMIDITY: Average house, most lush growth at 30 percent or more.

WATER: Average or slightly more moist.

SOIL: Standard indoor mixture with optional addition of leaf mold (3:1). Repot before stress signals appear.

PROPAGATION: Cuttings. Aluminum plant will root well in water.

*Anethum graveolens*, see **HERBS, Dill**

**ARALIAS**—Members of the ginseng family. Tropical and temperate foliage plants with simple or compound leaves. Beautiful and hardy stand-bys. They include aralia, fatsia, and tree ivy, English ivy, schefflera, and less common others.

**Aralia**           *Dizygotheca*
**False Aralia**      *elegantissima*
The aralia is an airy and elegant tropical plant from the New Hebrides. Although potentially as tall as 10 feet, it is still lovely as a young plant. The dark green and leathery, spreading compound leaves have strongly notched fingerlike parts and form a striking outline. Several plants are often potted together to give greater breadth to older plantings and these are frequently used as arrestingly graceful elements of office design. To prevent lower-leaf drop, avoid drafts, water with great consistency, and slowly acclimate larger specimens to normal house humidity. Older plants will acquire a bark-covered main stem.

LIGHT: Diffused indoor light. Adaptable to brighter light, but go slowly.

TEMPERATURE: Average house.

HUMIDITY: 30 percent or more. Mist liberally

or place over dry well for most luxuriant growth.

WATER: Slightly more than average. Evenly moist for most rapid growth, but false aralia will make a healthy adjustment to average watering if you are consistent. Spray foliage when watering and watch for red spider mites.

SOIL: Standard indoor mixture with additional leaf mold or humus (3:1) or more frequent dilute fertilizing than the average.

PROPAGATION: Cuttings in spring which require high humidity and warmth (70°–80°).

*Araucaria excelsa*, see **Norfolk Island Pine**

Areca palm, see **Butterfly Palm**

*Artemisia dracunculus*, see **HERBS, Tarragon**

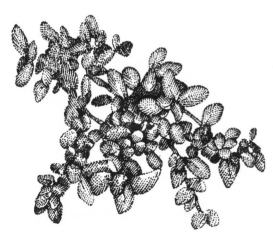

**Artillery Plant**     *Pilea microphylla*
The popular name of this plant refers to the fact that ripe pollen will shoot forth in great gusts if the plant inhabits a sunny location or, in any event, if you knock a stem at the proper time. The leaves are minute and provide a fernlike appearance. Stems are much branched and move upright for a few inches before they cascade; larger specimens thus

have an unusually beautiful crown shape. Cuttings will root actively in sand or rich soil at any time and it is best to achieve the benefits of pinching by taking frequent cuttings. Artillery plant is a *Pilea* and a member of the nettle family.

LIGHT: Bright indirect to almost dim light. Growth will be weak and spindly if the light is too poor.

TEMPERATURE: Average house.

HUMIDITY: Average house, most lush growth at 30 percent or more.

WATER: Average or slightly more moist.

SOIL: Standard indoor mixture with optional addition of leaf mold (3:1). Repot before stress signals appear.

PROPAGATION: Cuttings.

**Asparagus Fern**     *Asparagus sprengeri*
**Emerald Feather**     *A. plumosus*
Members of the lily family and relatives of the asparagus vegetable rather than of the true ferns, these are tough, radiantly green African foliage plants. A. *sprengeri* displays cascading branches of needlelike leaves. Bare shoots sometimes emerge and extend to a foot or more before they fill in; if after sev-

eral weeks these shoots do not become thick with bushy needlelike leaves, and if they bother you, you may certainly cut them off. Mature, satisfied plants sometimes produce short sprays of tiny and fragrant white blossoms; these are followed by bright red berries for winter cheer. The asparagus fern known as emerald feather, A. *plumosus*, has a remarkably delicate plumelike leaf. Some varieties will climb, but A. *plumosus nana*, the most commonly available, merely arches with grace. Keep in mind that asparagus ferns are directly related to outdoor vegetables and require more nitrogen in the soil than most indoor plants; foliage will yellow if the soil is insufficiently rich. Cut off yellowed fronds and fertilize.

LIGHT: Bright sunny to average indoor light.

TEMPERATURE: Average house; A. *plumosus* is more sensitive to lower humidity brought on by winter heating.

HUMIDITY: Average house. Good ventilation.

WATER: Average to evenly moist.

SOIL: Standard indoor mixture.

FERTILIZER: More frequently than normal, perhaps every six weeks during periods of active growth. Needs nitrogen.

PROPAGATION: From planted seeds or berries. Division in spring or fall.

### Aspidistra    *Aspidistra elatior*
### Cast-iron Plant

Native to China and a member of the lily family, aspidistra has long been appreciated for an uncanny ability to withstand enormous neglect. Thought indispensable since Victorian times as the forgotten man-in-the-corner, aspidistra displays heavy glossy leaves of a green which may be dark enough to appear black. Although the plant will stay alive with abuse, it is strikingly attractive if given good care. Varieties with yellow-spotted leaves (A. *elatior punctata*) or white-striped

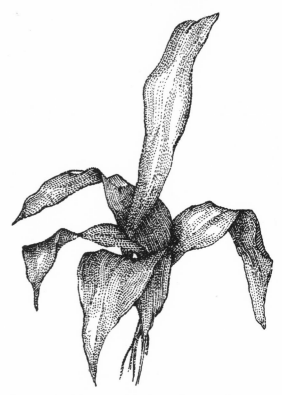

leaves (A. *elatior variegata*) may be seen, but they are not quite so handsome, I think, as the pure green.

LIGHT: Bright indirect light to shady.

TEMPERATURE: Average, but avoid excessive winter heat.

HUMIDITY: Average.

WATER: Average to evenly moist. A heavy drinker. Wash foliage well to discourage scale and maintain the glossy look.

SOIL: Standard indoor mix with additional leaf mold or humus (3:1) for better growth.

PROPAGATION: Division of root mass in early spring. Most attractive plants seem to be in 6-inch pots.

*Asplenium bulbiferum*, see **Mother Fern**

*Asplenium nidus*, see **Bird's-nest Fern**

*Asplenium viviparum*, see **Mother Fern**

**Baby Tears**     *Helxine soleirolii*
**Irish Moss**
Baby tears is a luxuriously dense, tiny-leafed creeper from the Mediterranean and, surprisingly enough, a member of the nettle family. It will creep as long as it can find moist, rich soil and will then delicately cascade. *Helxine* makes a superb ground cover in a terrarium planting, but will also do fabulously well in a pot if the room humidity is high.

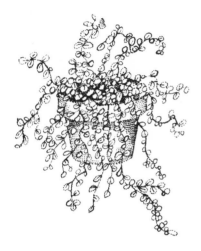

LIGHT: Average to dim or shady.

TEMPERATURE: Average house, but best under 75°.

HUMIDITY: High humidity. If you mist, do so often but lightly. The fragile stems will rot if the air is too drippy.

WATER: Evenly moist. Keep pot over sand-filled dry well.

SOIL: Standard indoor mixture with additional leaf mold (3:1).

PROPAGATION: Cuttings rooted in sand or division of the clump.

**Bamboo**     *Bambusa nana*
A member of the grass family, this cultivated bamboo provides an interesting contrast to the other plants in a home. It is native to the Orient, and may reach up to 10 feet. Cut it

back when you are overwhelmed.

LIGHT: Sunny to average indoor light.

TEMPERATURE: Average.

HUMIDITY: Average. Needs plentiful fresh air.

WATER: Evenly moist.

SOIL: Standard indoor mixture plus leaf mold or humus (3:1). High-nitrogen fertilizer for this green giant.

PROPAGATION: Division in spring.

*Bambusa nana*, see **Bamboo**

**Bear's-paw Fern**     *Polypodium aureum*
**Hare's-foot Fern**     and others
One of the so-called footed ferns, *Polypodium* displays fronds emerging from a hairy, creeping rhizome. The rhizomes are above-ground rootstalks that support the current foliage and meanwhile move out to root in other suitable spots. The fronds of these ferns are large and dramatic and may be almost blue green; spore cases are golden; rhizomes are buff or cinnamon colored. The plants are striking, most effectively planted in moss-lined wire baskets so that the creeping rhizomes may creep over the sides and their bizarre form may be enjoyed to full advantage.

LIGHT: Bright indirect to almost dim light. Delicately diffused light is best.

TEMPERATURE: Average to cool. Sensitive to lowered humidity from winter heating.

HUMIDITY: Average house, preferably 30 percent or more. Good circulation of air but no drafts.

WATER: Evenly moist. Allow topsoil to dry out lightly. Requires excellent drainage.

SOIL: Standard indoor mixture with additional leaf mold (3:1) and perhaps sphagnum moss in the soil or as basket lining.

PROPAGATION: No runners. Rhizome sections may be rooted in moist sand and planted separately. See chapter 4 for details of planting, and see FERNS for more general information.

**Bird's-nest Fern**    *Asplenium nidus*
A less delicately cut plant than most ferns, this attractive variety displays entire smooth, broad fronds with wavy margins rising in a rosette from the dark-haired center (the bird's

nest). The brightness of green color and its unusual form make this a popular plant.

LIGHT: Bright indirect to almost dim light.

TEMPERATURE: Cool preferred (40°–70°). Bird's-nest fern is particularly sensitive to artificial heat and frond edges will brown quickly when the air is too dry.

HUMIDITY: 30 percent or more. Avoid wet leaves in winter. Avoid drafts of any kind.

WATER: Evenly moist. Allow topsoil to dry only lightly. Drainage must be excellent.

SOIL: Standard indoor mixture with additional leaf mold (3:1).

PROPAGATION: Remove offsets.

**Blood Leaf**    *Iresine herbstii*
                  *I. lindenii*
Iresine is a beautiful red-leafed foliage plant from South America which has graduated from life as an outdoor bedding plant to a position in the house. It does very well indoors if it has enough light to maintain the striking crimson leaves. Pinch vigorously for full, bushy plants. Good for color in window boxes and baskets.

LIGHT: Bright direct sunlight or very bright indirect. (Outdoors they can make do with shade.)

TEMPERATURE: Average, best growth when cooler, so your sunniest spot may be too hot.

HUMIDITY: Average.

WATER: Heavy users; in other words, the interval between required soakings will be shorter than for your other plants.

SOIL: Standard indoor mixture.

PROPAGATION: Cuttings.

**Boston Fern** *Nephrolepis exaltata*
**Sword Fern** or *N. exaltata*
**Drapery Fern** *bostoniensis*

Currently the most popular of ferns for its luxuriant visual effect, Boston fern and its relatives are rather hardy plants. They are fast-growing both in length of individual fronds and in outward central growth of the root mass. Sword fern is upright, Boston is cascading; each has many popular ruffled or more finely serrated developed varieties (Fluffy Ruffles, Boston Whitmanii). If their cultural requirements are satisfied, they will take over the room. A well-satisfied, mature, and slightly cramped Boston fern will send out runners to root and form new plants. These appear as light green, fuzzy, bare fronds; you may cut them off if you dislike them, tuck their ends back into the pot soil, or root them for new plants (see chapter 3). Please refer to FERNS for more general information.

LIGHT: Bright indirect to almost dim light. Delicately diffused indoor light is the best.

TEMPERATURE: Average to cool. Sensitive to artificial heat in winter because of lowered humidity.

HUMIDITY: Average house, preferably 30 percent or more. Requires good circulation of fresh air, but no drafts.

WATER: Evenly moist. Allow topsoil to dry out only lightly. Requires excellent drainage.

SOIL: Standard indoor mixture with additional leaf mold (3:1).

PROPAGATION: Runners. Division of root mass in spring.

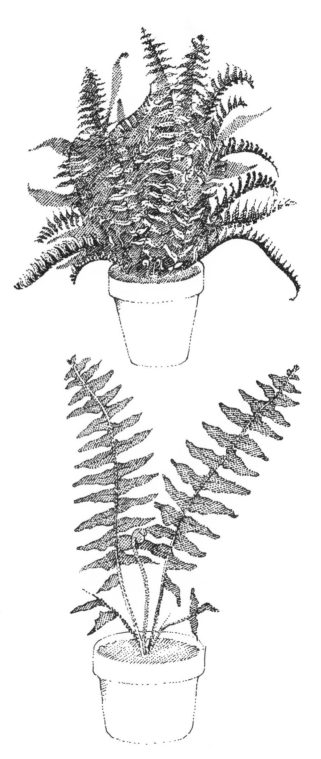

Brake fern, see **Table Fern**

*Brassica hirta*, see **HERBS, Mustard**

**Butterfly Palm**    *Chrysalidocarpus*
**Golden Feather**       *lutescens*
  **Palm**
**Areca Palm**
Butterfly Palm hails from Mauritius, will finally reach up to 25 feet, and will accept brighter than normal light. It grows outward in a clumpy fashion, displays feather- or streamerlike fronds, and has the excellent habit of refusing to shed lower fronds. The leaf stalks are normally almost yellow.

LIGHT: Semisunny to average indoor light.

TEMPERATURE: Average house; warmth is fine if humidity is not too low.

HUMIDITY: Average house or slightly higher, 30 percent or more.

WATER: Evenly moist, allow topsoil to dry out only lightly. Hold back on water during winter rest period.

SOIL: Standard indoor mixture with firm, almost heavy texture.

PROPAGATION: Division of clump. Seeds sown in spring.

**Button Fern**    *Pellaea rotundifolia*
A funny little fern with fat, rounded leaflets lined up along the main center vein. The plant is sturdier and fleshier than most ferns. Its cultural requirements are similar to those of Boston fern (see p. 157); yet because of its less delicate texture it will thrive with slightly lower humidity.

**Caladium**    *Caladium bicolor*
**Elephant Ears**
Foliage plants from tropical Mexico, caladiums offer extravagant indoor colors. Each leaf is shaped much like an arrowhead or elephant's ear and may be almost paper thin. The many named varieties of new color combinations glory in green, white, pink, yellow, bronze, and/or red. Caladium is grown from tubers.

LIGHT: Bright indirect to average indoor light.

TEMPERATURE: Warm. Avoid drafts.

HUMIDITY: 30 percent or more.

WATER: Evenly moist during growing season of spring to fall. After leaves fade, reduce water until soil is dry and foliage dies down. Store tubers in dry sand or in their pots until spring. Storage location must be warm, not below 55°–60°.

SOIL: Standard indoor mixture with additional leaf mold, peat moss or manure (3:1). Best soil is rich and slightly acid. Fertilize weekly until end of summer, then stop in order to allow tubers to ripen for next year's growth.

PROPAGATION: Divide tubers into separate clumps in the spring. If you are starting new tubers, here's what you do: In March or April, you should pot tubers ½-inch deep and supply even moisture and warmth (best results

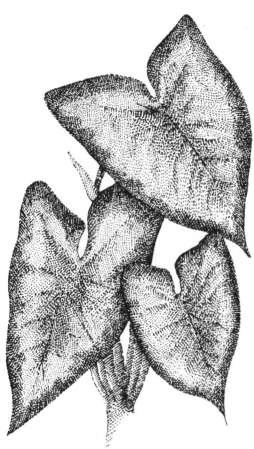

*Chamaedora elegans bella*, see **Parlor Palm**

*Chamaerops humilis*, see **European Fan Palm**

| **Chinese Ever-green** | *Aglaonema modestum* |
|---|---|
| | *A. simplex* |

A hearty member of the aroid family, Chinese evergreen presents a profusion of large, waxy green leaves set on a slender cane stem. Its kinship with dieffenbachia, and philodendron, pothos, and spathiphyllum is clear; this is a permanent, undemanding plant and a good one for beginners. Unassuming white flower stalks may appear and are followed in winter by red berries. Most attractive when planted several per pot.

LIGHT: Bright indirect to almost dim light.

TEMPERATURE: Average house.

HUMIDITY: Average house.

WATER: Average water. May be grown in plain water for long periods, but best results seem to come when grown in soil with thor-

around 80°) to prompt the new foliage. Obviously, a soil-heating cable is necessary for this kind of job. Begin in a 3-inch pot with leaf mold predominating; pot-on to 6-inch size when roots fill the first pot, and use the soil mixture above.

*Carum carvi*, see **HERBS, Caraway**

*Caryota*, see **Fishtail Palm**

Cast-iron plant, see **Aspidistra**

Catmint, see **HERBS, Mint**

Catnip, see **HERBS, Mint**

*Ceropegia woodii*, see **String of Hearts**

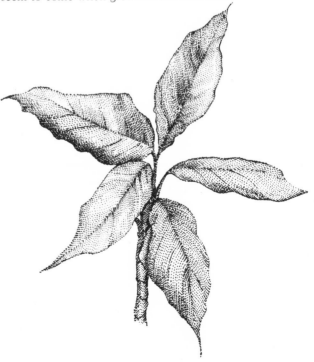

ough soaking, followed by a distinct drying-out period.

SOIL: Standard indoor mixture.

PROPAGATION: Tip cuttings or cane sections in spring or summer. Air layering of older plants.

**Chinese Fan**          *Livistona chinensis*
   **Palm**

This fan-shaped palm requires a lot of room. It has a broad lateral spread and may grow up to 30 feet high—so when yours begins to touch the ceiling, call up the local conservatory and make your donation. The Chinese fan palm is more fussy than others about fresh air and also requires the higher levels of humidity.

LIGHT: Subdued average indoor light to almost dim.

TEMPERATURE: Average house.

HUMIDITY: Slightly higher than average (50 percent or more). Ample fresh air but no

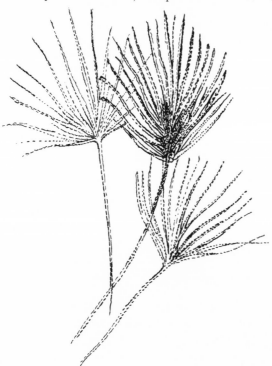

drafts. Use sphagnum moss to cover topsoil, provide dry well under plants, and/or mist.

WATER: Evenly moist, allow topsoil to dry out only lightly. Hold back on water during winter rest.

SOIL: Standard indoor mixture with a firm, almost heavy texture.

PROPAGATION: Removal of offset "suckers." Seeds.

*Chlorophytum elatum*, see **Spider Plant**

*Chrysalidocarpus lutescens*, see **Butterfly Palm**

*Cissus antarctica*, see **Kangaroo Ivy**

*Cissus rhombifolia*, see **Grape Ivy**

**Cocos Palm**          *Syagrus weddelliana*
**Weddell Palm**

A small variety of palm from Rio de Janiero, cocos displays beautiful feather- or streamer-shaped fronds. It is often seen as a seedling in terrarium plantings.

LIGHT: Average indoor light to almost dim.

TEMPERATURE: Average house; warmth is fine.

HUMIDITY: Average house or higher (30 percent or more).

WATER: Evenly moist. Allow topsoil to dry out only lightly between waterings. Reduce water during winter rest.

SOIL: Standard indoor mixture.

PROPAGATION: Seeds sown in spring.

**Coleus**          *Coleus blumei*
**Painted Nettle**

A giant in the house-plant boom, this attractive plant is a member of the mint family and native to Java. The striking colors of the foliage intensify with better light. This is a fast-growing plant and requires constant

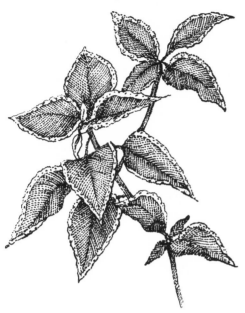

Creeping charlie, see **Swedish Ivy**

**Creeping Fig**         *Ficus pumila*
                        *F. radicans*
A small, creeping plant with heart-shaped leaves—very different from the larger figs. Creeping fig will climb if provided with a damp surface or will spread out if given moisture and space. Most useful in terrariums.

pinching to assure bushy growth. Flower spikes should be pinched out as soon as they form; I happen to like the delicate (known in the trade as "insignificant") blue flowers, but they demand a considerable amount of the plant's energy so do not let the plant finish its flowering cycle if you are not totally satisfied with the lushness of the present foliage growth.

LIGHT: Bright direct or indirect light. The better the light, the greater the color intensity. But beware of leaf drop with the scorchingly hot sun.

TEMPERATURE: Average house.

HUMIDITY: Average house. Provide ample ventilation and practice avid but gentle leaf washing to discourage mealybugs.

WATER: Average to moist. Coleus uses a lot of water.

SOIL: Standard indoor mixture.

PROPAGATION: Cuttings at any time. Seeds sown in late winter or in spring.

Corn plant, see **Dracaena**

LIGHT: Bright indirect to almost dim.

TEMPERATURE: Average house.

HUMIDITY: Average house, best at 30 percent or more. A dry well of pebbles or sand will encourage luxuriant creeping.

WATER: Average to evenly moist, do not allow to dry out completely. Keep leaves clean.

SOIL: Standard indoor mixture.

PROPAGATION: Stem cuttings.

**Croton**         *Codiaeum variegatum*
                  *pictum* and others
Croton comprises a group of fabulously colored foliage plants from the tropics. Species, varieties, and sports are numerous—with a profusion of color combinations, markings, and leaf shapes; but all are called croton. Mature leaves may be of different colors than young ones; rarely will two leaves be identical, even on the same plant. Unless kept at even warmth and high humidity, croton will

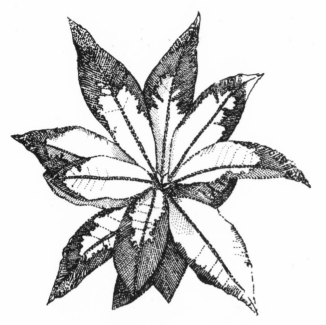

drafts will cause extensive leaf drop. Spray foliage regularly to discourage red spider mites and mealybugs.

WATER: Average to evenly moist.

SOIL: Standard indoor mixture with additional leaf mold (3:1).

PROPAGATION: Cuttings in warmth (above 70°) and high humidity. Larger plants may be air layered.

*Cyperus alternifolius*, see **Umbrella Plant**

*Cyrtomium falcatum rochefordianum*, see **Holly Fern**

*Davallia bullata mariesii*, see **Rabbit's-foot Fern**

*Davallia fejeensis*, see **Rabbit's-foot Fern**

Devil's ivy, see **Pothos**

drop leaves with gay abandon. For this reason croton is a difficult and often disappointing plant. Perhaps a poor choice for a limited collection; try it first in a frequently ventilated terrarium.

LIGHT: Bright direct or indirect light. Abundant sunlight will encourage the more striking colorations of the leaves.

TEMPERATURE: Average house to warm.

HUMIDITY: High, 40 percent or preferably more. Requires plenty of fresh air, but any

**Dieffenbachia**      *Dieffenbachia* var.
**Dumb Cane**
**Mother-in-law**
  **Plant**

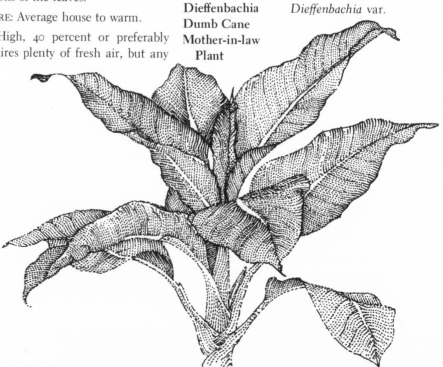

Dieffenbachias are handsome, cane-stemmed foliage plants. The plant's sap contains poisonous calcium oxalate and may cause a painful paralysis of the tongue if leaves or stems are chewed; hence, the common names. Even young dieffenbachias appear massive and grand; older plants will inevitably develop barren lower stems. The most common varieties display white or yellow veining or white-flecked patterns on the pointed oblong leaves. Easy to care for and permanent.

LIGHT: Bright indirect to average indoor light. Direct sun will cause burn spots on leaves; better light brings greater contrast of colors.

TEMPERATURE: Average house, warmer without problems.

HUMIDITY: Average house, but growth more luxuriant at 30 percent or more. Spray foliage liberally to discourage pests and encourage natural gloss of leaves.

WATER: Average. Soak well, then allow topsoil to become dry.

SOIL: Standard indoor mixture.

PROPAGATION: Air layer large plants. Remaining cane stem may be sectioned. Tip cuttings from younger plants in high humidity.

*Dizygotheca elegantissima*, see **Aralia**

**Dracaena**
**Corn Plant**

*Dracaena sanderiana*
*D. fragrans*
*D. marginata*

Reliable and decorative members of the lily family and primarily native to tropical Africa, the dracaenas display long, slender leaves emerging centrally from a cane stem. Older plants often become quite bare and tough below but, if clustered with several per pot, they are still impressive. Varieties include plants with deep green leaves striped with white (*D. sanderiana*), large, soft, scarflike leaves banded in cream or yellow (*D. fragrans* —a Victorian stand-by), or bladelike leaves

touched at the margins with red (*D. marginata*). Permanent and simple plants.

LIGHT: Bright indirect to dim light.

TEMPERATURE: Average house.

HUMIDITY: Average house.

WATER: Average. Soak well, then allow topsoil to become dry.

SOIL: Standard indoor mixture.

PROPAGATION: Seeds. Tip cuttings. Air layering of larger plants and cane section of bare stem.

Drapery fern, see **Boston Fern**

Dumb cane, see **Dieffenbachia**

Elephant ears, see **Caladium**

Emerald feather, see **Asparagus Fern**

**English Ivy**
*Hedera helix* and var.
There are close to a hundred named varieties of English ivy, some with white or yellow

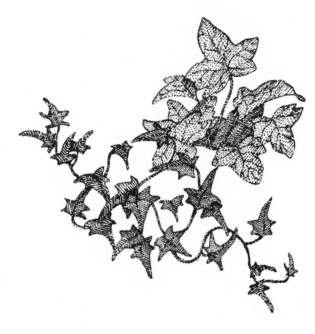

through the green, some scalloped or ruffled at the edge, large-leafed varieties and small. All are admirably sturdy and attractive plants. Troubles with English ivy can usually be traced to excessive room heat and/or low humidity. Of the more popular varieties are heart-leafed, Hahn's, canary, and needle-point. Pinch all vigorously, as they grow outward and threaten to get leggy. Winding barren stems back over available topsoil and pinning them down to root will achieve a fuller appearance for older plants.

LIGHT: Average indoor light. Anything but direct bright sunlight or the shadiest other extreme.

TEMPERATURE: Cool (40°–75°). In winter try for an unheated location; beware of the drop in humidity in heated rooms. Cool temperature and higher humidity are the keys to success. Red spider mites are devoted to English ivy; scale may also make an appearance.

WATER: Average to evenly moist. Allow an occasional drying-out period if you are generally keeping the soil quite moist.

SOIL: Standard indoor mixture with optional addition of leaf mold or more peat moss (3:1). Maintain loose soil texture.

PROPAGATION: Cuttings.

**European Fan Palm**  *Chamaerops humilis*

With the broad lateral spread characteristic of fan-shaped palms, *Chamaerops* requires a lot of room. While it may thrive in brighter-than-normal locations, it also prefers a cooler temperature range (50°–70°).

LIGHT: Semisunny to subdued general indoor light.

TEMPERATURE: Average house, cooler preferred.

HUMIDITY: Average or slightly higher (30 percent or more).

WATER: Evenly moist, allow topsoil to dry out lightly between waterings. Reduce water during winter rest.

SOIL: Standard indoor mixture with firm, almost heavy texture.

PROPAGATION: Removal of offsets or "suckers." Seeds.

False aralia, see **Aralia**

*Fatshedera lizei*, see **Tree Ivy**

**Fatsia**  *Fatsia japonica*

Fatsia is an aralia that is an admirable foliage plant with lobed, dark green, and glossy leaves. It may become enormous, and obviously is native to Japan.

LIGHT: Bright, indirect to average indoor light.

TEMPERATURE: Average, best growth when cool.

HUMIDITY: 30 percent or more.

WATER: Average to evenly moist. Consistency.

SOIL: Standard indoor mixture.

PROPAGATION: Terminal stem cuttings in spring.

## FERNS          *Polypodiaceae*

By dint of volumes written, ferns are to horticulture what William Shakespeare is to literature. The airy beauty of the ferns captures the heart and then we fern fanciers try everything to have them flourish indoors. It has been my experience that they will indeed flourish, that the most difficult aspect of their care involves finding the most suitable location at the start.

Ferns require consistent care. They prefer higher-than-average humidity, moderately warm temperatures (60°–70°), constantly available moisture in the soil, and a rich, loose planting mixture.

They do not need to be watered daily, just often enough to assure that roots will find water when they need it. So you water, as always, when you can feel from the topsoil that the roots have made use of the water from last time. Their delicate roots will rot in standing water; so any fern planting must emphasize good drainage and a porous soil texture. They need a spot that offers indirect or filtered light. In brighter indirect light the frond color will be a milder green and in nearly dim light the green will be thicker and darker. Remember that house-plant ferns are native to the tropics. This means they are well adapted to the degree of warmth in a home, but that they require more humidity than they generally find there. Ferns were perhaps more reliable as house plants before every home had central heating and its consequent dry air. The more finely cut and lacy is the foliage, the more water vapor is lost from the increased surface area of the fronds, and the more careful you must be to maintain adequate relative humidity.

The sitting or hanging site for a fern must emphasize protection from the bumps of passing people and the vicissitudes of draft-producing open windows or proximity to sources of drying heat.

Should any fronds become damaged or unattractively old, cut them off at their base near the soil. Yellowing of fronds may be caused by too much light, standing water, injury (from clumsy people, animals, wind, or whatever), or the need for fertilizer. Fern roots burn promptly with overly strong doses of fertilizer; many growers therefore pot in rich soil, spread a slow-release form of fertilizer on top of the soil, and tell new owners *not* to feed the plant. If you feel the fern's original supply of food has been exhausted and repotting with newly rich soil is not indicated, merely water the fern well and then water again with a very dilute fertilizer solution. You may use a high-nitrogen fertilizer since ferns do not flower. They reproduce by runners, plantlets, offsets, or spores.

When you become highly confident of your fern-nurturing abilities, you might try your hand at raising new ones from spores. Ferns are primitive plants, present on the globe for the last three hundred million years. You need not worry that they are too fragile to endure. The spores are the little brown dots produced in a regular pattern on the backs of the fronds. Gather them after they have ripened and are dark and almost dry; cut off the fertile frond and place it on a piece of hard paper and weight it and wait a few days for the spore cases to open and release the spores. Provide a loose, rich, damp soil and tamp it down to a smooth surface; lightly tap the spores onto the soil and cover the planting with plastic or glass. Everything used must be sterilized: soil, water, container, and tamper. Germination time varies with the individual ferns, from days to months. Eventually, if sterility is maintained and consistent moisture provided, you will have your own home-grown ferns.

General care for all ferns must include vigilance against scale insects. Scales will cluster in irregular patterns along the midvein on the back of the fronds and on the stalks. Do not confuse them with the regularly arranged spore cases. One situation indicates excellent health, the other is trouble. Deal with the trouble promptly and inspect ferns regularly to rout scale attacks before they become invasions.

For specific cultural requirements of an individual fern, see entry under its common name.

*Ficus benjamina*, see **Weeping Fig**

*Ficus elastica*, see **Rubber Plant**

*Ficus lyrata*, see **Fiddle-leaf Fig**

*Ficus pandurata*, see **Fiddle-leaf Fig**

*Ficus pumila*, see **Creeping Fig**

*Ficus radicans*, see **Creeping Fig**

**Fiddle-leaf Fig**      *Ficus lyrata* or
                          *Ficus pandurata*
A beautiful and popular plant of permanent stature. The leaves are large and glossy and of a peculiar, waving, lyrical shape; they have never reminded *me* of a fiddle, but the name is euphonious and some think it fits. Lower-

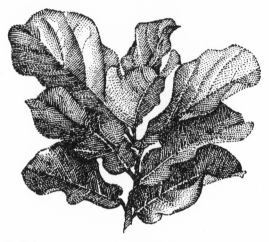

leaf drop is common under difficult conditions. Frequent pinching will encourage a bushy plant. Consistent care will achieve a large plant of impressive good looks.

LIGHT: Bright indirect to almost dim.

TEMPERATURE: Average house.

HUMIDITY: Average house, best at 30 percent or more. A dry well or sphagnum moss to cover topsoil is helpful.

WATER: Average to evenly moist. Never allow the soil to dry out completely or lower leaves will begin to fall. Clean leaves regularly with dampened sponge or firm spray of plain water.

SOIL: Standard indoor mixture.

PROPAGATION: Stem cuttings. Air layering of larger specimens.

**Fishtail Palm**      *Caryota* ssp.
This feather-shaped palm will accept brighter-than-normal locations, even a bit of direct sun. It is a beautiful indoor plant when young enough to fit beneath the ceiling.

LIGHT: Semisunny to almost dim light locations.

TEMPERATURE: Average house.

HUMIDITY: Average house or slightly higher (30 percent or more).

WATER: Evenly moist, allow topsoil to dry out only lightly between soakings. Reduce water during winter rest.

SOIL: Standard indoor mixture with firm, almost heavy texture.

PROPAGATION: Seeds sown in spring. Division of varieties that increase outwardly in a clump.

**Fittonia** *Fittonia verschaffeltii*
**Nerve Plant** var.

A lovely and beguiling native of Peru, fittonia is a creeper and a trailer. It demands high humidity or will brown and curl at the leaf tips; so perhaps it is best suited to a terrarium situation for average homes. The varieties available are striking plants: oval, bright green leaves with fine white veins or dark green leaves with scarlet veins. Both are knockouts.

LIGHT: Average indoor to almost dim light.

TEMPERATURE: Average house, preferably warmer. Watch the relative humidity at higher temperatures.

HUMIDITY: 50 percent or more.

WATER: Average to evenly moist.

SOIL: Standard indoor mixture with additional leaf mold or peat moss (3:1).

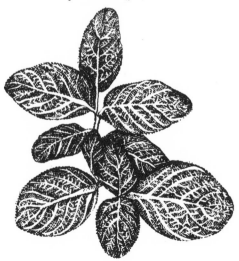

PROPAGATION: Cuttings in sand with warmth (70°–80°) and high humidity.

Freckle-face, see **Pink Polka Dot**

**Friendship Plant** *Pilea involucrata*
**Panimiga**

Friendship plant is a *pilea* that boasts an easily branching, compact habit; its leaves are slightly hairy and minutely quilted or pebbled in appearance. The color is a bronzed or reddish green with minute, pale green flowers clustered at the center of each terminal shoot. This is an easy plant to nurture, if it is provided proper light and a moist and loose-textured rich soil. It does quite well in a terrarium.

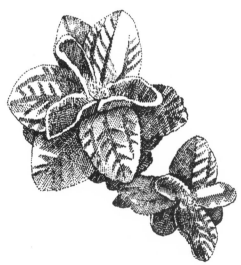

LIGHT: Average to almost dim.

TEMPERATURE: Average house.

HUMIDITY: Average house, most lush growth at 30 percent or more.

WATER: Average or slightly more moist, allowing topsoil to dry out lightly between soakings.

SOIL: Standard indoor mixture with addition of leaf mold (3:1).

PROPAGATION: Cuttings rooted in sand.

**Grape Ivy**        *Cissus rhombifolia*

Indeed a member of the grape family, this vine has attractive, glossy, three-part leaves. The metallic shine of the leaves, the curling tendrils, backup leaves at branch axils, and compact, cascading habit make this a popular plant. Although not as naturally leggy as other ivies, grape ivy will occasionally drop lower leaves. In this event, pinching and/or the winding of barren stems back over available spots of soil and pinning the stems down will result in a fuller appearance.

LIGHT: Average indoor light. Avoid direct sun.

TEMPERATURE: Average house, but 75° is tops in winter.

HUMIDITY: Average house.

WATER: Average to evenly moist. Opinions differ widely on the water requirements of *Cissus*. Begin by keeping the soil evenly moist and allowing an occasional drying-out period; then vary your plan as you see fit. The more water available, the more rapid growth will be, but take sensible precautions to avoid waterlogging the soil. Wash foliage vigorously and inspect undersides of leaves at frequent intervals to rout red spider mites and scale insects.

SOIL: Standard indoor mixture.

PROPAGATION: Cuttings. Grape ivy requires warmth (70°–80°) and high humidity to produce roots.

Golden feather palm, see **Butterfly Palm**

*Gynura aurantiaca*, see **Velvet Plant**

Hare's-foot fern, see **Bear's-paw Fern**

Hearts entangled, see **String of Hearts**

*Hedera helix*, see **English Ivy**

*Helxine soleirolii*, see **Baby Tears**

## HERBS

Herbs at the kitchen window seem to be one of the archetypes of the cozy home. If you have the time, don't fight the feeling. There is, however, a common notion that herbs thrive on neglect and poor soil, perhaps because so many were considered "weeds" until they were finally tasted. In fact, they require top conditions for luxuriant tasty growth. It has been my experience that most herb plants go rapidly downhill as soon as they are the least bit neglected. Unlike the other indoor plants, they have not been carefully and slowly adapted away from their natural outdoor preference. Any home-grown, indoor herb will be more tender and heady in its aroma than the market or garden variety. But even at best they seem short-lived and, whenever weakened, become a haven for whiteflies. I've found I enjoy my herb collection thoroughly when I view it as a round-robin, rather temporary group. As the wild things

say to Max: "We'll eat you up, we love you so."* As far as I'm concerned, sweet basil for pesto is as much a staple as toothpaste.

In general, herbs require a sunny location, relatively high humidity (30–60 percent) and a well-drained, rich, loose soil. Most must be kept evenly moist. Their temperature range is 50°–75°, with a nighttime drop of from 10° to 15° for best growth. They will not do well in a heated room, particularly if the thermostat is left up at night. Herbs require a great deal of pinching beyond the normal harvest; if unguided most will become quite leggy since even the sunniest window does not compete with the light intensity of an unsheltered garden. Turn them regularly for even growth. Wash the foliage liberally at each watering. Since they are humidity lovers, you might group them or arrange them in a decorative tray above a dry well. Herbs do exceedingly well in a window box in good weather. Obviously you must avoid chemical pest sprays if you plan to eat your produce, although rotenone and pyrethrum are supposedly safe if used sufficiently in advance of the harvest.

* Maurice Sendak, *Where The Wild Things Are.*

To dry your herbs, cut them before they flower, tie the stems in bunches, and hang them upside down in an exceedingly well-ventilated, dim location. The airier the drying place the faster the herbs will dry and the better they will taste. Brighter light will rob them of their good green color. When they are unquestionably free from moisture, strip the leaves if you wish and pack them in airtight bottles. Leaves harvested for drying are generally most flavorful if picked in midsummer.

Here are some of the favorites and their peculiarities, if any. To sample their flavors before you buy, rub a leaf with your thumb and then smell your thumb. It is the slight bruising of the plant tissue that releases the aroma.

**Bay**        *Laurus nobilis*
Cooler temperature (50°–60°), prune to keep as a bush or small tree. Buy young plants in fall.

**Caraway**        *Carum carvi*
Plant seeds in spring or fall. Caraway is a biennial: you have two years before the plant goes to seed again.

**Chives**        *Allium schoenoprasum*
Warmer temperatures are fine. Clip chives vigorously to promote bushy growth. The plant takes a three-month rest period, after which you should divide the clump and repot. The chive flowers are beautiful but, if you're raising the plant for eating purposes, pinch them out before they can develop.

**Dill**        *Anethum graveolens*
Annual, cooler temperature preferred, feed sparsely and keep clipped to 12 inches. Seeds planted in spring for summer use (pickles) or in early September for winter (potato soup).

**Marjoram**        *Marjorana hortensis*
Perennial, plant seeds at any time, discard or prune severely in winter, cut back any

flowers. A lovely, small-leaved trailing plant; try a mass of it in a hanging basket.

**Mint**          *Mentha* var.
Also related:
**Catnip** or      *Nepeta cataria*
**Catmint**
Partial sun, cooler temperatures preferred. Pinch vigorously, shear flowers. The family includes spearmint, peppermint, pennyroyal, bergamot. Perennials.

**Mustard**        *Brassica hirta*
Annual, sow seeds at any time (darkness required), discard plant when dying down. Cooler temperatures preferred.

**Oregano**        *Origanum vulgare*
Cut back severely in fall. Treat as for marjoram; they're of the same family. Perennial, but oregano gets woody and will need to be replaced at least every three years.

**Parsley**        *Petroselinum crispum*
Cut back vigorously. Best plants are dug from garden in late summer and acclimated to a sunny winter window. Seeds may be planted any time; soak them at least twenty-four hours, germination is quite slow. Clip flower heads and discard plant when growth slows down.

**Rosemary**       *Rosmarinus officinalis*
Prune as necessary, at least a few inches once a year. Perennial and slow grower. Needs alkaline soil; add lime or wood ashes to top-soil monthly. Feed often. Leaf drop from warm temperatures and need for more alkaline condition.

**Sage**          *Salvia officinalis*
Cut vigorously for bushy growth. Needs a lot of water, but watch for mildew on the pebbly leaves. Perennial: seeds or cuttings.

**Sweet Basil**    *Ocimum basilicum*
and less common varieties:
**Purple Basil**
**Lemon-scented**
  **Basil**
**Lettuce-leafed**
  **Basil**

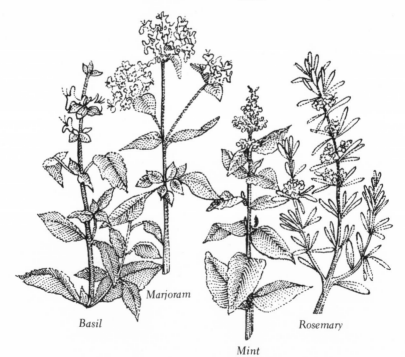

*Marjoram*

*Basil*

*Rosemary*

*Mint*

Annual, seeds planted in fall or spring, discard tired plants. Fertilize at least monthly. Plant seeds sparsely and pinch vigorously for bushier, leafier (therefore tastier) plants.

**Tarragon**  *Artemisia dracunculus*
A marvelous flavor and one of the most amazing Latin names in the book. Partial sun and rich soil preferred. Take cuttings; divide plant annually to prevent dying out at the center. Grows from rhizomes.

**Thyme**  *Thymus vulgaris*
Sandy, slightly alkaline soil and less than average water preferred. Perennial: seeds or summer cuttings. Pinch for bushiness and discourage flowers.

**Holly Fern**  *Cyrtomium falcatum rochefordianum*
The holly fern displays sharply toothed, hollylike leaflets arranged evenly along a robust and furry center stalk. The foliage is dark green, glossy, and firm, and the uncurling of new fronds from the center appears as a bold ritual. Each new frond is slightly longer than the one before.

LIGHT: Average indoor to dim light.

TEMPERATURE: Average to cool (35°–70°).

HUMIDITY: 30 percent or more.

WATER: Evenly moist. Allow topsoil to dry out only lightly.

SOIL: Standard indoor mixture with additional leaf mold (3:1).

PROPAGATION: Division of rhizomes in spring.

*Howea belmoreana*, see **Kentia Palm**

*Howea forsteriana*, see **Kentia Palm**

*Hypoestes sanguinolenta*, see **Pink Polka Dot**

Inch plant, see **Wandering Jew**

*Iresine*, see **Blood Leaf**

Irish moss, see **Baby Tears**

## IVY AND FRIENDS
Not all plants generally referred to as ivy are botanically related, but many have similar growing requirements. The cuttings of all but grape ivy provide avidly rooting replacement parts; grape ivy usually requires soil heat and high humidity to root. Pinch ivy plants with great abandon. All can benefit from winding barren stems back over available spots of the topsoil and pinning them down for a fuller appearance. Be quite conscientious about washing the foliage with a hard spray of water and inspecting the undersides of the leaves at frequent intervals. Scale is the classic enemy, but watch out for red spider mites on *Cissus* and mealybugs on *Plectranthus*.

For the specific cultural needs of each ivy, see the entry under its common name.

Japanese fern ball, see **Rabbit's-foot Fern**

Japanese yew, see **Podocarpus**

Java fig, see **Weeping Fig**

**Kangaroo Ivy**  *Cissus antarctica*
**Kangaroo Vine**
A beautiful, rambling vine, with large, oval, toothed leaves, kangaroo ivy provides us with a hearty and favorite plant. It is fast growing, will cascade or climb, and is absolutely spectacular when planted in a large pot and given a rough trellis to climb. As with the other ivies, pinch vigorously; if necessary, you may wind barren stems back over available spots of soil and pin them down to root there for a fuller appearance.

LIGHT: Semisunny to average indoor light.

TEMPERATURE: Average house, but beware of furnace-induced lower humidity in winter.

TEMPERATURE: Average house.

HUMIDITY: Average or slightly higher (30 percent or more). Dry wells, misting, and/or sphagnum moss used to cover the topsoil are well-rewarded humidifying improvements. Avoid drafts.

WATER: Evenly moist, allow topsoil to dry out lightly between waterings. Spray or wash foliage regularly. Reduce water during winter rest period.

HUMIDITY: Average house, growth most luxuriant at higher levels (30 percent or more).

WATER: Average to evenly moist. The more water available, the more rapid growth will be. However, allow an occasional distinct drying-out period to avoid waterlogging the soil. Wash foliage vigorously and inspect the leaves and stems at frequent intervals for red spider mites and scale insects.

SOIL: Standard indoor mixture.

PROPAGATION: Cuttings rooted in soil or water.

| | |
|---|---|
| **Kentia Palm** | *Howea* or *Kentia belmoreana* |
| **Sentry Palm** | *H.* or *K. forsteriana* |
| **Paradise Palm** | |

These palms are particularly hardy, slow growing, and stout at the base. They are the ones most commonly used for renting out to weddings, hotels, and the like. They are native to Lord Howe Island off the coast of Australia.

LIGHT: Subdued average indoor light to shady or almost dim.

SOIL: Standard indoor mixture with a firm, almost heavy texture.

PROPAGATION: Removal of offsets or "suckers" at base of older plants. Seeds sown in spring.

*Laurus nobilis*, see **HERBS, Bay**

**Leather Fern**     *Polystichum*
                     *adiantiforme*

An admirable smaller fern of upright type, leather fern boasts triangular dark green fronds usually 1 to 1½ feet in length. The texture of the leaflets is indeed leathery and firm.

LIGHT: Bright indirect to almost dim light. Delicately diffused indoor light is the best.

TEMPERATURE: Average to cool.

HUMIDITY: Average house. Because of the firm texture of the fronds, leather fern will manage at lower levels; however growth will be most luxuriant at 30 percent or more. Requires circulation of fresh air but no drafts.

WATER: Average to evenly moist. Water when topsoil begins to be slightly dry. Excellent drainage.

SOIL: Standard indoor mixture with additional leaf mold (3:1).

PROPAGATION: Division in spring.

Lemon-scented basil, see **HERBS, Sweet Basil**

Lettuce-leafed basil, see **HERBS, Sweet Basil**

*Livistona chinensis*, see **Chinese Fan Palm**

**Maidenhair Fern**     *Adiantum* var.

Maidenhair ferns are the most challenging of the ferns as house plants. Consider that their foliage is more intricately and finely cut than any other fern and you will appreciate the difficulty of maintaining a perfect nurturing balance of air temperature, humidity, and water in the soil. Should any calamity strike—drafts, a blast of hot air from the furnace, or a sudden drop in temperature—all fronds may wither and die. Maidenhairs are perhaps best suited to indoor culture in terrariums, but if you care to try them out and about, remember that if the fronds all topple you may sim-

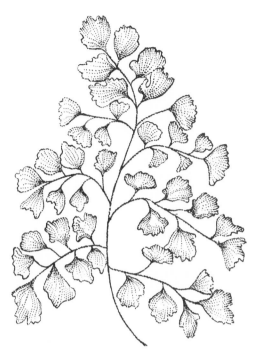

ply cut them off at the soil level and, if the root ball is healthy, the fern will soon renew itself.

Maidenhair varieties comprise a seemingly endless list. All display bright black, wirelike center stems. The small, delicate leaflets are generally wedge-shaped and ruffled at their borders. The foliage is extremely fine and so are the roots; the planting medium must be rich, soft, spongy, and constantly moist. The plant requires a distinct resting period in winter; water less, move the plant to a cool location, and expect a few older fronds to die out.

LIGHT: Indirect or filtered light.

TEMPERATURE: Average to cool (45°–70°).

HUMIDITY: 50 percent or more for best growth. Mist regularly but lightly and set plants on dry wells.

WATER: Keep evenly and consistently moist.

SOIL: A rich, porous medium which will hold oxygen in the soil, but may be kept constantly moist. Standard indoor potting mixture (1 part), combined with peat moss, sphagnum moss, or leaf mold (3 parts). Straight peat moss, leaf mold, or shredded fir bark may also be used.

PROPAGATION: Division of root clump in spring. Repotting best done only in spring.

**Maranta**          *Maranta leuconeura*
**Prayer Plant**          var.
**Old Rabbit Tracks**

These unusual plants are native to the tropical rain forests of South America and like their places warm, moist, and almost shady. It is rare to see a home-grown maranta without brown leaf tips from excessively dry air. A terrarium is one solution, but the foliage of this plant is so striking the most growers want to try for more public display. The leaves are broad and green with darker, almost brown, blotches between the veins, moving out from the midrib (*M. leuconeura kerchoveana*). The more rare *M. leuconeura massangeana* displays silver and red stripes moving out to the leaf borders. Both varieties close up for the night like hands in prayer.

LIGHT: Filtered indoor light to almost dim.

TEMPERATURE: Average house, warm nights (65°–70°) preferred.

HUMIDITY: 30 percent or more. Misting and/or dry wells will stave off browning at the tips.

WATER: Evenly moist but hold back on water when the plant takes a marked winter rest.

SOIL: Standard indoor mixture with additional leaf mold (3:1). A rich, loose soil as for begonias.

PROPAGATION: Offsets. Division at spring repotting.

Marble queen, see **Pothos**

*Marjorana hortensis*, see **HERBS, Marjoram**

*Mentha*, see **HERBS, Mint**

Mexican breadfruit, see **Monstera**

**Monstera**          *Monstera deliciosa*
**Swiss-cheese**
  **Plant**
**Shingle Plant**
**Mexican**
  **Breadfruit**

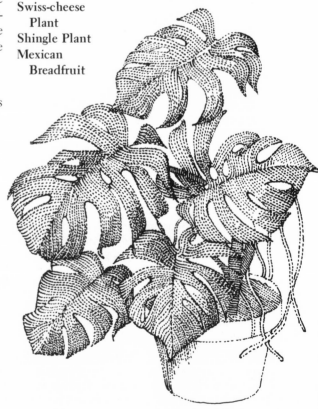

Monstera is a simple plant whose greatest claim to fame is that it is usually lumped in together with the philodendrons and incorrectly called *Philodendron pertusa*. Its large, oval leaves develop deep indentations and holes as they mature, and the plant is an avid climber. Younger plants are so quick to begin their upward path that the leaves come fast upon each other and offer a shingled-roof effect. See PHILODENDRONS for full discussion of cultural requirements.

### Mother fern
*Asplenium bulbiferum*
or *A. viviparum*

These graceful, upright ferns are most famous for their progeny. Small baby ferns are borne upon the top side of mature fronds. As the plantlets become larger and heavier, the frond bends down or breaks off to the forest floor. The plantlets root quickly and new growing sites are established. Obviously you may do the same at home: cut the plantlet-bearing frond away from the mother plant; pot in a 2- to 3-inch pot with a bit of the frond below the soil level as an anchor; provide humidity and warmth for best results.

Mother fern is of the same genus as bird's-nest fern and cultural requirements are similar.

LIGHT: Bright direct to almost dim light.

TEMPERATURE: Average house, cool preferred (40°–70°).

HUMIDITY: 30 percent or more. Avoid wetting the foliage in winter; it may cause fronds to brown. Avoid drafts.

WATER: Evenly moist. Allow topsoil to dry only slightly between waterings. Excellent drainage required.

SOIL: Standard indoor mixture with additional leaf mold (3:1).

PROPAGATION: Remove plantlets on bearing fronds.

Mother-in-law plant, see **Dieffenbachia**

Mother-in-law's Tongue, see **Sansevieria**

Mother of thousands, see **Saxifraga**

*Neanthe bella*, see **Parlor Palm**

*Nepeta cataria*, see **HERBS, Mint**

*Nephrolepis exaltata bostoniensis*, see **Boston Fern**

*Nephthytis*, see **Syngonium**

Nerve plant, see **Fittonia**

### Norfolk Island Pine
*Araucaria excelsa*

An old-fashioned favorite, its stoic constitution and symmetrical good looks should not be surprising since this house plant is indeed a small pine tree. Stiff needles, resinlike sap, and even cones are part of the package. Be advised that Norfolk Island is in the South Seas and don't expect this pine to make do with life on the back porch as if it were the northern forest primeval.

LIGHT: Bright general or average indoor light to almost dim.

TEMPERATURE: Cool, not over 65° in winter, preferably lower.

HUMIDITY: 30 percent or more.

WATER: Keep evenly moist with occasional light drying-out periods of the topsoil.

SOIL: Standard indoor mixture. Will need repotting only every several years, but top dress the soil each spring. To top dress, you merely remove as much of the topsoil as will come out of the pot without difficulty and replace it with fresh.

PROPAGATION: Seeds. Terminal cuttings from top of older plants; tips of side branches will root, but produce new plants of a decidedly unbalanced shape.

*Ocimum basilicum*, see **HERBS, Sweet Basil**

Old rabbit tracks, see **Maranta**

*Origanum vulgare*, see **HERBS, Oregano**

Painted nettle, see **Coleus**

## PALMS

Palms are easily nurtured and long-lived indoor plants; the graceful nature of their spreading fronds makes them desirable indeed. You need not be afraid to buy the more expensive larger plants; they are fabulously beautiful and, moreover, will endure. Although twenty years ago palms were on their way out, they currently risk becoming a clichéd theme of interior décor. The most common mistake, however, is to treat them as desert plants; the indoor specimens originate in the humid tropics and cannot be allowed to get too dry. The tips of the fronds will brown if the air is hot and dry (particularly in winter), and lack of moisture in the soil will encourage older fronds to lose their grip. Cut off older fronds as they yellow, and you may also use a sharp scissors for cosmetic trimming of brown leaf tips. Carefully inspect a palm before you buy it: do not buy a palm that has already had its tips trimmed, for it seems there is no point in beginning with less than the best. Check also for insects with the understanding that scales favor palms and red spider mites and mealybugs will roost if the air has been dry.

Individual palms are discussed under their own common names, but certain cultural requirements apply to all. Palms thrive at low levels of light. Too much light will cause the fronds to change from their natural great fat green to a lighter green and finally to an almost yellow color. If you don't mind the paler green, at least be on guard for the lower relative humidity in brighter, hence warmer, rooms. Humidity is best kept at 30 percent or more. Dry wells, misting, and/or a thick layer of sphagnum moss over the topsoil are well-rewarded humidifying efforts. Air that is too dry will cause tips to brown and newly emerged furled fronds may refuse to unfurl. Palm fronds should be sponged or sprayed liberally with plain water at regular intervals to remove dust and to discourage the bugs. Ample fresh air is appreciated. Drafts are not.

Palms prefer a cramped and seemingly disproportionately small pot. You need repot them as infrequently as every three years, even less with older plants. The soil should be quite firm and somewhat rich. Florists usually sell "made-up" pots with an older specimen in the center and a few younger plants around it to hide the less graceful barren older stalk; try it yourself, it's a good idea. When repotting a palm, you may find that the growing roots have entwined at the base of the root ball and are lifting the plant out of its pot. If this is the case you can trim the basal roots somewhat to provide a better level and deeper planting. A palm that has been root trimmed needs a month or so of recuperative special treatment with increased humidity and protection from bright light. Mature pot-bound plants which do not yet demand repotting will benefit from a dilute fertilizing solution applied once a month during the active growing season (March to October).

Palms should be kept evenly moist in the same way as ferns; it is important to keep in mind their tropical origin. Allow the topsoil to dry out only lightly between waterings. However, due to the heavy texture of the soil, standing water does great damage to the roots. Too much water will cause the fronds to yellow. Pay particular attention to this from late autumn to early spring; palms observe a distinct rest period and you must then water only enough to keep the plant alive until new growth emerges.

All efforts with palm-propagation techniques involve months of care before you can see emergent new growth and several years before you have an attractive, reasonably sized plant. So it is not surprising that most conservatories and commercial growers choose to import their palms as young plants from tropical suppliers. However, it can be done. Consistent high humidity and high temperatures are required.

Here are the options for propagating your own:

1) Older plants may develop "suckers" at their base; if these shoots have formed roots and can be removed from the plant without damage, they can be potted for individual new plants. Pot them in a mixture of sand and peat moss (1:1), provide them with high humidity (70 percent) and high temperatures (85°–95°), and wait.

2) Some palms increase outwardly at their base; if this increase is considerable you may opt for division at repotting time. Provide dim light, extra humidity, and extra warmth for several weeks to allow the plant a period of recuperation.

3) You may also plant seeds for new palms. With the exception of cocos palms, and *Neanthe bella*, young plants will look quite unexciting for up to three years, but you may nevertheless enjoy the project. The seeds are planted ½-inch deep in moist, humus-rich soil; this may be all peat moss, a combination of vermiculite and peat moss (1:1), or standard indoor mixture with additional peat (3:2). Provide even moisture, high humidity (best near 75 percent), warmth (70°–80°, never over 85°), and average to almost dim light. After two to three months the seeds should have sprouted; after two years, if all goes well, the new plants may be a foot high.

Panimiga, see **Friendship Plant**

Paradise palm, see **Kentia Palm**

**Parlor Palm**          *Chamaedora bella* or
**Neanthe bella**          *Neanthe bella*

A smaller variety from Mexico and Guatemala, the *Neanthe bella* or parlor palm reaches 3 feet in height. It is more tolerant than most of dry indoor air. It regularly flowers in winter; if you have two plants, one of each sex, the tiny, yellow flowers may be followed by dark green and black fruits. Plant the seeds from such properly fertilized plants.

LIGHT: Subdued average indoor light to almost dim.

TEMPERATURE: Average house.

HUMIDITY: Average house.

WATER: Average to evenly moist. Allow topsoil to dry out only slightly between waterings. Hold back on water during winter rest periods. Spray or wash foliage regularly.

SOIL: Standard indoor mixture with firm, almost heavy texture.

PROPAGATION: Removal of "suckers" at base of older plants. Seeds sown in spring.

*Pellaea rotundifolia*, see **Button Fern**

| **Peperomia** | *Peperomia* ssp. and var. |
| **Watermelon** | *P. argyreia* or |
| **Begonia** | *P. sandersii* |

All relatives of table pepper, the many peperomias are rewarding and easy-to-care-for plants. The most common leaf shape is a pointed oval, although almost anything is possible within this large group: leaves that are quilted, hairy, shiny, striped, or blotched; small, delicate foliage or large and heavy leaves; an upright or a trailing habit. Any small enough are well suited for a terrarium or dish garden.

LIGHT: Bright indirect to almost dim light.

TEMPERATURE: Average. Warmer spots are all right.

HUMIDITY: Average house. Slightly higher humidity will encourage more luxurious, spreading growth.

WATER: Average. Take care not to water until topsoil is dry. Most peperomia varieties have succulent leaves, so beware of overwatering.

SOIL: Standard indoor mixture.

PROPAGATION: Leaf cuttings from those plants

that grow from a central crown. Tip cuttings from branching varieties.

*Petroselinum crispum*, see **HERBS, Parsley**

## PHILODENDRONS

A massive and interesting group of plants that are easy to care for and known to all. They will maintain themselves with forgetful keepers, but if given good care philodendrons will take over the house. It is only a pity that some very satisfying varieties are rarely offered commercially. Leaves may be green, red, almost black, variegated with cream, mottled with silver; they may be solid, indented, finely cut, or filled with holes; leaf size ranges from a few inches to several feet in length. Generally the plants are classified as climbing or self-heading. The climbers are long-stemmed and branching and may reach up to 20 feet if allowed support and optimum growing conditions; you may use the standard totem poles or devise your own rough, moist surface to which the aerial roots may attach themselves. The self-heading varieties will not climb; all leaves emerge from a central crown at soil level and the plant grows ever wider rather than taller.

The philodendrons are native to the lower levels of the jungles of Central and South America and, consequently, are well suited to filtered or dim light, periods of torrential rain, wind, and sudden drought.

The holes in larger leaves of climbing types are reportedly there to save the leaves from tearing in the fierce wind of tropical storms. The holes are present only in older leaves, and if you have not provided a climbing support even then they may not appear. Supports must be kept constantly moist to encourage the aerial roots to take hold. Even self-heading varieties may grow aerial roots and if you don't like them sprawling about, you may wind them back and tuck them into the pot's soil or have at them with a scissors and chop them off.

LIGHT: Bright indirect to almost dim light.

TEMPERATURE: Average house.

HUMIDITY: Average house, but 30 percent or more preferred.

WATER: Evenly and abundantly moist for best growth.

SOIL: Standard indoor mixture with optional addition of leaf mold or humus (3:1). A tight pot will do for long periods.

PROPAGATION: Cuttings from climbing varieties. Offsets from self-headers. Warmth and added humidity will speed the rooting process, but most will root admirably well in water. Air layer larger branching varieties.

**Piggyback Plant**   *Tolmiea menziesii*
**Pick-a-back Plant**
Piggyback is a plant particularly enjoyed by children and larger people for its distinctive habit of producing baby plantlets right on top of mature leaves. These form at the juncture of the leaf stem and will root readily for new,

independent individuals. In nature they would merely sit until their weight brought the older leaf to the soil; but you may hasten the process if you like. Even without this interesting habit, the pebbly soft texture of the leaves and full, open crown shape of the plant make it a popular one. With any graying, yellowing, or mottling effect developing on the leaves, inspect promptly for red spider mites. The most common error made with piggyback is to place it in hot rooms or hot, direct-sun locations. It is native to the Pacific coast, from northern California to Alaska, and can tolerate below-freezing temperatures sooner than it can adapt to dry heat.

LIGHT: Bright indirect to almost dim light.

TEMPERATURE: Average house, cooler preferred (20°–75°). Beware of low humidity when the furnace is on; perhaps piggyback might enjoy winter in the (unheated) porch or bathroom.

HUMIDITY: 30 percent or more. Despite the fuzzy leaves, misting is fine since the normal weather of the northern Pacific coast is primarily ocean fog. But misting is certainly not required.

WATER: Evenly moist with vigorous and fre-

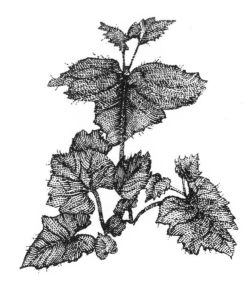

quent plain-water spraying. This will discourage mealybugs and mites as well as providing sufficient humidity even without misting.

SOIL: Standard indoor mixture with additional leaf mold (3:1).

PROPAGATION: Root babies in soil or water (see pp. 68–71).

*Pilea cadierei*, see **Aluminum Plant**

*Pilea involucrata*, see **Friendship Plant**

*Pilea microphylla*, see **Artillery Plant**

## PILEAS

The pileas are interesting and unusual plants, and include aluminum plant, artillery plant, and friendship plant. These popular cultivated indoor species hardly look related, but indeed they are. They are members of the sizable nettle family (as is baby tears), and each described herein has long been a favorite stand-by. Care for all is basically the same. For specific cultural requirements, see entries under individual plant names.

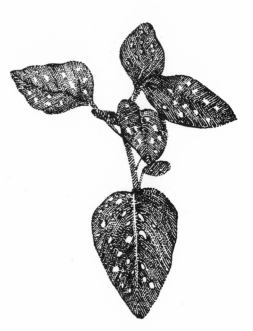

SOIL: Standard indoor mixture with additional leaf mold or peat moss (3:1).

PROPAGATION: Cuttings at any time. Seeds. If the spikes of lavender flowers are not pinched out, the plant may die back for a rest. Greatly reduce water until new growth begins. Plant the seeds.

| | |
|---|---|
| **Pink Polka Dot** | *Hypoestes* |
| **Freckle-face** | *sanguinolenta* |

A silly plant from Madagascar, *Hypoestes* derives its common names from the pink splash marking on its dark green leaves. The leaves are pointed long ovals; the stem is upright. Pink polka dot is most commonly offered as a novelty or terrarium plant, but can be grown up to 2 feet with liberal pinching for a fuller look.

LIGHT: Bright direct to bright indirect light. If the light is inadequate the freckle marks will fade and decrease in number as the plant's chlorophyll production must be increased.

TEMPERATURE: Average house.

HUMIDITY: 30 percent or more.

WATER: Evenly moist.

| | |
|---|---|
| **Pittosporum** | *Pittosporum tobira* |
| | and |
| | *P. variegatum* |

A rugged and attractive tropical shrub with shiny thick leaves, pittosporum may be grown for its foliage, its fragrant white flowers, as a responsive bonsai candidate, or as a seedling in a terrarium. The leaves are of a dense green color; in the variegated variety, they are edged with creamy white.

LIGHT: Bright indirect to almost dim light.

TEMPERATURE: Cool temperatures preferred, particularly in winter.

HUMIDITY: Average, but more luxuriant growth at 30 percent or more. Wash the foliage regularly and well. Requires good circulation of fresh air.

that will tolerate small amounts of gas in the atmosphere without suffering undue harm.

LIGHT: Bright indirect to almost dim light.

TEMPERATURE: Cool preferred, particularly in winter.

HUMIDITY: Average, but 30 percent or more preferred. Good ventilation and circulation of fresh air is required.

WATER: Moderately to evenly moist.

SOIL: Standard indoor mixture.

PROPAGATION: Seeds. Cuttings of nonwoody stems.

WATER: Average or slightly more moist.

SOIL: Standard indoor mixture.

PROPAGATION: Frequent pruning and pinching is much appreciated. Cuttings are successful if from young growth.

*Platycerium bifurcatum*, see **Staghorn Fern**

*Plectranthus australis*, see **Swedish Ivy**

**Podocarpus**          *Podocarpus neriifolia*
**Southern Yew**        *P. nagi*
**Japanese Yew**        *P. macrophylla maki*
Podocarpus derives its popular names from the facts that its leaves are quite yewlike (slender green fingers about 4 inches long), that it is native to Japan, and that it is grown as a hardy outdoor evergreen shrub or tree in the South and other mild regions of this country. Potted specimens remain small for years and are appreciated as bonsai plants or for general indoor appeal. Seedlings do well in a cool terrarium. Podocarpus is also a plant

*Polypodiaceae*, see **FERNS**

*Polypodium aureum*, see **Bear's-paw Fern**

**Pothos**          *Scindapsus aureus*
**Devil's Ivy**     *S. pictus argyraeus*
**Marble Queen**
This native of the Solomon Islands is another member of the ubiquitous aroid family,

among whose members are those other reliable favorites—Chinese evergreen, dieffenbachia, philodendron, spathiphyllum, and syngonium. *Scindapsus* has long been confused with *Pothos*, and indeed, "pothos" is now retained as the common name. The plant looks much like a heart-leafed philodendron and will climb if encouraged. The leaves are a bit coarser, waxy, and the green is blotched with yellow or cream for a devilish look. The leaves grow quite large with maturity.

LIGHT: Bright indirect sun to almost dim. The better the light the more dramatic the variegation of the leaves.

TEMPERATURE: Average house, although tropical warmth is preferred.

HUMIDITY: Average house, 30 percent or more. But most luxuriant growth at the higher levels, as befits a plant from the tropics.

WATER: Average to evenly moist. Beware of standing water. Pot with excellent drainage. If you opt for a moist soil, allow a thorough drying out at regular intervals before the next soaking. Hold back a bit on water in colder weather.

SOIL: Standard indoor mixture with optional addition of leaf mold, humus, or peat moss

(3:1). S. *aureus* does better without the additional enrichment. A tight fit of the pot is appreciated so do not rush with repotting.

PROPAGATION: Cuttings. Division. Pinch vigorously; barren top stems may be wound back onto available soil and pinned down to root.

Prayer plant, see **Maranta**

*Pteris cretica*, see **Table Fern**

*Pteris ensiformis*, see **Table Fern**

Pteris fern, see **Table Fern**

*Pteris serrulata*, see **Table Fern**

*Pteris tremula*, see **Table Fern**

Purple basil, see **HERBS, Sweet Basil**

**Purple Heart**        *Setcreasea purpurea*
Purple heart is a Mexican relative and look-alike of wandering Jew. The leaves are purple and covered with fine white hairs. It is a succulent and exotic in appearance. It will trail, but with a stronger, less supple stem than the more common wandering Jew.

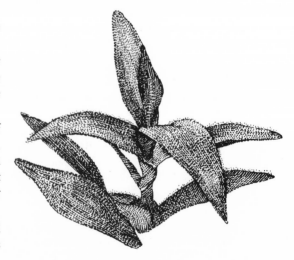

LIGHT: Bright direct to indirect light.

TEMPERATURE: Average but not over 75° in winter.

HUMIDITY: Average house.

WATER: Average water.

SOIL: Standard indoor mixture.

PROPAGATION: Cuttings at any time.

Purple velvet, see **Velvet Plant**

**Rabbit's-foot Fern**    *Davallia bullata mariesii* or *D. fejeensis* and others

This marvelous, bizarre fern from the Fiji Islands grows from a hairy, creeping rhizome in the manner of *Polypodium*. The fronds and rhizomes of rabbit's-foot fern are smaller, more finely cut, pointed, and almost sinewy. They need an open-basket planting or shallow pot over which the rhizomes may creep. They are striking plants, but a bit difficult to maintain.

LIGHT: Average indoor to almost dim.

TEMPERATURE: Cool (45°–70°).

HUMIDITY: High, 50 percent or more. Mist foliage and rhizomes frequently. As always, be most careful with humidity at the higher levels of acceptable temperature.

WATER: Evenly moist. The plant is deciduous, which means it observes a dormancy in winter and may shed all foliage. If the plant becomes bare, hold back all water until late winter or spring. New growth will begin to show and you then resume normal watering. The plant is often sold in its dormant stage as Japanese fern ball: you add water and a davallia appears.

SOIL: Standard indoor mixture with additional leaf mold or sphagnum moss. A tight fit in the pot encourages rhizomes to move out.

PROPAGATION: Spores are prominent. Division or rhizome cuttings. Place a section of the rhizome on moist sand, cover it with moist sphagnum moss, and provide warmth and high humidity.

Resurrection plant, see **Selaginella**

Rosary vine, see **String of Hearts**

*Rosmarinus officinalis*, see **HERBS, Rosemary**

**Rubber Plant**    *Ficus elastica*

This durable and broad-textured foliage plant hails from India and Malaya although it is

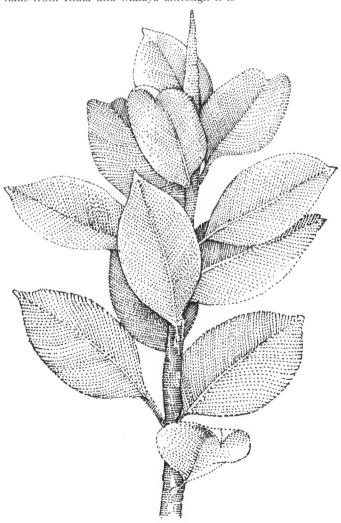

often credited to Brooklyn. It is a *Ficus*, and, as such, is related to fiddle-leaf, weeping, and creeping fig. Although the rubber plant is renowned for its ability to maintain itself under poor conditions, it is luxuriant with humidity and warmth. Lower-leaf drop is common under difficult conditions. Pinch frequently to encourage a bushy plant.

LIGHT: Bright indirect to almost dim.

TEMPERATURE: Average house.

HUMIDITY: Average house, best at 30 percent or more.

WATER: Average to evenly moist. Never allow the soil to dry out completely or lower leaves will begin to fall. Clean leaves regularly with dampened sponge or firm spray of plain water.

SOIL: Standard indoor mixture.

PROPAGATION: Stem cuttings. Air layering of larger specimens.

*Salvia officinalis*, see **HERBS, Sage**

*Sansevieria*, see **Snake Plant**

**Saxifraga**   *Saxifraga sarmentosa*
**Strawberry**
 **Begonia**
**Strawberry**
 **Geranium**
**Mother of**
 **Thousands**

Saxifraga is a beautiful foliage plant which also offers fine white spring flowers and year-round cascading red stolons. The stolons are reminiscent of strawberry plants and hence part of the common name; where begonia or geranium came in is only a matter of conjecture. The leaves are roughly rounded, fuzzy, deep gray green, and markedly veined above and reddish beneath. New plants begin at the end of each runner and are easily rooted. Saxifraga thus grows in a handsome, loose

rosette form, much like its relative the piggyback, but in a more cascading fashion. It is native to China and Japan.

LIGHT: Indirect, average to almost dim light. Saxifraga requires shading from the bright rays of the sun.

TEMPERATURE: Cool. It is best in an unheated room; while it can survive temperatures as low as 20°, it begins to fail over 70° and would do admirably at an average of 50° in winter.

HUMIDITY: 30 percent or more. Requires good ventilation and ample fresh air.

WATER: Average to evenly moist, with an occasional opportunity to approach dryness. Keep topsoil well aerated.

SOIL: Standard indoor mixture with additional leaf mold (3:1). A rich soil with loose texture.

PROPAGATION: Remove plants formed at end of runners and root in moist, sandy soil.

**Schefflera**  *Schefflera actinophylla*
**Umbrella Tree**

A graceful and striking foliage plant with tree-size potential, schefflera is a common sight in public buildings. There it is often stuck in a dark corner and covered with dust; however with frequent leaf washing and a bit more light, the plant is unusually attractive for its height and large, strong, palmately compound green leaves. Schefflera is native to Australia and Java yet more rugged than most tropicals.

LIGHT: Anything, but the strongest direct sunlight or the deepest shade. Even in deep shade, schefflera will manage to survive for some time, but the middle range is the safest.

TEMPERATURE: Average house.

HUMIDITY: Average house.

WATER: Average watering; let the topsoil dry to the touch between soakings. Spray foliage frequently for glossy leaves and to deter red spider mites and mealybugs.

SOIL: Standard indoor mixture.

PROPAGATION: Remove suckers from the base of mature plants and root these eager shoots in moist sand. Cuttings will root if the stem is not yet barky; taking frequent cuttings or pinching is an admirable way to have a bushy future tree.

*Scindapsus*, see **Pothos**

| **Selaginella** | *Selaginella emmeliana* |
| **Sweat Plant** | |
| **Spreading Club** | *S. kraussiana brownii* |
| **Moss** | |
| **Resurrection** | *S. lepidophylla* |
| **Plant** | |

Selaginella is a spreading tropical ground cover; it is most commonly planted in a terrarium to satisfy its preference for highly humid, indeed "sweaty" air. S. *emmeliana* is the most common of the group, with a bright green, delicate, fernlike branching habit. S. *kraussiana* will appear as a deep, soft cushion of forest moss, and its eagerness to root at every node makes it an excellent spreading ground cover for humid plantings. The variety from Texas known as resurrection plant (S. *lepidophylla*) will spring back to verdant beauty even from a fully dried mass of rolled

brown stems; all it asks is that its roots find water. However, the more popular emerald-green selaginellas are more demanding of a consistent environment.

LIGHT: Weak average to dim light.

TEMPERATURE: Average house or terrarium.

HUMIDITY: High, 50 percent or more.

WATER: Evenly moist.

SOIL: Standard indoor mixture with additional leaf mold or humus (3:1).

PROPAGATION: Cuttings will root eagerly in warmth and high humidity. Division of well-rooted, spreading clumps.

Sentry palm, see **Kentia Palm**

*Setcreasea purpurea*, see **Purple Heart**

Shingle plant, see **Monstera.**

| **Snake Plant** | *Sansevieria* |
|---|---|
| **Mother-in-law's** | *trifasciata* or |
| **Tongue** | *S. hahnii* |

Snake plant offers an unusual, even menacing, outline with succulent, knifelike leaves rising straight from the soil level and in a rosette form.

The more common and arresting *Sansevieria* will grow as tall as 5 feet and the rosette pattern is loose with rough, irregular growth outward as the plant matures. The low-growing bird's-nest types (*S. hahnii*) will be limited to under a foot with a meticulously tidy central form. The leaves may be plain green, or mottled with darker or lighter shades; some plants display cream or yellow marginal stripes. Fragrant flowers on tall spikes appear unpredictably on mature plants when they are grown in full sun. Snake plant is famous for its ability to withstand enormous neglect, anything but overwatering.

LIGHT: Anything you've got. Acclimate new plants slowly to the most extreme sunny location to avoid burn marks on the leaves.

TEMPERATURE: Average house.

HUMIDITY: Average house.

WATER: Allow soil to become quite dry between waterings. Take care not to overwater in winter.

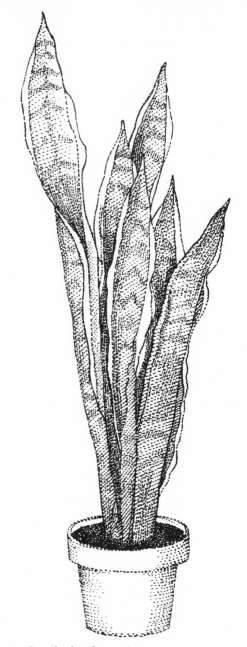

SOIL: Standard indoor mixture.

PROPAGATION: Division of plants with thickened bases. Cut sections of leaves will root in sandy soil (see p. 75); however, variegated varieties (*S. trifasciata laurentii*) may revert to plain green with the cut-leaf technique, so you might prefer the safety of division.

Southern yew, see **Podocarpus**

**Spider Plant**　　　*Chlorophytum elatum*
**Airplane Plant**

Spider plant is an easy-to-care-for and generally popular house plant; although from my experience it seems that people either love it or hate it, never in between. The slender, bladelike leaves emerge from a loose soil-level rosette and are green with a white stripe. Other varieties have been cultivated, but only the white-striped and solid green are currently common. Tall, slender shoots emerge and bear a smattering of attractive, small, white lilylike flowers which fade as new plantlets form along the aerial shoot. This airplanelike zooming habit and the development of the spidery small plants at the end of the racemes have prompted the popular names. *Chlorophytum* is a member of the widespread lily family and is related to asparagus fern, dracaena, and snake plant.

LIGHT: Bright indirect to almost dim light.

TEMPERATURE: Average house.

HUMIDITY: Average house.

WATER: Average water. Allow a distinct drying-out period between soakings. The spider

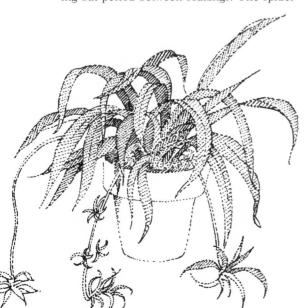

plant's roots are enormously expanded for water storage; they look very much like fat white icicle radishes and the plant will develop a wilted, flat look if it is consistently overwatered.

SOIL: Standard indoor mixture.

PROPAGATION: Division of larger plants. Rooting of new plantlets at ends of runners (see pp. 76–77).

Spreading club moss, see **Selaginella**

**Staghorn Fern**　　　*Platycerium bifurcatum*

The staghorn fern is an unusual and marvelous tree-clasping fern from Australia and New Guinea. It is expensive because it requires many years of greenhouse care before it assumes a massive and bizarre stature. The plant is supported by sterile, firmly-rooted, clasping fronds; these emerge succulent and green each spring and fade to a parchment-like buff by fall. The base fronds flare out at the top and remain open to receive the nourishment of rain and falling organic debris. The fertile fronds emerge from the center of the clasping base pad and are gray green, slightly fuzzy, and lustrous; they are deeply but broadly notched, looking a great deal like the antlers of a stag.

　　The plants are usually planted on a slab of wood and displayed for admiration of their epiphytic habit (see pp. 97–98). They are not difficult to maintain and will grow even broader as they mature. When necessary, add a heavier plank behind the former slab.

LIGHT: Average indoor light with some leeway on either side. No direct sun.

TEMPERATURE: Average house (40°–80°). Beware of low humidity on hot or heated days.

HUMIDITY: High preferred. Best growth at 50 percent or more. Provide ample fresh air and use regular firm spray of plain water to clean foliage and discourage scale insects.

WATER: Evenly moist with mild drying-out period of planting mixture. Thoroughly soak the planting by submerging it in sink or tub for 15–20 minutes. The plank may be watered on its wall if drips are no problem, but give it an occasional deep soaking as well.

SOIL: Osmunda fiber or sphagnum moss on bark.

PROPAGATION: Offsets, known as pups, will appear anywhere near the base of a mature plant. Remove the pups and root them in moist osmunda fiber or sphagnum moss with added warmth (70°–80°).

Strawberry begonia, see **Saxifraga**

Strawberry geranium, see **Saxifraga**

**String of Hearts**      *Ceropegia woodii*
**Rosary Vine**
**Hearts Entangled**

An attractive, small vine of opposing, heart-shaped leaves on a thin, wirelike stem, *Ceropegia* offers several surprises. Tiny round bulbs develop along the stem and can be popped back in the soil of the parent plant or

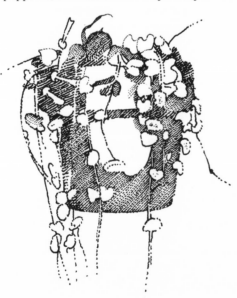

into individual pots for propagation. The flowers are purple or almost pink and make for a dainty, if odd, appearance in the summer months. The color of the leaves varies from silver on gray green when in shade to silver on bronze green when receiving full sun; the undersides of the leaves show similarly unusual metallic tones. My favorite spot for *Ceropegia* is on a high shelf where it may trail downward to the floor; it is also popular as a hanging-basket plant, but must be thickly planted. Pinching is most helpful to develop a fuller plant.

LIGHT: Bright direct sun to almost dim light.

TEMPERATURE: Average house.

HUMIDITY: Average house; dry air is no threat.

WATER: Average water. The leaves and stems are quite succulent, so allow a distinct drying out of the topsoil between soakings. Gradually reduce water in midwinter if the plant begins to wilt and display a desire to take a needed rest period; a month or two of near dryness and you may resume normal watering to induce new growth.

SOIL: Sandy soil. Standard indoor mixture with addition of sand (1:1 or 2:1). Cactus mixtures.

PROPAGATION: Cuttings rooted in sand. Tiny ball-shaped tubers removed and planted.

Sweat plant, see **Selaginella**

**Swedish Ivy**      *Plectranthus australis*
**Creeping Charlie**

Swedish ivy is a relative of coleus and equally fast growing, but it is thoroughly adaptable to whatever growing conditions you might have. Because of its urgency to grow, you must pinch and cut back constantly to maintain a bushy appearance; even then, you might have to refresh the top of the plant by inserting newly-rooted cuttings or by winding the barren parts of older stems around and pinning them down to root. The color, size, and depth of the plant's leaves will vary considerably with the light and humidity. Swedish ivy is a chameleon but shift it to new locations gradually to avoid burning, wilt, or dropping of the leaves.

LIGHT: Filtered direct or bright indirect to almost dim light.

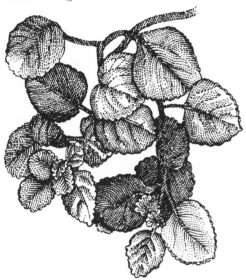

TEMPERATURE: Average house.

HUMIDITY: Average house, more for phenomenally rapid and succulent, deep growth. Wash foliage vigorously and inspect the plant regularly to keep it free from mealybugs and scale insects.

WATER: Swedish ivy uses a lot of water, but allow a severe drying-out period between every or every other soaking.

SOIL: Standard indoor mixture.

PROPAGATION: Voluminous cuttings. Seeds sown in late winter or spring.

Swiss-cheese plant, see **Monstera**

Sword fern, see **Boston Fern**

*Syagrus weddelliana*, see **Cocos Palm**

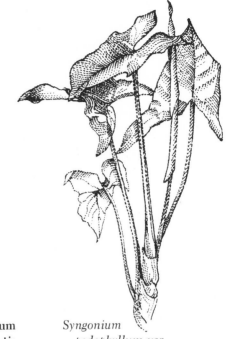

| **Syngonium** | *Syngonium* |
| **Nephthytis** | *podophyllum* var. |

A beautiful and reliable foliage plant, syngonium comes from the same family of aroids that includes philodendron, dieffenbachia, pothos, and numerous other indoor standbys. Nephthytis is a close African relative and most that are sold are in fact technically syngoniums. The large arrowhead-shaped leaves and variety of green mottling or white, silver, or yellow striations make this plant as attractive as it is durable. Trailing or upright forms.

LIGHT: Bright indirect to almost dim light.

TEMPERATURE: Average house.

HUMIDITY: Average house.

WATER: Average to evenly moist.

SOIL: Standard indoor mixture.

PROPAGATION: Cuttings.

| **Table Fern** | *Pteris cretica* |
| **Pteris Fern** | *P. ensiformis* |
| **Brake Fern** | *P. serrulata* |
| | *P. tremula* and var. |
| | and others |

An enormous genus of cultivated and discov-

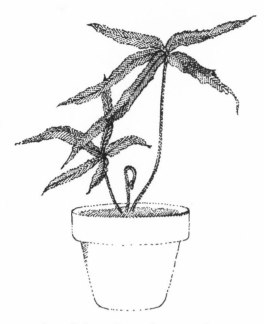

SOIL: Standard indoor mixture with additional leaf mold (3:1).

PROPAGATION: Spores, but may be sterile. Division.

*Thymus vulgaris*, see **HERBS, Thyme**

*Tolmiea menziesii*, see **Piggyback Plant**

*Tradescantia albiflora*, see **Wandering Jew**

**Tree Ivy**                    *Fatshedera lizei*
An aralia that is a cross between English ivy (*Hedera helix*) and fatsia (*F. japonica*), tree ivy is a hardy foliage plant with glossy ivylike leaves. Heavy pinching and cutting back are required for a bushy shrub.

LIGHT: Sunny to almost dim.

TEMPERATURE: Best growth when cool. Beware of furnace-induced lower humidity in winter. Does well outside if temperate.

HUMIDITY: 30 percent or more.

WATER: Average to evenly moist. Spray foliage when watering.

SOIL: Standard indoor mixture.

PROPAGATION: Cuttings taken at any time.

ered small ferns, *Pteris* ferns may be irregularly forked, crested, branched, or striped. Many varieties were developed in the estate greenhouses of Victorian England as head gardeners sought to surpass each other with new plants displayed down the center of the formal banquet tables, for example Victoria table brake (*Pteris ensiformis victoriana*). Taller species may be more centrally and regularly formed; *Pteris tremula dentata* may reach a height of 2–3 feet in an average supportive environment. Some *Pteris* ferns are quite small and appear as dwarf versions of jungle plants. The table ferns as a group are undemanding and reliable house plants.

LIGHT: Average indoor light.

TEMPERATURE: Average house, cool preferred.

HUMIDITY: Average house, higher humidity preferred. More luxuriant growth will be achieved with 50 percent or more. Wash foliage well with firm water spray to discourage scale.

WATER: Keep evenly moist. Allow the topsoil to dry only slightly between waterings.

**Umbrella Plant**   *Cyperus alternifolius*
A semiaquatic plant related to Egyptian papyrus (C. *papyrus*), umbrella plant displays um-
bels of grasslike leaves on narrow stems up to
4 feet tall. (Umbrella tree is *Schefflera*, see
above.) Dwarf, variegated, and broader-
leafed varieties and species are also cultivated.

LIGHT: Bright indirect to almost dim light.

TEMPERATURE: Average house, cool winter
preferred.

HUMIDITY: 30 percent or more. Provide ample fresh air.

WATER: Keep soil evenly moist. Wash foliage
regularly to deter red spider mites.

SOIL: Standard indoor mixture.

PROPAGATION: Seeds. Division at any time.

Umbrella tree, see **Schefflera**

**Velvet Plant**   *Gynura aurantiaca*
**Purple Velvet**
A colorful and desirable plant, velvet plant
boasts leaves and stems covered with bright,
fuzzy purple hairs. It is a Javanese relative of
the common garden daisy and occasionally
displays small yellow composite flowers. The
unusual coloration of the lush foliage is its
primary attribute, but velvet plant's preference for bright, sunny spots is also appreciated. Pinch vigorously for a bushy vine and
spray with plain water at regular intervals to
discourage pests; let the plant dry off before
the sun next hits.

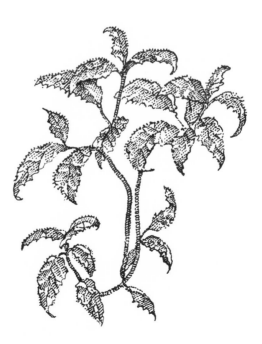

LIGHT: Bright, direct or indirect light.

TEMPERATURE: Average house. Beware of
very low humidity in heated rooms or near a
hot sunny window.

HUMIDITY: Average house.

WATER: Keep evenly moist.

SOIL: Standard indoor mixture.

PROPAGATION: Cuttings.

Victoria table brake, see **Table Fern**

**Wandering Jew**  *Tradescantia albiflora*
var. and
**Inch Plant**  *Zebrina pendula* var.
Any of the numerous *Tradescantia* or *Zebrina*
species or varieties may go by these popular
names. All are famous as cascading plants;
the small bladelike leaves may be all deep
green, light green striped with white, or deep
green striped with lavender and silver ("rainbow"), or of another less common combination. The stems are fleshy and fat and root
avidly at every node. Small, usually lavender
flowers may also appear.

LIGHT: Bright indirect to almost dim light.
Rainbow wandering Jew and most others do
best with abundant, softly filtered light.

TEMPERATURE: Average house; striped varieties are more sensitive to winter heat or hot
summer sun.

HUMIDITY: 30 percent or more for lush growth;
beware of drafts or blasts of hot, dry air.

WATER: Average to evenly moist.

SOIL: Standard indoor mixture.

PROPAGATION: Cuttings eager to root at any
time. Wind bare stems back over available
soil and pin them down for a fuller appearance. Cuttings may be inserted directly into
soil of parent plant.

Watermelon begonia, see **Peperomia**

Weddell palm, see **Cocos Palm**

**Weeping Fig**  *Ficus benjamina*
**Java Fig**
The status plant of the seventies, *Ficus benjamina* is also a temperamental beast. Large
specimens are quite expensive and you must
be prepared to treat them with enormous
consistency rather than timid hit-and-miss
techniques. A deluge of leaves may follow exposure to drafts, rapid changes in seasonal
temperatures (such as turning on the furnace

full-blast for the first time), drop in humidity, or severe drying of the soil. Occasionally some plants will drop their leaves for no apparent reason; this is a natural occurrence and new leaf buds should be forming promptly on the barren stems. Spray or sponge the foliage regularly and carefully to discourage the enemy—red spider mites.

LIGHT: Filtered indirect or average indoor light.

TEMPERATURE: Average to warm.

HUMIDITY: Average, higher preferred, 30 percent or more.

WATER: Average to evenly moist. Never allow the soil to dry out completely.

SOIL: Standard indoor mixture.

PROPAGATION: Air layering.

*Zebrina pendula*, see **Wandering Jew**

# 2

# Cacti & Succulents

## CACTI

I must admit at the beginning to a greater admiration than fondness for members of this desert group. Yet they are certainly remarkable plants, and once they've captured your attention, they may court your fancy with a thousand varieties you still must try. Like the reptiles, the cacti seem to have been here since time began. Their bizarre forms have developed in response to adverse conditions of extreme heat and unpredictable drought. The fleshy, thickened leaves have evolved as water-storing tissues; the thorns and prickles are there to discourage thirsty desert beasts.

Cactus plants require only minimal care and a bit of understanding. Choose plants that have a well-balanced shape and uniform color and that are free from scars. They may look cramped in their pots, but no matter; cacti prefer cozy quarters and most grow slowly enough to require spring repotting only every two or three years.

Popular and easy plants are: **Rat's-tail Cactus** (*Aporocactus flagelliformis*), with trailing thin stems and extravagant crimson flowers; **Sea Urchin Cactus** (*Astrophytum asterias*), a spineless, segmented, domelike plant; **Old Man Cactus** (*Cephalocereus senilis*), renowned for its covering of snowy white hair; **Peanut Cactus** (*Chamaecereus silvestrii*), with clusters of odd cylindrical branches emerging from the soil, all covered with soft white bristles; two types known as **Barrel Cactus** (*Echinocactus* and *Lobivia*), both with very dramatic and spiny barrel shapes; **Hedgehog Cactus** (*Echinocereus*) offers varieties of smaller size with soft spikes as well as brilliant, eager summer flowers; **Chin Cactus** (*Gymnocalycium*) includes many easy-to-grow varieties, long-lasting flowers, and ridiculous protuberances that look like double chins; **Pincushion Cactus** (*Mammillaria elongata*) belongs to an enormous group of the *Mammillaria* cacti, all easy to care for and very classic in their bulbous, fleshy, upright forms; **Prickly Pear, Bunny Ears,** and

**Beaver-tail Cactus** (*Opuntia* varieties), all with an odd branching pad form and the latter two without spines. All of these are normal or classic in their "cactus-ness"; they will thrive under the same hot and dry conditions.

LIGHT: Full sun to semisunny. If dry or burnt areas appear, the light is too strong. If the cactus becomes pale, the light is not adequate to the plant's needs. An incandescent light bulb is a simple way to boost light for cacti, since heat from the bulb is not a big problem.

TEMPERATURE: Average to warm. Flowering requires preceding cool winter conditions.

HUMIDITY: Average to dry. Good ventilation is required. Keep plants clean with a soft brush because excessive dust or kitchen grease caught in the hairy bristles may prove fatal. Occasionally you may use a firm spray of water to clean the plants; only be sure to let them dry thoroughly before they are again exposed to direct sun. This will also help discourage mealybugs, the chief cactus blight.

WATER: Water only when soil is thoroughly gritty and dry. This may be as infrequently as once a month. During the active growth of spring and summer, water perhaps once a week. In winter, allow only enough water to prevent shriveling of the leaves. Avoid cold water. A limp, soft cactus usually means overwatering and impending rot.

SOIL: The mixture must be loose and sandy or gritty. Excellent drainage is of prime importance when repotting. A standard indoor mixture may be combined half and half with sand or pieces of brick (no piece larger than a pea) or you may purchase prepared cactus mixtures.

PROPAGATION: Cuttings can be taken from branching types. Allow cactus sap to dry out and a callus to form (overnight or up to four days) before inserting the cutting in moist sand. Make a hole first and set the cutting into it. Bring the sand up for gentle contact, but do not shove, push, or bruise the cutting

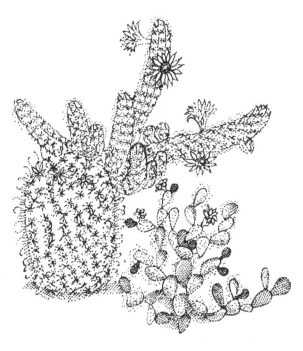

stem in any way. Do not water the planting until the sand is completely dry and do not cover the planting or otherwise add humidity. Rot is obviously the chief threat. Another useful technique is the removal of offsets from near the base of an older plant.

EXCEPTIONS:

**Mistletoe Cactus** (*Rhipsalis*) is a rare one. It appears to be a sculpture of self-fastening magnetized nails with thin pencillike branches emerging in clusters from the one before. Its cultural requirements differ as well. It thrives in high humidity and warmth. Some growers insist on its need for strong light; others have had success with near-shade. A porous, rich soil with added peat or sphagnum moss suits this maverick plant. *Rhipsalis* requires water whenever the topsoil becomes dry, which is exactly what one would expect; but water even less in winter to simulate a mild drought—water just enough to keep the stems from shriveling. Propagate by cuttings.

*Epiphyllum* includes the many varieties of **Orchid Cactus** and **Night-blooming Cereus.** All are spineless with flattened branching stems and roughly scalloped edges. Their blooms have made them famous. They are natives of tropical America, but require different treatment from their bulbous relatives. The only similarity is the insistence on excellent drainage (use up to an inch of drainage material under the soil).

LIGHT: Good to average indirect light. No direct sun, unless the location is also cool.

TEMPERATURE: Average, but resents excessive artificial heat in autumn and winter.

HUMIDITY: 30 percent or more. Mist daily or provide added humidity in other ways. If the air is too dry, flower buds will drop.

WATER: Water freely and keep evenly moist during spring and summer periods of active growth. In winter, offer only enough water to prevent shrinking of stems.

SOIL: Standard indoor mixture. Fertilize frequently with dilute solution during active growth.

PROPAGATION: Cuttings in spring or summer.

**Christmas Cactus** (*Schlumbergera bridgesii*) and **Thanksgiving Cactus** (*Zygocactus truncatus*) have cultural requirements similar to *Epiphyllum*. Since flowers are triggered by the plant's understanding of the time of year, be sure that no artificial light hits the plants in autumn and that for this season it experiences natural, cool weather. Until the flower buds form (in fall), keep the plant watered just enough to prevent shrinking of the stems. During flowering, water well and then let topsoil dry to the touch before another good soak. When flowers have faded, keep the plant fairly dry again until new shoots emerge, then as new growth gets underway, the plant again needs liberal amounts of water. Avoid drafts, fluctuation in humidity, or gas in the air; these conditions may cause buds to drop off.

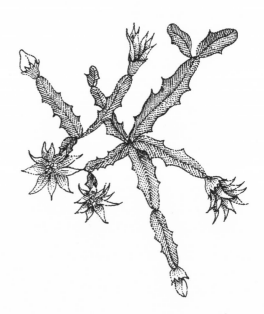

# SUCCULENTS

The plants listed in this section display a high degree of succulence, and by the great many similarities in their cultural requirements have come to be regarded as a group —they show a "botanical affinity" (as one of my favorite horticulturalists puts it), if not a botanically precise family relationship. Whereas any true cactus is a member of *Cactaceae* and almost assuredly native to the Americas, a plant exhibiting succulence may come from one of many plant families and any part of the world. *Succulence* is merely a descriptive term and indicates that the plant tissues are fleshy and thickened, covered with a resistant surface cuticle, and modified to store large amounts of water. They come from the desert or arid regions and have adapted to scarce rainfall, porous sandy soil, and hot, dry air. Cactus plants exhibit a particularly high degree of succulence. Ferns none at all. Any plant of any family that displays somewhat thickened, fleshy leaves has a greater ability to store water than another related, but thinly or delicately leafed one. Thus, you may take your cue to avoid overwatering. Swedish ivy, African violet, and peperomia exhibit a degree of succulence. You must therefore take care not to waterlog the soil. It also makes good sense that, because of the water stored in the succulent leaves, bruising the plant tissue may quickly lead to rot. Fern fronds do not rot; a bruised spot turns brittle instead. African violet, cactus, or jade plant will rot if the tissues are damaged and left to spread their moisture to the rest of the plant.

Notwithstanding these cautions, the succulents are reliably fine house plants. Their forms are interesting and exotic and their coloration covers a broad range of evocative pastels, as well as odd shades of green. Because of their desert origins the succulents are well suited to the hot, dry air of indoor living; they can go without repotting for years and thrive when cared for by an individual who hates to water. Their uncommon forms are striking and once you've become a devotee you will find hundreds of less-publicized varieties to expand your collection. They are easily propagated as well. Shallow dish plantings, hanging baskets, and wall-plank plantings are among the most effective to emphasize the dramatic succulent forms. Nearly all require the same conditions; eccentric pleasures will be noted in the discussion of individual plants.

LIGHT: Bright direct, bright indirect, or average indoor light. You may need to provide some protection from the hot blaze of direct summer sun. If you observe browning or even withering of the leaves, move the plant back. The better the light, the more striking will be the coloration and range of pastel suggestions in the foliage. If the light is too dim, the succulent will barely grow and risks the onset of rot.

TEMPERATURE: Average house, cool preferred. The best range is 46° at night to 75° during the day, with ten degrees difference between given day and night temperatures. In cooler locations, a succulent will get by with poorer light, since the cool temperatures simulate a winter season. In warmer locations, you will obviously observe a more frequent need for water.

HUMIDITY: Average to dry.

WATER: Water when the topsoil feels dry, hard, and gritty. Gradually reduce water when you observe a rest period coming on; generally this is in winter, but many succulents from South Africa are accustomed to a reverse of the seasons and some are plainly unpredictable. Watch the plant; spurts of new growth and intense greening of the foliage mark the beginning of a period of active growth and you may water more freely; a marked halt in growth indicates a seasonal rest and excess watering may rot the root ball. Succulents are normally fast-growing plants.

SOIL: Standard indoor mixture with additional sand, brick rubble, or mortar rubble (3:1).

PROPAGATION: Most of the succulents grow ever-wider rather than taller, and this is your cue that they may be propagated as for offsets or by division (see chapter 3). Those that grow taller and branch, such as jade plant, or those that grow longer, such as burro's tail, can be propagated by cuttings. Allow the cutting a day or two to dry out in a dim-light location; the cut surface will thus be able to form a callus before you plant it and be more resistant to rot. Insert an offset or a cutting in moist sand or very sandy soil taking care not to bruise the outer tissues; no pushing or screwing motions are allowed. Provide no added humidity and do not water the planting until the soil is nearly totally dry. Keep it in a bright, but not sunny, spot and it may be fully rooted within a week or two.

**Agave**        *Agave*
**Dwarf Century Plant**

Both a gray green (A. *miradorensis*) and a dark green, silver-striped (A. *pumila*) form are commonly seen. The flat, broad, rosette pattern of growth and spiked edges of the fibrous leaves give a distinctive appearance. Members of the amaryllis family and eager with offsets. Agaves prefer lots of sun.

**Aloe**        *Aloe*

A genus from South Africa with hundreds of known species, the aloes offer smooth tender leaves in rosette form and a habit of rapidly crowding their pots with offset growth. Winter bloom of red tubular flowers on a tall spike. The bitter sap of the aloe has long been regarded as a salve for burns or skin irritations.

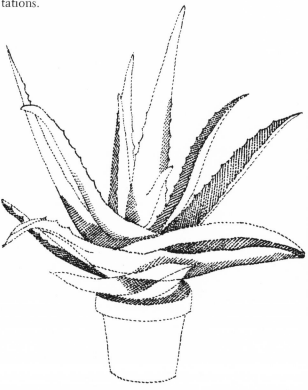

*Aptenia*, see **Ice plant**

Burro's tail, see **Sedums**

*Conophytum*, see **Stone Faces**

Coral beads, see **Sedums**

*Crassula*, see **Jade Plant**

Donkey tail, see **Sedums**

Dwarf century plant, see **Agave**

*Echeveria*, see **Hens and Chickens**

Good-luck leaf, see **Panda Plant**

*Haworthia*, see **Zebra Haworthia**

### Hens and Chickens *Echeveria*

*Echeveria* boasts some of the most exotic coloration of the succulents. Generally their form is of tender open rosettes with a cluster of smaller offsets crowded up to the base like a brood of baby chicks. Flowers are long-lasting and held well above the rosette, clustered on a colorful spike.

### Ice Plant *Aptenia*

From the succulent fig marigold family, A. *cordifolia* is a cascading plant with opposite heart-shaped leaves and small purple flowers that appear in early summer. Standard indoor mixture and a bit wetter soil are preferred. Can be propagated by division or cuttings from branched stems.

### Jade Plant *Crassula argentea*

An admirable plant which may reach shrub or small-tree size, jade plant is well known for its fat, thickened leaves and branching stubby growth. There are numerous smaller and low-growing *Crassula* species, notably string of pearls (*C. perfossa*) and scarlet paintbrush

(*C. falcata*). Some growers report best results with average watering, allowing the topsoil to dry, but not become gritty between waterings. Seeds are available for growing your own.

*Kalanchoe*, see **Panda Plant**

*Lithops*, see **Stone Faces**

Living stones, see **Stone Faces**

### Panda Plant *Kalanchoe*
### Good-luck Leaf
and many others

Many kalanchoes are grown, the most common being K. *blossfeldiana* which offers fleshy, green leaves spread out in a flat cup near the soil and raised clusters of tiny orange flowers in midwinter. It is a shrubby plant and will need more water than most succulents, but water only when the topsoil is dry.

*Sansevieria*, see FOLIAGE PLANTS, p. 186.

Scarlet paintbrush, see **Jade Plant**

### Sedums *Sedum*

An enormous genus of admirable succulents varying widely in shape and color. Burro's tail or donkey tail (*S. morganianum*) is popular for its pendulous habit and because it is careful to retain older leaves; however, it does break easily—so hang it out of the way of heavy traffic. Cuttings root quickly. Coral beads (*S. stahlii*) has reddish, fat, oval leaves crowding fast upon each other on branching stems.

### Sempervivum *Sempervivum*

Sempervivum is perhaps the hardiest of the succulents, as its name ("live forever") insists. Vigorous growths of offset plantlets appear around the parent plant. Sempervivum grows in a flat rosette of pale green leaves which are often edged with brown. A particularly good choice for shallow pans or planks.

Snake plant, see FOLIAGE PLANTS, p. 186.

**Stone Faces**        *Lithops* and
**Living Stones**      *Conophytum*
These small plants from South Africa have developed their ability to conserve moisture and camouflage themselves to the extent that they look simply like half-buried stones. The two leaves meet at the center and open in autumn to allow the emergence of a white, yellow, or orange blossom. Very gritty, sandy soil. Keep quite dry during winter and early spring. Seeds available.

String of pearls, see **Jade Plant**

Wart plant, see **Zebra Haworthia**

**Zebra Haworthia**    *Haworthia*
**Wart Plant**
Succulents of South Africa with thick, pointed, densely crowded rosette form. The zebra (*H. fasciata*) is perhaps the most popular, with wartlike raised stripes of white across the dark green. But dozens of other haworthias are also available. The "windowed" haworthias are pudgy, fleshy plants which grow nearly buried in the soil during drought; transparent "windows" have developed at the tips of the leaves to admit sunlight to the underground tissues. Lily family.

# 3

# Flowering Plants

There comes a time in the life of every indoor gardener when a longing for flowers presents itself, and undiluted green, no matter how lavish, seems tedious indeed. There are a great many beautiful flowering plants well-suited to indoor living and most boast foliage as desirable as the blooms, so you need not confine yourself to geraniums and African violets. I have purposely included some plants that are currently less often seen as the tides of mass retailing and fashion shift, hoping in this way that you will be able to satisfy your fancy completely even if it means a bit more shopping around.

Each flowering plant's specific growing requirements will be outlined. All general considerations for good health still hold and, if you are ready, here come a few more. Flowering plants do demand a greater sensitivity to their needs, but everything that sets apart their care from that of foliage plants can be understood inasmuch as they do more explosive, exuberant work and need a bit of a rest afterward.

It is also interesting to consider that when you are lusting for blossoms, certain critical levels in environmental conditions come into play. If a dieffenbachia develops brown tips because the air is too dry, that's certainly too bad, but life goes on much as it always did; however, the same lack of humidity may bring down every flower bud from a lipstick vine and strew them on the floor—to your unending dismay. So the fine points are worth a second glance. The main thing to remember is that most of these plants are quite easy to grow once you've discovered their stride.

Flowering plants generally require a nighttime drop in temperature of at least ten degrees. The cellular impetus to flower is triggered by the seasonal changes, so best results will be enjoyed by those growers who are not married to their furnace and air-conditioning thermostats. In some cases, buds will not set if the plant receives any artificial light at specific times of the year, but these are special cases and will be mentioned in the discussion of the individual plant. If buds do form but soon drop off, look to a low-humidity problem; in nearly all cases this is the source of the trouble.

The universal reason for a plant's failure to flower is that it is not receiving enough light. Every higher plant we know (ferns and true mosses not included here) does flower; some can never hope to find the required degree of light in our homes and in temperate regions, but they do flower *au naturel* in the tropical jungle—while home-bound and temperate, we think of these fellows as foliage plants.

Considering that many plants which thrive in outdoor shady places require the brightest indirect indoor light we can provide, it is not surprising that those which require the outdoor tropical sun for blooming cannot manage at all behind glass. Yet all the plants listed in this section will flower with reasonable indoor levels of light.

So if you are being disappointed by flowers refusing to appear on a listed "flowering" plant, consider that the light intensity in the plant's particular present location may not be sufficient. Secondly consider that the plant may need more nourishment. A pot-bound condition will hamper some plants to the extent that they cannot produce buds. Setting buds requires an adequate supply of nutrients in the soil, and when there are more roots in the pot than soil or when you have not been fertilizing regularly the plant will make use of the food it has for sure-fire foliage growth and bypass flowering. There are some flowering plants that blossom more freely in a root-bound mood but these will be noted specifically; generally when a plant is known to resent having its roots disturbed your best bet is to feed it with a very dilute solution at frequent intervals. Remember, too, to use a well-balanced fertilizer; a high-nitrogen fertilizer will boost foliage growth at the expense of flowering.

You will have the widest selection of flowering plants if you have a sunny and cool spot for the numerous beauties who need it. Sunny and cool is a difficult combination in most homes; an unheated sun porch or conservatory or a living room in which people wear sweaters would fill the bill. So look over the required growing conditions, make a sensible choice, and simply do the best you can. It is similarly ideal if you have a spot to store plants when they are not in bloom. A number of flowering plants observe a distinctly unattractive rest period after prolific blooming. If you have a cool room that receives good to average light, you may stow the sleepers there and concentrate on better-looking fellows in the living area. That's the ideal. For those who cannot stand a pot filled with odd-looking dormant stuff among the beauties, take a good look at the specifics on each plant and choose those which make do with a leafy mild rest period or can be raised anew each year from seeds, cuttings, or tubers.

You water flowering plants as you do any other, when they need the water. However, you will find that more of them are listed as being properly kept on the evenly moist side. Consider that the basic indoor favorites are from the hot tropics and grow there below the shade of higher trees and this is why they thrive in our warm houses and at comparatively low levels of light. It is also true that their seasonal flowering corresponds to native periods of abundant moisture in the soil and air. Many therefore require moderately high humidity for most luxuriant growth and a moist, but not sodden, soil. In general you will do well to follow this pattern: be prepared to supply abundant water when new shoot growth and/or buds are forming; if you let the soil dry out too much, the buds may simply be discouraged and drop off; water less once the flowers have opened if they are all of one large crop and no new buds are developing; this small work slowdown will allow the flowers to last longer; gradually give less water after a large spurt of flowering has been completed and thus satisfy the plant's need to rest.

Rest periods required by plants are little understood but play an important part in a plant's ability to survive and continue to be beautiful year after year. Foliage plants can sneak in a midwinter rest; they grow more slowly in response to the decreased intensity of the sun and are accommodated as you find the soil stays moist longer and therefore water the plants at less frequent intervals. Flowering plants may rest at any time of year that suits them, particularly after a period of abundant flowering. They are listed specifically for each plant, but you may develop a general idea of when they will occur and thereby increase your sensitivity without always having to resort to the book. You will know when the rest period is over; new foliage growth will begin with vigor and you may bring the plant to better light and water enthusiastically in anticipation of the delights to come. It is worth emphasizing that if your plant is not behaving in accordance with Hoyle, you should let it make its own rules. Every year there are new varieties and hybrids developed with more easygoing habits—such as shorter rest periods.

*Abutilon*, see **Flowering Maple**

*Acalypha hispida*, see **Chenille Plant**

**Achimines**          *Achimines longiflora*
**Monkey-face**        *A. patens* and others
  **Flower**
**Nut Orchid**

Achimines is a native of the tropical Americas and a popular choice for hanging pots, baskets, or a lightly shaded window box. The leaves are slightly hairy, their edges notched, and they appear in pairs on opposite sides of the stem. These small leaves themselves are attractive, but from July on into the fall the profusion of open-faced, long-throated, tubular blossoms give the plant a delicate but overwhelming beauty.

The many hybrids offer a color choice of white, rose, pink, red, lavender, purple, or blue flowers. Achimines has a graceful floppy habit and generally reaches a foot or two in height. It grows from a rhizome, a scaly underground rootstalk, and dies back to the rhizome after the flowering period. Sometimes small catkinlike rhizomes will appear at the leaf axils among the flowers; they look rather like miniature pine cones and can be planted for future growth. Achimines is a gesneriad; see GESNERIAD FAMILY, below, for more general information.

LIGHT: Abundant, bright, indirect light, but no direct sun. Many plants will also do well at lower levels of average indoor brightness.

TEMPERATURE: Average house.

HUMIDITY: Average to slightly higher, 30 percent or more.

WATER: Evenly moist in spring and summer. Fertilize with a dilute solution every two weeks during active growth.

REST PERIOD: A dormant period will begin when the flowers fade in the fall or at any time from lack of adequate moisture in the soil. Gradually reduce watering and store the rhizomes in their pot, nearly dry, and at a temperature as close to 50°–55° as you can manage. Or you may also remove the tubers from the soil in September, clean them off and store them in a dry paper bag or in dry sand until spring repotting.

SOIL: Standard indoor mixture with additional leaf mold (3:1). Repot each spring.

PROPAGATION: Plant purchased or harvested conelike rhizomes between January and April; plant six to a 6-inch pot or bulb pan, cover them with ½–1 inch of soil, and use bottom heat for most vigorous results. Pinch the shoots several times when they are 2–3 inches tall for a bushy plant. Larger rhizomes may be broken in two and potted separately. Seeds sown in winter will produce flowering plants the next summer. Leaf or stem cuttings are useful as well.

*Aeschynanthus*, see **Lipstick Vine**

**African Lily**          *Agapanthus africanus*
**Lily of the Nile**      *A. orientalis albus*

The African lily is indeed a member of the lily family and native to South Africa. It is a plant of easy, robust culture, grown from a bulb and displaying a central mass of long straplike leaves from which emerge the tall (2- to 3-foot) flower stems. The flowers are blue, porcelainlike, and clustered in masses; a single umbel may carry more than fifty individual tubular flowers. Dwarf species and varieties are available for smaller spaces and *A. orientalis albus* includes a white-flowered plant. African lily is generally planted in large pots, preferably strong tubs; the exuberant roots are quite powerful and will simply break their container if they find it wanting for space.

LIGHT: Bright indirect light; some direct sun is fine and average indoor light will also do. An amenable plant.

TEMPERATURE: Cool preferred.

HUMIDITY: Average house.

WATER: Plentiful water in spring and summer. Frequent feeding with a well-balanced fertilizer beginning in early spring and continuing until just after the flowers have faded for proper blooms this year and next. Gradually reduce water after flowers fade in late summer or early fall.

REST PERIOD: Store bulbs in pots and keep nearly dry during late fall and winter. A cool cellar is the classic site; a well-insulated garage will do equally well. The intent is to provide just enough water and light to maintain the large leaves in their semidormant state.

SOIL: Standard indoor mixture with additional leaf mold or humus (3:1). Plant bulbs in large pots or tubs (10-inch diameter).

PROPAGATION: Division in early spring. Plant purchased bulbs.

**African Violet**  *Saintpaulia*
Since this beauty from Tanganyika was first "discovered" in 1890, thousands of hybrids and varieties have resulted and now fill windowsills around the world. The lush rosette of semisucculent leaves and profusion of delicately colored flowers have endeared the African violet to many. The fancier has a good many choices; leaves may be fuzzy or smooth with scalloped, fringed, or wavy edges; flowers may be single, double, pink, blue, white, lavender, crested, bicolor, multicolor—and each year something new. African violets are members of the energetic gesneriad family and thrive when treated as the lush tropicals they are. If the conditions are satisfactory they will blossom year round and take over the house; if you have not yet found their stride, they can drive you to distraction. Common reasons for failure to flower include poor light, room temperature too high or humidity too low, too many crowns in one pot, the presence of unburned

gas in the air, or a discouraging dose of cold water. Plants flower best when they are slightly crowded in their pots and have only one crown. Cold water spots the leaves and may restrain flowering. African violets leaves must be kept clean and this is best done with a soft watercolor brush for dusting or a sink full of tepid water for an upside-down dip; whenever the leaves are wet, the plant must obviously be kept out of direct sun to prevent burn marks.

LIGHT: Bright light. No direct sun in summer; direct sun or bright indirect light in winter. Artificial light (incandescent or fluorescent) will boost dim sunlight for prolific flowering.

TEMPERATURE: Average house, preferably near 70°. If the temperature is too cool, the leaves will pale and curl downward.

HUMIDITY: Average house, 30 percent or more; higher in winter to compensate for the drying effects of artificial heat. Dry wells in trays for more luxuriant growth.

WATER: Average to evenly moist. Use water at room temperature only. Bottom water occasionally to ensure thorough wetting of the root ball.

SOIL: Standard indoor mixture or packaged African-violet mix. Frequent dilute feeding with a well-balanced fertilizer after the pot is filled with roots. Repot in spring or summer

when roots have completely overtaken the soil ball. Repot so that the crown is slightly above soil level to prevent rot of the fleshy stems. Cover the edge of clay pots with aluminum foil or plastic if leaf stalks touch the moist edge and begin to brown. Trim any old dying leaves with a clean razor cut close to the crown. Crown rot is easily avoided if the dense, succulent foliage is accorded a bit of respect.

PROPAGATION: Seeds. Leaf or stem cuttings. Division of multiple crowns. Removal of offset plantlets from base of parent plant.

*Agapanthus*, see **African Lily**

Angel-wing begonia, see **BEGONIAS, Fibrous-rooted**

**Anthurium**　　　*Anthurium andreanum*
**Tail Flower**　　　*A. scherzerianum*
**Flamingo Flower**
The anthurium is a distinctive member of the aroid family, grown primarily for its jaunty flower. The common names allude to this showy form; the true flower appears as a long, taillike spadix similar to that of its relative the garden calla lily—but it is surrounded by a flat heart-shaped spathe or bract that is glossy

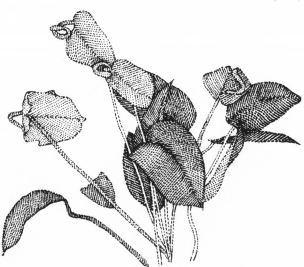

enough to resemble patent leather and may be coral, pink, white, or a brilliant scarlet. *A. andreanum* is most commonly seen as or often mistaken for an artificial plant. *A. scherzerianum* offers a curly pigtail spadix in addition to the brightly colored spathes. The leaves are large and shaped like elephant ears, a favored form among the aroids; leaf stalks are long and grow longer as the plant matures. Other anthuriums are suitable for indoor growth and feature velvety and prominently indented or veined foliage in lieu of such ostentatious flowers.

LIGHT: Average to almost dim light.

TEMPERATURE: Average to warm. The minimum for this tropical is 65°.

HUMIDITY: High humidity for best growth, 50 percent or more.

WATER: Evenly moist. Fertilize every two to four weeks with a dilute well-balanced fertilizer.

SOIL: A well-drained loose texture is the prime requirement. Osmunda fiber, leaf mold, or long-stranded sphagnum moss may be used separately or mixed with charcoal and sand.

PROPAGATION: Offsets from named self-heading species above. Vining anthuriums may be propagated from cuttings. (See PHILODENDRONS, p. 178, for the distinction between self-heading and vining habits.)

*Aphelandra*, see **Zebra Plant**

Apostle plant, see **Walking Iris**

**Azalea**　　　*Rhododendron indicum*
　　　　　　　*R. obtusum* and
　　　　　　　hybrids
Azalea is a beautiful woody plant native to cool regions of the Northern Hemisphere and a member of the heath family. It is a perennial, but its insistence upon cold (40°–50°) winter temperatures makes it difficult to hold over in the average home. The flowers are splendid; they may be red, pink, coral, sal-

mon, cerise, ivory, and/or pure white; they burst into bloom in January and with proper conditions will last through March. Frequent misting is beneficial not only to increase humidity, but to deter red spider mites as well. All parts of rhododendrons are poisonous so be careful if there are young children or pets about.

LIGHT: Abundant filtered or indirect light.

TEMPERATURE: Cool; 50°–55° is the ideal range, so attempt to maintain a temperature at least under 65°. Azaleas are unharmed by a light frost and indeed prefer their winter temperatures between 40°–50°. This is the most intimidating requirement of their proper indoor care.

HUMIDITY: Moderate to high, 40 percent or more. Extra humidity measures are quite well rewarded. Misting or dry wells coupled with periodic leaf washing will result in more luxuriant growth.

WATER: Keep the soil evenly moist, but not soggy.

SOIL: Rich, acid soil. See chapter 8 for discussion of acid-loving plants. May be repotted entirely with peat moss.

FERTILIZER: See chapter 8.

WHEN THE BLOOMS FADE: Allow the plants to approach dryness between soakings. Repot if necessary and prune the plant back if you feel the need to improve its shape. Thereafter pinch only as necessary to control any irregularly tall shoots. In late spring take the plant to an outside porch, or sink it in a semishady part of the garden. Surround such outdoor plantings with plenty of peat moss to promote cool soil temperatures and higher humidity. If an outdoor spot is not possible, aim for somewhere in the house that will not be too hot or dry. Return to regular watering and increase your humidifying efforts as the summer progresses. In the fall, bring the plant to a bright but unheated location; the tempera-

ture is best near 50° at this time. Water only when the topsoil is quite dry. Finally, in January to mid-February, bring the plant to a 60° location, begin to keep it evenly moist again, and resume regular feeding. Hope for new blooms.

Bag flower, see **Glory Bower**

**BEGONIAS**          *Begonia* ssp. and var.
Begonias comprise an enormous group of lovely flowering plants; the estimated number of species is from a thousand to fifteen hundred, and the varieties of those number upward of four thousand. Obviously everyone could find a begonia to suit any number of fancies. Their foliage is invariably beautiful and the cheerful airy clusters of blossoms well worth the minimal effort and encouragement they require. Begonias may best be grouped according to their growth habits, those growing from the common fibrous-root pattern, from rhizomes, or from tubers. They all show a preference for a lightly packed porous soil; indeed failure to flower can often be remedied simply by supplying a more loosely textured planting. Begonia roots are relatively

light may also do. Abundant filtered light is the ideal, but the possible range for success is broad. Put your new begonia where you want it and watch carefully for signs of too much or too little light.

TEMPERATURE: Average house.

HUMIDITY: Average to high, 30 percent or more for finest growth. Ample circulation of fresh, clean air.

WATER: Allow topsoil to dry between soakings. Fertilize with a well-balanced, slightly dilute solution every four to six weeks, more frequently if pot bound. Do not fertilize a resting plant.

SOIL: Standard indoor mixture with additional leaf mold or humus (3:1). A loose, rough texture is essential.

PROPAGATION: Cuttings, seeds.

**Rhizomatous begonias** grow from a rhizome and reveal their pattern with a thick, roughly notched, ground-creeping stem from which the leaves emerge. The rhizome lies on top of the soil and sends down shallow roots. The leaves and flower stalks rise from the eyelike nodes of the rhizome. Clusters of blossoms are held high above the plant and generally appear in late winter. White, delicate peach, pink, and rose are the most likely colors. The rex begonias are primarily rhizomatous and are grown for their unbelievable colors and exotic patterns of their leaves, hence the popular name, painted leaf.

LIGHT: Bright indirect to almost dim light.

TEMPERATURE: Average to warm, 70°–72° the optimum.

HUMIDITY: High humidity, 50 percent or more for most lavish growth. Mist frequently, but gently, with tepid water.

WATER: Evenly moist.

SOIL: Standard indoor mixture with additional leaf mold or humus (3:1). Loose soil texture.

shallow; a properly fitted pot would be smaller than you would expect for other plants. Whatever the growth pattern, begonias thrive in moist air and are sensitive to gas and other urban impurities. The best light is filtered or indirect sun and while some of the tougher fibrous-rooted begonias flourish with a few hours of direct sun daily, none can stay beautiful unless shaded from the glaring heat of hours in the direct summer sun. Since the number of species and varieties is enormous, watch your own begonia carefully and respect its need for a change in location or for a rest. Some bloom year round, with only the shortest of recovery periods.

**Fibrous-rooted begonias** include those with cane stems (such as angel-wing), the universal wax begonias (B. *semperflorens*), and many of the velvety hairy-leaved species. Pinch whenever possible for bushiest plants.

LIGHT: Bright indirect light, average indoor light, or almost dim. Some gentle direct sun-

PROPAGATION: Leaf cuttings. Slit-leaf technique for rex begonia. Seeds. Tip cutting from the creeping rhizome. Dormant nodes may be encouraged to become active by frequent misting of the rhizome or wrapping with moist sphagnum moss.

**Tuberous-rooted begonias** boast the winter-flowering Christmas begonia and the summer-flowering, outdoor-basket begonias among their ranks. These are not the easiest of house plants; the summer bloomers are discussed specifically in chapter 7. The bulbs must be replanted annually and they require an exacting combination of cool humid conditioning to promote luxuriant growth and vivid flowers.

LIGHT: Filtered or indirect light.

TEMPERATURE: Cool (60°–65°).

HUMIDITY: High, 50 percent or more for luxuriant growth.

WATER: Evenly moist. Fertilize regularly during growing season.

SOIL: Standard indoor mixture with additional leaf mold or humus (3:1). Loose, rich texture.

PROPAGATION: Division of tubers. Cuttings from young shoots in spring or fall. Seeds sown in early spring at 65°–70° and high humidity for summer bloom.

*Beloperone guttata*, see **Shrimp Plant**

Bermuda buttercup, see **Oxalis**

**Black-eyed Susan**    *Thunbergia alata*
Black-eyed Susan is a tender perennial vine from tropical Africa. The broad, bell-shaped flowers may be blue, apricot, or white, and are usually marked with a deep purple or black splotch in the center forming the eye. The vines may reach a length of 6 feet, will climb if provided with support and encouragement, or cascade floorward if left alone. They are striking when used in hanging pots

or baskets or for a window box. You may treat black-eyed Susan as an annual and sow new seeds each spring. Or, since it is indeed perennial, you may cut the plant back nearly to the soil after its period of heavy blooming, let it rest, and wait for reemergent robust growth.

LIGHT: Bright direct or indirect sunlight.

TEMPERATURE: Average house.

HUMIDITY: 30 percent or more for luxuriant growth.

WATER: Evenly moist, slightly less during rest period after heavy bloom. Spray foliage liberally to deter red spider mites.

SOIL: Standard indoor mixture.

PROPAGATION: Seeds sown in late winter or early spring. Pinch vigorously. Flowering may begin in as little as three months.

Bleeding heart vine, see **Glory Bower**

**Bougainvillea**    *Bougainvillea*
                    ssp. and hybrids
Bougainvillea's small white true flowers are not too exciting, but the brilliant paperlike complex bracts which enclose them are fabulous. The bracts are most commonly a vi-

brant purple, but they may also be crimson, tangerine, or white. Flowering is active through spring and summer. Bougainvillea is another tropical plant from Brazil and a member of the four o'clock family of outdoor-garden fame. It is a forceful shrub, reaching 8–10 feet in the garden, and must be cut back, pruned, and pinched to keep it tame and bushy indoors. Pinch new summer and fall growth most vigorously for abundant spring blossoms. The base of older vines will be quite woody; sharp spines sparsely dot the stems.

LIGHT: Bright, direct sun.

TEMPERATURE: Average house; warmth is fine.

HUMIDITY: 30 percent or more.

WATER: Average water, allowing the topsoil to dry out between soakings. Bougainvillea is a heavy drinker. Fertilize with a dilute solution at frequent intervals through the end of the active growing season. In October or so, reduce the amount of water, do not fertilize, cut back severely, and repot the plant if necessary.

SOIL: Standard indoor mixture.

PROPAGATION: Seeds sown in spring. Cuttings of 6-inch length root easily in early summer.

**Browallia**     *Browallia speciosa*
**Sapphire Flower**     *major* and others
Browallia is a lovely, gently trailing plant with deep green leaves and a profuse free-flowering habit. The flowers are generally sapphire or violet blue and 2 inches across, although dark blue (*B. viscosa*) or smaller blue and white (*B. americana*) varieties are also seen. Sapphire flower is most memorable in a hanging tub or planter; it is an annual and a South American member of the nightshade family which also offers the ornamental pepper and Jerusalem cherry for indoor cultivation; pinch small browallias well for bushier plants and more profuse bloom.

LIGHT: Direct bright sun to indirect filtered light.

TEMPERATURE: Average temperature, but a rather narrow range for best development and flowers. Keep winter temperature below 75°; temperatures below 65° will result in very slow growth.

HUMIDITY: Average or higher, 30 percent or more for luxuriant growth.

WATER: Average.

SOIL: Standard indoor mixture with additional leaf mold (3:1).

PROPAGATION: Cuttings in spring. Seeds sown between June and August will be ready for winter and spring bloom; seeds sown in February will produce blooming adults by July. If you are planting indoors with plans to get seedlings out as inexpensive bedding plants (or in window boxes), plan on eight weeks from seed to the rough outdoors. Plant four small plants to a 6-inch standard or fern pot or six to an 8-inch bulb pan.

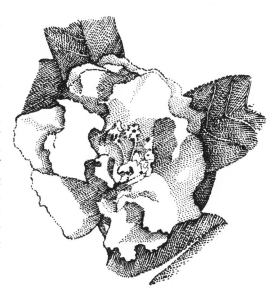

### Camellia — *Camellia japonica* / *C. reticulata*

The camellia has been a popular indoor plant for more than a century. It is native to China and Japan, and is a member of the tea family. The glossy, leathery green leaves of the shrub are beautifully highlighted by the large, waxy white flowers. The flowers may appear from November to March and are long-lived if the temperature is cool enough to suit them. The flowers may be pink, orange, red, or variegated, but white is the classic.

Cool temperatures are the most difficult aspect of proper care. Camellias are famous for dropping their buds. A location that is too hot or too dry is the most common cause, although you must also look to insufficient light or inconsistent watering if bud drop is plaguing your plants. A cool sun porch is the ideal location for camellias and it is quite common to grow them in tubs so that they can be moved to the outdoor garden, shaded, and packed with peat moss for a cooler summer. Flower buds begin to form in late summer and you should remove all tiny side buds if you wish fewer but larger flowers; the professionals call this "debudding."

LIGHT: Bright light; direct sun in winter, filtered or indirect light in summer.

TEMPERATURE: Cool, 40°–60°. Pay particular attention to cool winter temperatures to hold the flowers for as long as possible.

HUMIDITY: Moderate to high, 50 percent or more. Provide ample fresh air, but avoid drafts.

WATER: Keep soil evenly moist.

SOIL: Rich, acid soil. See chapter 8 for discussion of acid-loving plants. Excellent drainage is essential.

FERTILIZER: See chapter 8. Fertilize from March through August.

WHEN THE BLOOMS FADE: Repot if necessary; generally camellias are potted large enough to last them three or four years. Prune the plant to remove overly extravagant or irregular growth. Camellias are best summered outdoors to avoid the heat and dryness of the house. Plunge them into a cool part of the garden where they will receive filtered or dappled sunlight and will be protected from hot winds; surround them with moist peat moss for further insulation. If you have the plants standing on the porch or in the house, pack them with moist peat moss as well. Water regularly and sprinkle the plants with the hose or mist them with a spray bottle daily. Bring them in when the weather cools and place them in a bright and unheated location.

**Campanula**      *Campanula isophylla*
**Star of**           and var.
  **Bethlehem**
**Italian Bellflower**
**Falling Stars**

Campanula is a profusely flowering plant suitable to hanging baskets or pots and most attractive with its alternate grayish green leaves, tender stems, and prolific summer and autumn blooms. The flowers are bell-shaped which makes a great deal of sense for a plant in the bellflower family. *Campanula isophylla* is from Italy and although technically the name star of Bethlehem belongs to another plant (*Ornithogalum*) it has stuck for some time; the white flowers of the *alba* variety indeed resemble a cascade of falling stars. The *mayii* variety offers blue flowers. Other species provide double whites or smaller, intense blue blossoms. Trim the bellflowers to keep them from sprawling and pinch new spring growth vigorously for a fuller plant.

LIGHT: Gentle direct sun (winter) to bright indirect light (summer and early fall).

TEMPERATURE: Average, but sensitive to temperatures above 75° in winter.

HUMIDITY: 30 percent or more.

WATER: Average to moist, allow topsoil to dry out slightly between generous soakings. Frequent dilute fertilizing during active growth.

SOIL: Standard indoor mixture with additional leaf mold or humus (3:1). Repot with fresh soil in spring.

REST PERIOD: When blossoms fade at end of autumn, trim the plant back and find a suitable bright but cool (near 50° is best) winter location. Keep it on the dry side during bleak weather. Repot in early spring, resume normal care, and pinch vigorously through June.

PROPAGATION: Cuttings in spring. Seed sown in early spring; pinch seedlings to control leggy sprawl.

Candy-corn plant, see **Manettia**

Cape primrose, see **GESNERIAD FAMILY**

**Chenille Plant**      *Acalypha hispida*

Chenille plant is a bit difficult because of its tropical preference for consistently warm temperatures and high humidity; but it is a decorative and unusual plant and well worth the effort. The flowers are quite small and are clustered on fat fuzzy tassels which may be 4–6 inches long. These showy strings of myriad flowers may be pink, purple, or bright, bright red. The leaves are large pointed ovals and attractive; they share axils with the flower spikes. Prune chenille plant quite severely in the spring for finer summer bloom. If you have trouble with chenille plant, remember

Clivia         *Clivia miniata*

**Clivia**         *Clivia miniata*
**Kafir Lily**

The Kafir lily is a tender, evergreen tropical plant from South Africa. Its glossy, deep green, straplike leaves are impressive in both texture and size and a well-grown plant will take over a fair share of a room. The blossoms are trumpet-shaped and clustered in a lilylike stalk high above the plant; they may be yellow, orange, salmon, or scarlet. The plant is grown from a bulb and is a robust and reliable favorite. Although somewhat similar to African lily (*Agapanthus*), clivia has a rougher, bolder texture.

LIGHT: Bright indirect light to almost dim.

TEMPERATURE: Average, cooler preferred.

HUMIDITY: 30 percent or more.

WATER: Evenly moist. Clivia does not do well if ever allowed to dry out thoroughly; on the other hand, do not overwater or allow accu-

that the spurge family also offers croton and poinsettia as two other sources of aggravation and extreme beauty for indoor gardeners.

LIGHT: Bright indirect light. Direct sun if not accompanied by burning summer heat.

TEMPERATURE: Average to warm. No cooler than 60° for proper growth.

HUMIDITY: Average to high, 40 percent or more. Misting is an excellent idea; a sudden drop in humidity will be costly to lower leaves.

WATER: Average to moderately moist. Infrequent fertilizing.

SOIL: Standard indoor mixture. Good drainage is required. Repot in spring and trim roots if necessary, following with convalescent treatment.

PROPAGATION: Cuttings in spring or fall, rooted in sand.

Christmas begonia, see **BEGONIAS, Tuberous-rooted**

*Clerodendrum*, see **Glory Bower**

mulation of standing water in the root ball. Be careful to use only tepid water as the large bulbous roots are sensitive to sudden cold. Clivia is a heavy drinker.

SOIL: Standard indoor mixture with additional manure or bone meal as a light enrichment. Leave clivia pot bound until it is unmanageable; top dress in spring by scraping away as much topsoil as you can and replacing it with fresh. When you do repot, take care not to disturb the roots.

PROPAGATION: Division when the root mass is enormous. Division will generally interfere with flowering so it is best to put it off until absolutely necessary.

REST PERIOD: In late fall the plant becomes semidormant. Give less water but not so little that the heavy leaves might wilt. A temperature close to 55° will benefit next year's blossoms. Do not fertilize until January when the plant is brought back to warmth, watered freely, and fertilized with a dilute solution every week or two.

**Columnea**     *Columnea* ssp.

The columneas provide numerous handsome trailing plants for indoor growth, with striking foliage as well as generous flowers. Columnea is a gesneriad and you will find a more lengthy general discussion under that name. The leaves appear in pairs on opposite sides of the stem. They are generally narrow, deep green, and waxy, although bronze leaves with red hairs or tiny green leaves with coppery hairs are also among the popular possibilities. Blooming is profuse from spring through fall. The flowers are deep-throated and brilliant red, yellow, orange, or pink. Upright forms are known although the long cascading varieties are the most common. The period of bloom may be nearly endless, most plants resting for two or three months in the dullest part of winter. An admirable hanging plant.

LIGHT: Bright indirect to average indoor to al-most dim light. The most common waxy-leafed, trailing columneas will thrive in abundant indirect light.

TEMPERATURE: Average house. Beware of temperatures above 75° because of the attendant drop in humidity; the plant does come from the tropics.

HUMIDITY: Average to high, 50 percent or more for luxuriant foliage growth and unending flowers.

WATER: Average to almost evenly moist. The plant will require abundant and frequent watering during active growth. Take care that only tepid water is used.

SOIL: Standard indoor mixture (3 parts) with additional leaf mold or humus (1 part) and osmunda fiber or sphagnum moss (1 part). A rich, well-drained, porous soil.

PROPAGATION: Tip cuttings in spring. Seeds sown with warmth and high humidity provided.

Dizzy lizzy, see **Impatiens**

**Episcia** *Episcia reptans* and
**Flame Violet** many others
Episcia is grown as much for its luxuriant foliage as for its colorful flowers. The leaves have a pebbled surface with intricate silver veining; they may range from a muted green to bronze; they may be hairy or hairless; many appear quite quilted. The plant follows a strawberrylike habit, sending out stolons from which new plantlets arise; episcia is thus well suited to a shallow hanging pot or basket and is duly impressive when used as a ground cover in a warm, slightly shaded conservatory or large window box. The flowers are tubular, flaring out to an open five-lobed face with petal edges often delicately fringed; they may be yellow, pink, blue, lavender, or, most commonly, bright red. The flowering is at its

height in midsummer. Episcias should be pinched and cut back regularly if you want them bushy. They are yet another of the robust gesneriads and are thus related to African violet, columnea, lipstick vine, achimines, and gloxinia.

LIGHT: Bright indirect to almost dim light. Average indoor light in a room with plenty of windows suits most episcias quite well.

TEMPERATURE: Average house; does better with winter heat than without in cold climates.

HUMIDITY: Average or slightly higher, 30 percent or more for rapid growth.

WATER: Average to evenly moist. Tepid water only. Fertilize frequently with a dilute solution in spring and summer; not at all in late fall or winter. The plant rests from November to January; attend to this slowing of growth and water less.

SOIL: Standard indoor mixture with additional leaf mold or humus (3:1).

PROPAGATION: Tip cuttings in spring rooted with high humidity and warmth. Root plantlets formed on stolons at any time.

Fairy rose, see **Rose**

Falling stars, see **Campanula**

Firecracker vine, see **Manettia**

Flame of the woods, see **Ixora**

Flame violet, see **Episcia**

Flamingo flower, see **Anthurium**

**Flowering Maple** *Abutilon* var. and
**Parlor Maple** hybrids
Flowering maple is a lovely plant—more popular before the days of central heating than it is now, but well worth a try. It does best near 60°, which goes by the name of

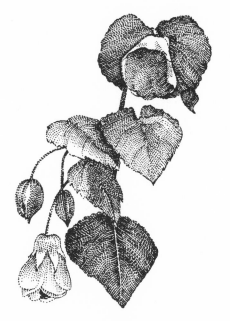

rapidly; pot-on until the most desirable pot size is reached and then fertilize frequently and keep the plant slightly pot bound for blooming.

LIGHT: Bright direct winter sun to bright indirect summer light.

TEMPERATURE: Average to cool.

HUMIDITY: Average house, more in winter to compensate for drying effect of artificial heat. Mist whenever the humidity falls or provide dry wells or other humidity-increasing devices.

WATER: Average to moderately moist. Flowering maple will require abundant water in warm weather.

SOIL: Standard indoor mixture. Fertilize frequently with a dilute solution when the plant begins to crowd the pot.

PROPAGATION: Cuttings in spring or fall, rooted in sand. Seeds may be sown winter or spring; spring seeds may be grown outdoors in their pots and brought indoors in fall for winter bloom.

"average to cool" house temperature; *Abutilon* is still another plant preferring bright winter sun and yet a cool location. This plant takes its common names from the maplelike shape of the drooping, textured, soft, fuzzy leaves. It is not related to the maple, but is a member of the mallow family (hollyhocks, etc.) and native to tropical South America. The flowers are papery thin, shaped like miniature hoop skirts, and held on narrow stems at leaf axils; extensive hybridization has brought us nearly everblooming plants whose blossoms may be yellow, orange, salmon, pink, red, or white. The plant is quite graceful and of an easygoing nature, but, since it grows to the proportion of a shrub in its natural habitat, it will tend to be tall and straggly unless preventive measures are taken. Choose your measures. Fresh cuttings may be taken each year for renewed plantings; or prune older plants quite severely in early fall to encourage bushy growth for the next crop of flowers. Flowers emerge from terminal growth; so the more branching you can encourage, the more potential blossom sites you will have; pinch vigorously. The plant grows

| Fuchsia | *Fuchsia speciosa* |
|---|---|
| **Lady's Eardrops** | hybrids |

Fuchsia is another flowering beauty which requires cool winter temperatures for proper growth. That people have had success with its culture may be surmised from the fact that there are thousands of named varieties (from *F. fulgens* and *F. magellanica* hybrids). Fuchsia blooms from late spring through early autumn and the pendulous graceful flowers may be red, pink, lavender, white, violet, blue, salmon, purple, or more generally a combination of two. Flowering is from new tip growth; so active pruning and pinching of young plants at any time and of established plants in late winter (January and on) will achieve fuller plants with greater potential for extravagant flowering. The fuchsia has a shrubby inclination and therefore pruning is essential to keep a plant of house pro-

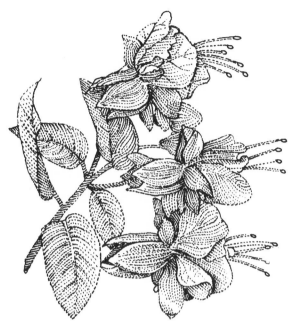

portion from turning to pure wood. Fuchsias are unmatched for hanging planters or baskets on a sheltered porch; they are also one of the more suitable candidates for extensive side pruning and an indoor future as a trained house-plant tree.

LIGHT: Abundant light, but fuchsias must have shade from the hot sun.

TEMPERATURE: Average to cool. A cool temperature (60°–68°) is particularly important in winter and early spring. Consistency is also a factor; sudden change in temperature is a common cause of bud drop.

HUMIDITY: Average, but higher humidity preferred for most luxuriant growth, 50 percent or more. Fresh air must be available to discourage mold and fungus growths.

WATER: Evenly moist during active growing season. Fuchsias require a great deal of water and frequent dilute fertilizing when in growth.

REST PERIOD: After the last fall flowers fade, remove the plant to a cool (45°–50° is fine) and perhaps dimmer-light location and water

only enough to keep the woody stems plump; prune the plant back to under a foot. Do not fertilize. In late winter (January), you may begin to increase the water and bring the plant to a warmer spot (still not over 68°). When buds swell and new growth is active, prune away all scraggly growth and dead wood. Pinch vigorously until midspring.

SOIL: Standard indoor mixture.

PROPAGATION: Cuttings in spring or summer, rooted in sand. Seeds are available.

**Gardenia**          *Gardenia jasminoides*
The famous gardenia is an evergreen shrub with deep green glossy leaves and beautiful, intoxicatingly fragrant, white flowers that appear in November. It is native to China, a member of the madder family, and quite irascible. Leaves will drop from any sudden changes, particularly in temperature. Leaves will yellow from insufficient acid in the soil (chlorosis) or from temperatures that are unseasonably cool. Mealybugs and scale are common invaders, so inspect gardenia plants frequently and deal with the guests promptly.

LIGHT: Bright light: direct sun or bright indirect light in winter, less intense light in summer.

TEMPERATURE: Cool, 60°–70° in spring and summer, 45°–55° from November to March.

The ideal nighttime temperature for greenhouse gardenias is 62°. Do the best you can; again the unheated but insulated sun porch is the ideal spot for home-grown plants.

HUMIDITY: Average, 30 percent or more. Ample fresh air required. Increase humidifying efforts through misting or dry wells in hot weather.

WATER: Keep soil evenly moist.

SOIL: Rich, acid soil. See chapter 8 for discussion of acid-loving plants.

FERTILIZER: See chapter 8.

WHEN THE BLOOMS FADE: Continue to water and fertilize regularly. In late spring, repot gardenias if they are crowded in their pots and prune back any plant that has grown irregularly out of bounds. If the size of the plant suits you, be content to remove any suckers (extra shoots at the base) or wayward stems. Pinch gardenias through August to maximize next year's blooms. The plants may be summered in a filtered-sun location outdoors or they may stay in if you can keep them cool and moist. Water regularly and vigilantly in hot weather. From November through March they need good light and a temperature as close to 50° as you can manage.

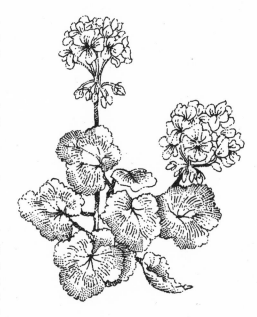

### Geranium      *Pelargonium hortorum* and others

A simple, stocky plant from South Africa, geranium now covers the globe. The "common," "house," or "zonal" geranium (*P. hortorum*) is so named for a horseshoe-shaped zone of brown across the green leaf. Heavy clusters of red, white, or pink flowers, an upright, thick set of branching stems, and an impervious nature have made this an unbelievably popular plant. Variegated white leaves, fancy leaves, and miniatures are also offered. *P. domesticum* is a developed type of the zonal plant and goes variously by the names of Lady Washington, Martha Washington, or "show geranium." Their leaves are all green, ridged, and crisp. Flowers appear in late spring; the distinctive dark spots on the pansylike petals are known to all. These varieties are more difficult to grow, requiring a winter temperature of 50°–60° to set buds, which neatly limits their culture to coastal areas. They must be pinched vigorously until late February and cut back and repotted after the end of summer blooms. The scented geraniums (*P. speciosa* var.) are not terribly showy. They need less sunlight than the others and offer scented leaves from lemon, cinnamon, and apple to rose. They are required for recipes calling for a rose-geranium leaf at the bottom of the jar of apple jelly and as floating leaves in the crystal finger bowl; other than that, they are also admirable plants. Ivy geranium (*P. peltatum*) is a hanging or trailing plant with glossy, ivylike leaves; it is a summer bloomer but not as free-flowering as the common geranium. Ivy geranium prefers a cool summer and somewhat more humid air; it is a fine plant for the outdoor window box or hanging basket.

Whiteflies and red spider mites are the chief enemies of geraniums. Leaf washing is fine to deter red spider mites, but bear in mind that ample ventilation is required to avoid fungus development.

LIGHT: Bright direct sun to bright indirect light.

TEMPERATURE: Average to cool (45°–70°).

HUMIDITY: Average or slightly higher, 30 percent or more. Ample fresh air and frequent ventilation is definitely required to avoid fungus growths on the leaves.

WATER: Average watering, alternating a mild drying-out period with thorough soaks. Reduce water if mold or leaf spots appear. Avoid wetting the leaves unless you are thoroughly washing them and taking care they dry well. Yellowing of the foliage generally indicates overwatering and wet feet. Light fertilizing required.

SOIL: Standard indoor mixture with additional leaf mold (3:1 or 3:2). The planting must be well drained to avoid wet feet and the soil texture must be firm. Geraniums seem to flower best when slightly pot bound and in a pot no larger than 6 inches. Scratch bone meal into the topsoil of a pot-bound plant at the rate of one teaspoon per 6-inch pot.

PROPAGATION: Cuttings in spring or fall. Pinch young plants vigorously. Seeds are available but the gene pack is enormous and you have no idea what variations you will get; so most growers therefore prefer cuttings or young plants from named varieties.

## GESNERIAD FAMILY
Gesneriaceae

The gesneriad family offers a staggering number of house plants with attractive foliage as well as showy, colorful, and long-lasting blooms. In addition to those described in detail here—achimines, African violet, columnea, episcia, and lipstick vine—this group includes *Kohleria*, gloxinia (*Sinningia*), cape primrose (*Streptocarpus*), *Nautilocalyx*, temple bells (*Smithiantha*), *Rechsteineria*, and the new *Gloxinera*. Some of the names may be foreign to the tongue, but the plants have been widely enjoyed for years. It is no surprise that there are gesneriad societies around the globe.

The gesneriads are native to various wide-flung but tropical regions. They grow beneath the shelter of taller trees in the organically rich, loose-textured, and moist jungle soil. Consequently they require abundant filtered light, a warm environment (68°–80°), and humid air; growth is rampant at 50–60 percent relative humidity, but most gesneriads will make do with a bit less. The soil mixture must be rich and porous. African-violet mixes or the standard indoor mixture with additional leaf mold and sphagnum moss (3:1:1) would be proper choices; I prefer the latter, particularly for the heavy-vining columnea and lipstick vine. The plants of this family are heavy water users; plan to water when the topsoil approaches dryness and use water as close to room temperature as possible for these jungle plants. Spray the foliage frequently and forcefully if the plants are not hairy-leafed; red spider mite is a problem that can be easily avoided with lots of plain water. Cyclamen mite is the enemy of African violet and other crowned species; watch new plants carefully, use only sterilized soil, and read up a bit on cyclamen mite (see chapter 5).

Fertilize the gesneriads with a dilute solution of a well-balanced fertilizer and apply it frequently during periods of active growth. Rest periods vary considerably with the different species and the numerous varieties and hybrids of each. Many of the family rest only during the dull winter months, others off and on through the year. Water less and do not fertilize until new growth picks up. Repotting is most commonly slated for spring.

*Gloxinera*, see **GESNERIAD FAMILY**

Gloxinia, see **GESNERIAD FAMILY**

| **Glory Bower** | *Clerodendrum* |
| **Bag Flower** | *thompsonaes* |
| **Bleeding Heart** | *C. fragrans* |
| **Vine** | and others |

The common name of this evergreen and shrubby vine from West Africa alludes to its vibrant bloom. Glory bower is a vigorous plant; it will bloom at 18 inches tall and in greenhouses it may grow higher than 10 feet. The true flowers are not the glory, but the large inflated bracts of white and red are stunning.

LIGHT: Bright direct sun to bright indirect light.

TEMPERATURE: Average, but cool in winter.

HUMIDITY: Average, higher preferred, 30 percent or more.

WATER: Average to evenly moist. Abundant water and frequent dilute fertilizing will be required from spring to fall.

REST PERIOD: After blooms fade in fall, the vine may drop most of its leaves. Reduce watering, bring it to a cool place (below 60° at night) and, after a few weeks of quiet, prune it down to a desirable size. A rest of two or three months is sufficient, after which you may renew active watering and return the plant to its window location.

SOIL: Standard indoor mixture with additional leaf mold (3:1).

PROPAGATION: Cuttings taken in late spring or summer. Suckers removed from base of older plants.

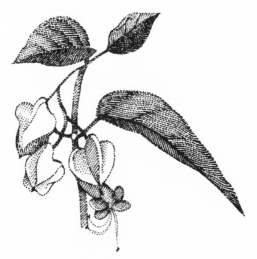

| **Hoya** | *Hoya carnosa* |
| **Wax Plant** | *H. bella* |
| **Porcelain Flower** | |

Hoya is a climbing or trailing vine which produces clusters of fragrant, firm, pinkish white flowers with a red star at the center of each. It is a plant of easy habits and its only peculiarity concerns the spur or supporting stem of the flower cluster; do not remove this spur after the flowers fade, as next summer's flowers will begin there as well. When buds are forming, water the plant less and do not move it or bump into it lest the buds change their collective intent and drop to the floor. Small pots (6 inches and under) seem to

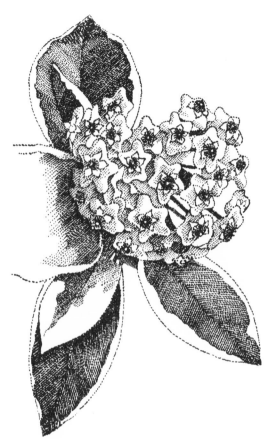

house the best blooming hoyas. Aerial roots will make their appearance and the plant is an avid climber if encouraged. *Hoya bella* is also commonly available and is similar to but smaller than *H. carnosa*. They are members of the milkweed family and native to Australia, among other spots.

LIGHT: Abundant bright light, but no direct summer sun.

TEMPERATURE: Average house.

HUMIDITY: Average but some additional humidifying efforts (misting, dry well, or humidifier) are beneficial in late winter and early spring.

WATER: Average, allow the topsoil to dry out well between soakings.

REST PERIOD: Keep hoya rather dry in winter, watering only enough to prevent shriveling of the leaves and stems. A cool spot (50°–60°) is ideal but added seasonal humidity makes a year-round location possible.

SOIL: Standard indoor mixture with additional leaf mold or humus (3:1).

PROPAGATION: Tip cuttings from young plants in spring. Air layer larger individuals.

**Impatiens**              *Impatiens sultanii*
**Patient Lucy**          *I. holstii* and hybrids
**Patience Plant**
**Dizzy Lizzy**
**Zanzibar Balsam**
**Touch-me-not**

This easy and good-looking plant-of-the-many-names is a tropical member of the balsam family. The botanical name *Impatiens* refers to its seed pods which literally shoot out their contents when ripe. What is singularly patient about the plant is that it prefers a pot-bound condition; indeed it will drop leaves with abandon if its roots are disturbed. Violent, vigorous, and nonstop pinching seems to be required to maintain bushy lower stems. The leaves are a glossy dark green and barely toothed or fringed at the edges; some hybrids also offer white variegation of bronzelike tones. The five-petaled flowers are hardy and deeply colored; scarlet is the norm but pink, orange, purple, rose, and white may also be found. Impatiens is a popular outdoor ground cover for areas in poor light or even deep shade.

LIGHT: Abundant bright light to average indoor light, but no direct summer sun.

TEMPERATURE: Average house.

HUMIDITY: Average to slightly higher, 50 percent or more for luxuriant growth and less lower-leaf drop. Red spider mite is the most common problem, much less troublesome with higher humidity and frequent spraying of the foliage.

WATER: Average to evenly moist. Fertilize with a dilute solution of a well-balanced fertilizer at frequent intervals during active growth.

SOIL: Standard indoor mixture.

PROPAGATION: Cuttings rooted in water or sand, most hardy in spring or summer. Seeds harvested or purchased and planted in late spring for summer blooms.

Italian bellflower, see **Campanula**

| **Ixora**<br>**Flame of the**<br>   **Woods** | *Ixora coccinea* and<br>many hybrids |
|---|---|

Ixora is an unusual, hardy, and lovely plant from the East Indies. It is related to gardenia (madder family) but by no means as temperamental. This evergreen shrub of glossy, deep green leaves is nearly everblooming with dense clusters of small tubular flowers appearing in early spring. The classic color is scarlet or "flame," but numerous hybrids offer yellow, rose, dark red, orange, and pink. Being of a shrubby natural intent, ixora requires frequent pinching and pruning to maintain bushiness and ample lower-stem growth under indoor conditions.

LIGHT: Bright direct sun to bright indirect light.

TEMPERATURE: Average, warmer rather than cooler in winter (65°+).

HUMIDITY: Average or slightly higher, 30 percent or more for proper growth.

WATER: Evenly moist. Fertilize frequently with a dilute solution; no fertilizer during mild winter rest period.

SOIL: Standard indoor mixture.

PROPAGATION: Cuttings in spring rooted in sand or peat moss with warmth and higher humidity provided.

Kafir lily, see **Clivia**

Lady's eardrops, see **Fuchsia**

Lady Washington, see **Geranium**

Lily of the Nile, see **African Lily**

| **Lipstick Vine** | *Aeschynanthus*<br>*lobbianus*<br>A. *pulcher* |
|---|---|

The lipstick vine is a dazzling plant, a trailing epiphyte from Java and the East Indies. It is another gesneriad. This tropical beauty is most often grown in a hanging pot; the stems may be 2 feet long or longer, and when covered with scarlet flowers they are striking indeed. Leaves are opposite, waxy, a deep lustrous green, and thickly crowded on the stem. The flowers unfold from a tubelike beginning (*à la* lipstick) to reveal an open-lipped, two-part blossom that is orange, scarlet, or red with a bit of yellow inside the throat. The calyxes are firm and of a reddish or bronze tone.

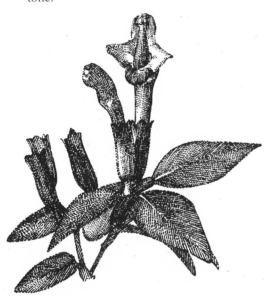

LIGHT: Abundant indirect light, but avoid direct summer sun.

TEMPERATURE: Average house, warmer rather than colder.

HUMIDITY: Average to high, 50 percent for most luxuriant growth. A drop in humidity will discourage blossoms.

WATER: Average water, allow the topsoil to dry out between thorough soakings. In spring and summer, the lipstick vine is a heavy drinker. Fertilize frequently during active growing season. Wash foliage thoroughly with a frequent plain-water spray to discourage red spider mites and maintain lustrous leaves.

## Manettia
## Firecracker Vine
## Candy-corn Plant

*Manettia bicolor* or *M. inflata*

Manettia is a fast growing, easy, free-blooming vine from Brazil, Paraguay, or Uruguay. The flowers appear in late winter or early spring; they are tubular scarlet blossoms with yellow petal tips, a colorful and exuberant addition for this dreary time of year. The vine will trail or climb if encouraged; individual stems of the vine may reach a length of 4 feet, although they are generally shorter. Better blooming often accompanies a slightly pot-bound condition.

LIGHT: Abundant bright indirect light, but no direct sun. Average indoor light will often do.

TEMPERATURE: Average house, but not over 75° in winter.

HUMIDITY: Average to slightly higher, 30 per-

cent or more for most extravagant growth. Ample fresh air is required.

WATER: Evenly moist. Firecracker vine is a heavy drinker. Fertilize with a regular dilute well-balanced solution during active growth.

SOIL: Standard indoor mixture.

PROPAGATION: Cuttings in spring or summer.

Martha Washington, see **Geranium**

Miniature rose, see **Rose**

Monkey-face flower, see **Achimines**

*Nautilocalyx*, see **GESNERIAD FAMILY**

*Neomarica*, see **Walking Iris**

Nut orchid, see **Achimines**

**Oxalis**          *Oxalis* ssp. and var.
**Wood Sorrel**
**Bermuda Butter-**
  **cup**

Oxalis is a charming, small, bulbous plant with cloverlike foliage and long-stemmed delicate flowers. The blossoms are most commonly yellow (as in "buttercup"), but white, red, lavender, or pink are also seen. Leaves fold and flowers close up at night and on very cloudy days. Remove all flowers or yellowed leaves as they begin to fade. Oxalis blooms profusely; some varieties are everblooming, others prefer fall and winter, a few choose spring or summer.

LIGHT: Bright direct winter sun to bright indirect summer light.

TEMPERATURE: Average to cool, 60° is a good average for hardiest growth.

HUMIDITY: 30 percent or more.

WATER: Average watering. Oxalis will require abundant water during active growth.

REST PERIOD: Allow this tuberous plant to rest after a period of heavy bloom. Gradually re-

duce water and then store the pot quite dry and in a cool place for two or three months. Then return the plant to its normal spot and resume watering. However, do not do this to everblooming varieties! These should instead be repotted annually in summer or fall and trimmed back at that time to promote renewed bushy growth.

SOIL: Standard indoor mixture with optional additional mortar rubble (3:1) to promote alkalinity of the soil. It is essential that the planting provide excellent drainage.

PROPAGATION: Plant tubers in early fall; place three or four in a prepared 5-inch pot (or six to a 6-inch pot) and barely cover their tops with soil. Water sparingly for the first month or more until growth appears. Then increase watering to fit the plant's lively needs. Offsets may also be removed from established plants at repotting time and treated as separate new individuals. Those plants with rhizomes can be divided.

Painted-leaf begonia, see **BEGONIAS, Rhizomatous**

Parlor maple, see **Flowering Maple**

**Passion Flower**      *Passiflora* ssp.
The passion flower is not the easiest of flowering plants to grow, but many people feel it is well worth the effort. Its spring flowers may be 5 inches across and bright blue, fiery red, white, or pink. It is an avidly climbing vine native to the southern United States and on to South America; active tendrils will make use of even a bit of string to support the plant. The plant grows rapidly, and once it has reached a 10-inch pot it should be top dressed each year and left where it is. Cut young shoots vigorously and often to maintain a bushy plant.

LIGHT: Bright direct sun to bright indirect light.

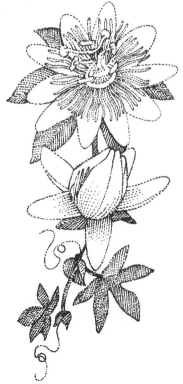

TEMPERATURE: Average house.

HUMIDITY: Average to slightly higher, 30 percent or more.

WATER: Keep evenly moist. From March onward through the period of active growth, passion flower requires abundant water. Fertilize every week or two during the growing season with a dilute well-balanced solution.

REST PERIOD: Gradually reduce water after blooms fade. Water less in winter and do not fertilize. In January, cut the plant back nearly to the soil, top dress by replacing as much of the topsoil as you can, and begin active watering to encourage new growth.

SOIL: Standard indoor mixture with additional leaf mold or humus (3:1). Excellent drainage is essential for proper growth.

PROPAGATION: Cuttings, most vigorous in early spring, are rooted in sand. Seeds.

Patience plant, see **Impatiens**

Patient Lucy, see **Impatiens**

*Pelargonium*, see **Geranium**

Porcelain flower, see **Hoya**

Pygmy rose, see **Rose**

*Rechsteineria*, see **GESNERIAD FAMILY**

Rex begonia, see **BEGONIAS, Rhizomatous**

*Rhododendron*, see **Azalea**

| **Rose** | *Rosa chinensis minima* |
| **Miniature Rose** | *R. roulettii* |
| **Pygmy Rose** | and others |
| **Fairy Rose** | |

Miniature roses (grown to 6 inches in height) come from China and offer delicate replicas of the outdoor hybrid tea roses. Their flowers may be white, yellow, pink, rose, red, or violet; they generally bloom from late spring on into fall. Buy your first plants in January in

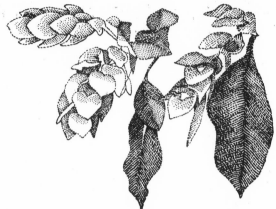

4-inch pot size, then cut them back almost to half.

LIGHT: Bright direct sun to bright indirect light.

TEMPERATURE: Average (55°–70°).

HUMIDITY: Average to slightly higher, 30 percent or more for best growth. Fresh clean air is quite important for fine flowers and to avoid mildew diseases.

WATER: Moist but not sodden. Fertilize frequently with a dilute well-balanced solution during active growing season.

REST PERIOD: Cut the plant back sharply after the blooming period, down to 4 inches or so in height. Store in a cool (45°) and slightly dimmer location during November and December for a better crop of next year's flowers; water much less to suit the plant's semidormant stage. In January, bring the rose back to a sunny window, cut it back again almost to half, and remove all old twiggy or straggly growth, and resume full watering and feeding.

*Saintpaulia,* see **African Violet**

Sapphire flower, see **Browallia**

Scented geraniums, see **Geranium**

*Schizocentron elegans,* see **Spanish Shawl**

**Shrimp Plant**        *Beloperone guttata*
Shrimp plant is a lovely, fast-growing plant from Mexico and Central America whose curled coppery-tipped flower sheathes fancifully resemble hanging shrimp. The true flowers of *Beloperone* are white and tiny, but they are held within a showy bract of overlapping paperlike parts which may be red, chartreuse, copper, or pinkish brown. It is a plant of easy culture and long-blooming habit, with plentiful "shrimp" from late fall through spring. The leaves are light green, the stems are wiry, and the plant requires a great deal of pinching and pruning to keep it bushy. Cut it back heavily in September for more prolific winter display. The blooms appear at the tips of the stems so the more branching you are able to induce the better. Shrimp plant does tend to be quite stubborn about developing bare legs and consequently many growers choose to renew it annually from cuttings; in any event, pinch new growth heavily.

LIGHT: Bright direct sun to bright indirect light.

TEMPERATURE: Average house.

HUMIDITY: Average to slightly higher, 30 percent or more preferred.

WATER: Average, allow topsoil to become moderately dry between soakings. The plant is a heavy drinker and the roots require plenty of water at all times—this despite periodic topsoil dryness. So never let the soil get bone-dry.

SOIL: Standard indoor mixture. A particularly well-drained planting is necessary for best growth and minimal lower-leaf drop.

PROPAGATION: Cuttings at any time.

*Sinningia*, see **GESNERIAD FAMILY**

*Smithiantha*, see **GESNERIAD FAMILY**

**Spanish Shawl** *Schizocentron elegans*
Another attractive plant from Mexico, Spanish shawl is a small, somewhat succulent creeper; nodes will root to any damp soil they find, and then the plant will cascade gracefully over the sides of the pot. The hairy green leaves are held on red stems and masses of red flowers appear in June. Spanish shawl has perhaps been more popular at other times than it is now, but I would think it worth trying any plant whose Latin name ends in *elegans*.

LIGHT: Bright direct sun to bright indirect light.

TEMPERATURE: Average to cool, not over 72° in winter. Here is another beauty that likes a sunny but cool spot; do your best.

HUMIDITY: Moderate to high, 50 percent or more for most luxuriant growth.

WATER: Keep constantly moist, but not water-logged.

SOIL: Standard indoor mixture.

PROPAGATION: Cuttings in spring, rooted in sand with warmth and high humidity provided.

**Spathiphyllum** *Spathiphyllum*
**Spathe Flower** *clevelandii*
*S. floribundum*
Spathe flower is a tough tropical plant from South America and a member of the aroid or calla family which brings us so many other reliable indoor specimens—Chinese evergreen, caladium, dieffenbachia, nephythytis, philodendron, and pothos. The spathiphyllum has long been appreciated for its shiny, dark green foliage as well as for its long-lasting white spathes which surround the fragrant fingerlike flowers. The plants bloom at the first hint of spring. *S. clevelandii*, most commonly seen, grows to 2 feet and offers wide lancelike leaves which seem almost stemless and dramatically frame the small white spathes. *S. floribundum* is a smaller plant (to 1 foot high) which is grown primarily for its velvety foliage.

LIGHT: Indirect light, from almost bright to almost dim. Direct sun will burn the thin leaves.

TEMPERATURE: Average to warm, 65°–75° is the best daytime range.

HUMIDITY: Moderate to high, 50 percent or more or mist daily for best growth.

WATER: Evenly moist.

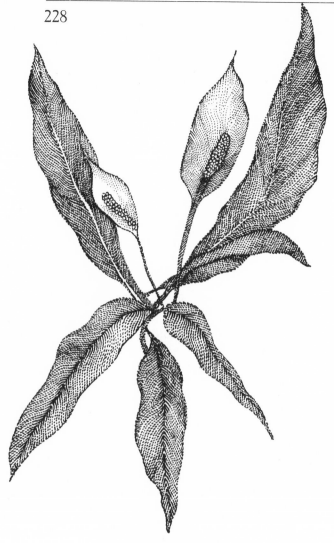

Touch-me-not, see **Impatiens**

**Walking Iris**      *Neomarica gracilis*
**Apostle Plant**     *N. northiana*
**Twelve Apostles**   *N. caerulea*
Surprisingly enough, walking iris is not mis-
named, and is indeed a member of the iris
family. The bladelike leaves are light green
and up to 2 feet long. The small iris flowers
are born on leaflike scapes; they offer a delightful freshness to late winter days. Three or
four of the short-lived fragrant flowers appear
at each tip and, when they are gone, a new
plantlet takes their spot and eventually bends
the tip of the scape down to the soil and the
plantlet roots promptly. Hence the name
walking iris. Legend has it that twelve leaves
will form around the center scape and none
will turn brown until the flowers appear; this
is not exactly true, but explains the popular
names twelve apostles or apostle plant. *Neomarica* is a dependable, easy plant, not
bothered by pests and unperturbed by a bit of
cooking or heating gas in the atmosphere.
*N. gracilis* offers white flowers with blue
centers; *N. northiana* white with brown, yellow, and violet; *N. caerulea* is primarily blue.

SOIL: Standard indoor mixture with additional
leaf mold or humus (3:1).

PROPAGATION: Division of rootstalk at spring
repotting. Young plants require warmth (70°–
80°) and high humidity to thrive.

Star of Bethlehem, see **Campanula**

*Streptocarpus*, see **GESNERIAD FAMILY**

Tail flower, see **Anthurium**

Temple bells, see **GESNERIAD FAMILY**

*Thunbergia alata*, see **Black-eyed Susan**

LIGHT: Bright direct winter sun to bright indirect summer light.

TEMPERATURE: Average to cool, not above 72° in winter.

HUMIDITY: 30 percent or more.

WATER: Average to evenly moist.

SOIL: Standard indoor mixture with optional addition of sharp sand (3:1).

PROPAGATION: Pin down plantlets formed at tips of flower scapes. Divide rhizome stalks at spring repotting.

Wax begonia, see **BEGONIAS, Fibrous-rooted**

Wax plant, see **Hoya**

Wood sorrel, see **Oxalis**

Zanzibar balsam, see **Impatiens**

**Zebra Plant**   *Aphelandra squarrosa louisae*
*A. aurantica roezlii*

Zebra is a flashy individual, native to the tropics of Brazil. While it can be grown indoors, it needs peculiar conditions and you might have to settle for enjoyment of this striking beauty on a temporary plane. The leaves are of a rich green, prominently veined with white; the resplendent spike of yellow or yellow orange flowers and waxy bracts appears in the fall. Prune after the flowers fade

and see if you can keep the plant from reaching unkempt legginess. Pinch and mist.

LIGHT: Bright indirect sun. Abundant light, but *Aphelandra* cannot take any intense direct sun.

TEMPERATURE: Average house, warm is fine.

HUMIDITY: 30 percent or more. Hot and humid (50 percent) is the very best.

WATER: Evenly moist. Zebra plant requires heavy watering. Leaves will go limp when the soil is still almost moist.

SOIL: Standard indoor mixture with additional leaf mold and peat moss (3:1:1).

PROPAGATION: Air layering of older barky-stemmed plants. Young plants may be used for tip cuttings in the spring; warmth (70°–80°) and high humidity required for rooting.

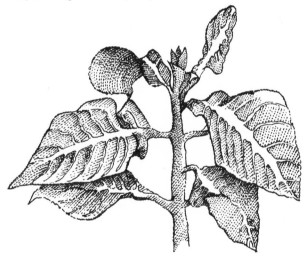

# 4

# Gift Plants

Whenever you receive a florist's specialty plant, you have two choices: try to keep it going forever or enjoy it briefly until you toss it out. This latter is the most carefree and often the most sensible tack. The popular gift plants are specialty items primarily because they do require exacting greenhouse conditions to produce their impressive displays. But some are relatively easy annuals and I will run through the list so that you will know how to maintain their "new-bought" beauty for the longest possible time and then know what your options are once the blooms are gone. The main idea is that you ought not to feel guilty when you are walking a defunct cyclamen to the garbage can. Besides which, as florists' plants become less and less expensive and purchased cut flowers become more so, it seems even easier to throw out the faded potted beauties without a qualm. Notwithstanding the element of challenge, you might contemplate whether the time involved to ensure another crop of poinsettias or whatever might be spent with greater satisfaction on a more unusual flowering plant.

*Calceolaria*, see **Pocketbook Plant**

*Capsicum*, see **Ornamental Pepper**

Christmas pepper, see **Ornamental Pepper**

**Chrysanthemum**     *Chrysanthemum hortorum* var.
Chrysanthemum is a handsome woody plant and perhaps the most popular of foil-wrapped

gifts. The blossoms court a wide range of colors and may vary in size from the small, daisylike button flowers to the giant pompons. Chrysanthemums for indoor use are generally raised annually and they do best if they spend most of their time outdoors. They are "short-day" plants, which means that buds set only when the days are short and nights not less than fourteen hours long. Thus their period of natural bloom is from

fall to midwinter, although professional growers will trick them with black-out shades and force them to flower at other commercially appropriate times of the year.

LIGHT: Abundant light, but with protection from strong direct sun.

TEMPERATURE: Average to cool (60°–70°) to prolong blooms.

HUMIDITY: Average to moderate, 30 percent or more. Ample ventilation and circulation of fresh air, but avoid drafts.

WATER: Keep evenly moist, but not soaking. Either remove the foil wrapper or be sure to punch a hole in the bottom to prevent standing water.

FERTILIZER: Young plants raised from cuttings are fertilized weekly throughout summer and fall, but only after they have become pot bound. Do not feed chrysanthemums after the flower buds have begun to show color, and consequently do not feed when in bloom.

SOIL: Standard indoor mixture. Texture very firm.

WHEN THE BLOOMS FADE: After the plant has withered, cut it back to 2 inches from the soil. Place it in a cool basement or cold frame (no frost) or an unheated sun porch. Keep it barely moist until spring. When the ground is warm enough, plant the chrysanthemum directly into the garden soil. Take cuttings as soon as the tip growth is established and/or pinch vigorously through mid-July. "Debud" if you like, as described below with the treatment of cuttings. The plant is ready to be dug up and brought in when the flower buds have formed; or, of course, you may leave it in the garden. Soak the area well the day before and pot the plant snugly to fit its compact root system. Give it a bit of shelter for a few days and then place it in a cool, sunny indoor spot. Enjoy the chrysanthemum indoors until it withers again and on you go.

If you follow this basic plan but have no garden, be sure the chrysanthemum receives no artificial light after sunset from August on; its ability to set flower buds is governed exclusively by photoperiodism, the relative length of night and day.

PROPAGATION: Cuttings in spring, rooted in sand and planted five per 8-inch pot or individually and potted-on until a 6–10-inch pot size is reached in early June. Mist young plants and begin to fertilize and pinch them vigorously as soon as their growth is well established. "Debud" if you like large flowers: remove all but one or two main stems and all side buds so that the ones on top will become impressively large flowers; also remove any flower buds which appear before the middle of August because they will not be as hardy as later arrivals.

You may also obtain new plants by removing the suckers that form at the base of older plants; tease these away gently from the main plant so that the attached roots will come along. Seeds are planted in early fall for flowering plants a year later.

**Cineraria**        *Senecio cruentus*

Cineraria is another member of the composite family and a native of the Canary Islands. It is generally between a foot and two in height and the many hybrids offer a range of flower color of everything but yellow. The small daisylike flowers are most often a vibrant lush blue; they are so numerous and closely packed that the large, soft-textured, piggybacklike leaves are nearly obscured from view. The flowers last only a few weeks; the plant is discarded after its floral display; but it is inexpensive and well worth the thrill. The period of natural bloom begins in late fall through early spring, depending on the variety; cineraria is another "short-day" plant.

LIGHT: Abundant indirect or direct light, but requires protection from strong direct sun.

TEMPERATURE: Cool to prolong blossoms, 55° at night to 65° daytime.

HUMIDITY: 30 percent or more. Ample fresh air, but beware that drafts will cause lower leaves to droop, drop, or yellow.

WATER: Evenly moist. Cineraria is a heavy drinker and wilts easily; in warmer rooms and on sunny days it may need to be watered more often than daily.

FERTILIZER: Frequent feeding with a dilute well-balanced solution from the time the plants are established until after flowers have faded.

SOIL: Standard indoor mixture.

WHEN THE BLOOMS FADE: Throw out the plant. Although not technically an annual, cineraria is treated as one. It is too difficult to keep or nurture without a greenhouse and most professional growers even prefer to begin each year with new seed.

PROPAGATION: Plant seeds in May for fall-flowering varieties, in August through October for spring-flowering plants. The dwarf varieties are perhaps best for indoor gardening. The seedlings require good light, frequent feeding, and cool temperatures. The cooler their summer location, the hardier the plants will be; in fact, if the night temperature does not fall below 60°, there will be no blossoms; 45° at night is the ideal. The young plants will require ample root space and frequent repotting. They are not to be root bound at any time and are ideally ready for the final shift to a 6- or 7-inch pot in January (or in August for fall varieties).

**Cyclamen**        *Cyclamen indicum*
**Persian Violet**    *C. persicum*
            *giganteum*

Cyclamen is a tuberous perennial plant, but extremely difficult to maintain from year to year as a lush house specimen. It is primarily the fault of our indoor heat, so if you have no unheated sun porch or greenhouse, simply enjoy the gift from the florist as long as you may. The blooming period is long and, if your rooms are on the cool side, the individual flowers are tenacious. Cyclamen blooms naturally from October through April, with February its most glorious time. The foliage of the neatly crowned plants is fleshy and deep green; the tender heart-shaped leaves are often patterned with white or silver. The flowers are large, held on high stems, and are a velvety white, pink, red, or lavender, boasting frilled edges or plain. Remove any dying leaves carefully; twist and then pull them off from the base to avoid crown rot of this fleshy beauty.

LIGHT: Bright indirect light to almost dim. Protect the plant from direct sun.

TEMPERATURE: Cool, 50° at night to 60° during the day is the ideal range.

HUMIDITY: High preferred, 50 percent or more. Good ventilation and circulation of fresh air around each cyclamen plant is an important aid to its continued good health.

WATER: Evenly moist but not soggy. The plant requires abundant water during active growth and blooming. Be sure to remove foil wrappings or punch a drainage hole in the bottom of the foil. Take care not to wet the succulent tender foliage, as it is very subject to spotting or rot. You might therefore prefer bottom watering, double potting, and/or an extradeep dry well.

FERTILIZER: Feed frequently with a mild, dilute well-balanced fertilizer when the plant is crowded in its pot and during active growth.

SOIL: Standard indoor mixture with additional leaf mold or humus (3:1). Cyclamen is properly potted with half of the crownlike corm above the soil level. Soil texture should be loose.

WHEN THE BLOOMS FADE: Cyclamen will rest anytime from April through June or July. Keep the plant on the dry side after the flowers fade, watering just enough to prevent shriveling of the fleshy leaves. When the plant dies down, either walk it respectfully to the wastebasket or follow this plan: Do not water at all to allow the tuber to cure or ripen; it is accumulating and storing food for next year's blossoms. When you can gently rub off all foliage without damaging the corm, the plant is ready to be repotted or top dressed,

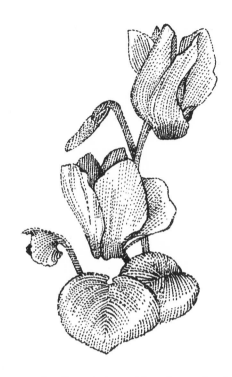

watered well, and plunged into the garden for the summer. Take care to repot with the corm at the same level, half out of the soil. Cool temperature and protection from strong summer sun are the primary requirements for next year's success. A cool greenhouse, lath house, or humid but cool sun porch would do equally well; a night temperature from 40°–50° will produce the strongest future results. In September, repot the tuber without changing its soil level. Keep the planting barely moist until growth begins and then treat it as one normally would.

PROPAGATION: Seeds may be planted in August for flowering plants eighteen months later. Transplant the seedlings into rich soil and an inch away from each neighbor; pot-on when the leaves are touching and continue in this way. Winter temperatures of 40°–50° will encourage the best growth. Beware of thrips and the infamous cyclamen mites; indeed professional growers spray weekly to deter these insidious deforming creatures.

**Easter Lily**     *Lilium longiflorum*
Easter lily is a bulbous plant so let the foliage die back naturally if you wish to retain the bulb for future outdoor flowers. When the stalk yellows, reduce the watering gradually until the soil is completely dry. Pull the top off with a gentle twisting motion and store the bulb in a cool, dark, dry place until the outdoor weather has warmed up. Plant the bulb 6–8 inches deep in a humus-rich and light soil bed and hope for the best next year. It cannot be forced for indoor use again.

LIGHT: Bright, but no direct sun.

TEMPERATURE: As cool as possible to prolong existing blooms.

HUMIDITY: Average or slightly higher preferred, 30 percent or more.

WATER: Average to evenly moist, allow a distinct but mild drying-out period between soakings.

FERTILIZER: Feed frequently with a dilute solution once the plant is in the garden.

SOIL: Standard indoor mixture with additional leaf mold (3:1). Good drainage is essential.

WHEN THE BLOOMS FADE: See above. A spring gift plant may bloom again outdoors in the fall.

*Euphorbia pulcherrima*, see **Poinsettia**

**Hydrangea**     *Hydrangea macrophylla*
This plant is often given as a gift, but is is not well suited to future life in the house. If you wish to plant it in your garden, wait until all danger of local frost is past.

LIGHT: Bright, but no direct sun.

TEMPERATURE: As cool as possible to prolong existing blooms.

HUMIDITY: Average or higher preferred, 30–50 percent.

WATER: Evenly moist.

FERTILIZER: Feed with a frequent dilute solution once planted in the garden.

SOIL: Standard indoor mixture with additional leaf mold or peat moss (3:1).

WHEN THE BLOOMS FADE: Cut the plant back considerably and provide it with a sunny and well-drained garden site, morning sun preferred.

**Jerusalem Cherry**     *Solanum pseudocapsicum*
Jerusalem cherry is a member of the nightshade family; it is thus closely related to the pepper plant and its cultural requirements are the same. It grows as a small shrub with dark pointed leaves and red fleshy berries. The beautiful berries are poisonous so this is a poor plant for homes with pets and small children. Jerusalem cherry will drop leaves and fruit with gay abandon if the humidity drops or if there is unconsumed gas in the air. It is also subject to a gray yellowing of the leaves, stems, and fruits; this is a mold condition, so take extra care that ventilation is adequate.

LIGHT: Bright direct winter sun to bright indirect light.

TEMPERATURE: Cool, 55°–65° is fine, but the fruits or "cherries" will last longer if nights are as cool as 40° and days not over 65°.

HUMIDITY: Average to moderate, 30 percent or more. Do not mist Jerusalem cherry because of its tendency to develop gray mold. Ample fresh air is beneficial in this regard. But avoid drafts.

WATER: Average to evenly moist.

FERTILIZER: Average.

SOIL: Standard indoor mixture.

WHEN THE BLOOMS FADE: Discard the plant.

PROPAGATION: Seeds may be sown in January and February. Average temperature is fine for

dried with great success. Although a woody perennial in the tropics, the ornamental pepper is best treated as an annual in our temperate regions. Harvest the fruits and discard the plant and raise next year's crop from seed if you will.

LIGHT: Bright direct winter sun to bright indirect light.

TEMPERATURE: Cool, 55°–65° is fine, but the peppers will last longer if nights are as cool as 40° and days not over 65°.

HUMIDITY: Average to moderate, 30 percent or more. Ample fresh air is beneficial, but avoid drafts.

WATER: Average to evenly moist.

FERTILIZER: Average.

SOIL: Standard indoor mixture.

WHEN THE BLOOMS FADE: Discard the plant.

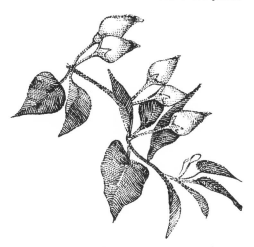

seedlings. Pinch the young plants vigorously for well-branched growth. Plant the seedlings individually and pot-on rapidly up to 5- to 7-inch pot size. The plants are best summered outdoors, pots sunk into the garden soil. They are brought in and repotted if necessary in early autumn (September to October) for winter bloom.

Lady's pocketbook, see **Pocketbook Plant**

*Lilium longiflorum*, see **Easter Lily**

**Ornamental Pepper**   *Capsicum annuum*
**Red-pepper Plant**   *C. frutescens* var.

**Christmas Pepper**

The ornamental pepper is native to South America, a member of the nightshade family and a vividly welcome fall and winter guest. The foliage is deep green; starlike white flowers appear before the peppery fruits which may be red, cream, or purple. The ornamental pepper is closely related to garden peppers, tomatoes, and potatoes; the peppers are edible but very hot and can be

PROPAGATION: Seeds may be sown for ornamental pepper in May and June. Average temperature is fine for seedlings. Pinch the young plants vigorously for well-branched growth. Plant the seedlings individually and pot-on rapidly up to 5- to 7-inch pot size. The plants are best summered outdoors, pots sunk into the garden soil. They are brought in and repotted if necessary in early autumn (September to October) for winter bloom.

Persian violet, see **Cyclamen**

**Pocketbook Plant** *Calceolaria*
**Lady's Pocket-** *crenatiflora*
**book** *C. herbeohybrida*
**Pouch Flower**
**Slipperwort**

The pocketbook plant is a charming and silly plant that appears in the shops in spring and is extremely hard to resist; it has in fact been a popular house plant since the late 1800s. The leaves are soft, thin, and downy. Great clusters of flowers appear with a distinctive and fanciful pouchlike shape; the lower lip is yellow or orange, inflated, and speckled with red, brown, or maroon dots. Although the flowers last less than a month, the unusual form and colorful design of the blooms make the plant well worthwhile. *Calceolaria* is a member of the figwort family, native to the cool Andes regions.

LIGHT: Bright indirect light to average indoor light.

TEMPERATURE: Average to cool, 60°–70° will do, but lower night temperatures (down to 45°) will prolong the flowers.

HUMIDITY: 30 percent or more. Ample fresh air.

WATER: Keep moist but not soggy. Bottom water or top water, but be sure to drain the plant well to avoid crown rot.

SOIL: Standard indoor mixture.

WHEN THE BLOOMS FADE: Discard the plant; it is an annual.

PROPAGATION: Seeds are sown in April for next year's bloom. Soak the seeds for an hour or two to soften the hard outer casings. Provide warmth (over 70°) and moderate to high humidity. Pinch the established seedlings and pot-on as the plants crowd their pots. Frequent, dilute, well-balanced fertilizing is necessary—but only after January when the plants should have been shifted to their final pots.

**Poinsettia** *Euphorbia pulcherrima*

The cheerful and distinctive poinsettia is known to all. The large, soft, notched, and pointed leaves and the explosively colorful flower bracts have made this Mexican native popular for the last hundred years. The true flowers of the plant are tiny and yellow; the impressive bracts or modified leaves are most commonly bright red, but may also be pink or white. Poinsettia is a "short-day" plant; the buds set when the night is fourteen hours long (October and on in the Northern Hemisphere) and the bloom appears naturally in late winter and spring. Professional growers use black-out curtains at any time of the year to simulate the natural autumn photoperiod and to have plants available for other popular commercial seasons. There will be no flowering if the least bit of light strikes the plant to interrupt the full period of darkness at critical preblooming times. To prolong the beauty of a newly received poinsettia, be sure that the light is abundant but neither direct nor hot, that the plant stays well watered, protected from chills, drafts, and sudden drops in humidity, and that the temperature is consistently between 60° and 72°. Poinsettia blithely drops bracts, flowers, and lower leaves with any sudden change in its environ-

ment. The leaves of the plant are poisonous, so take precautions in regard to small children and pets. If you are growing a plant beyond its first new-bought season, keep an eye out for scale and mealybugs.

LIGHT: Bright direct winter sun to bright indirect summer light. Abundant light, but avoid a blistering exposure. If you are interested in blooms the following year, be sure that no artificial light strikes the plant during autumn; keep it in an unlit room or move it each evening at dusk.

TEMPERATURE: 60°–72°. Avoid chills and drafts. If necessary, move the plant away from the window each night if the temperature there might fall below 60°.

HUMIDITY: Average to moderate, 30 percent or more. Poinsettia is quite sensitive about dry air and will drop leaves and bracts with any sudden downward fluctuation of the humidity.

WATER: Keep evenly moist during blooming.

FERTILIZER: None during blooming. From spring until blossoms appear, feed frequently with a mild, dilute well-balanced fertilizer solution.

SOIL: Standard indoor mixture. Excellent drainage is essential; remove foil wrappers or poke a hole in the bottom of the foil to circumvent root rot. When repotting, provide ample drainage material before adding the soil.

WHEN THE BLOOMS FADE: You have a number of choices depending upon your ambitions for next year and perhaps the availability of outdoor garden space: (1) Discard the plant; there will be more at the supermarket next year. (2) When the bracts fall, move the poinsettia to a light but more evenly cool location—60° is the ideal—and keep it only barely moist. Repot the plant in the spring and set it out in the garden. Because of a naturally roaming pattern of root growth, bury

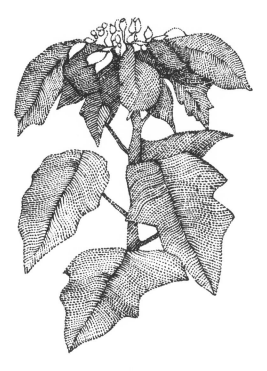

the pot with a thick layer of clinkers or chips beneath it and turn the pot regularly to keep the roots from hurrying to the center of the earth. Choose a location that receives good morning sun, but is also protected from the wind. Pinch vehemently until July; take cuttings if you wish. Keep the plant well watered and fed and prune out all but a few main shoots. It should be brought in before the nights get cool in the fall, provided with the standard indoor conditions, and sheltered from any artificial light after October 1. Decrease the water slightly after November until the blooms appear in order to harden the growth. (3) After the bracts have fallen and the leaves begin to yellow, gradually allow the plant to become dry. Store it until spring in a cool (50°–60°) location with average to almost dim indirect light. In late April or early May, cut it back to bare woody stems 3–6 inches long and repot; you will be able to remove a great deal of the old soil since the plant is semidormant. Then provide a sunny window, a temperature between 60° and 72°, and water again. Mist the poinsettia stems frequently to encourage the willing leaf nodes to break through the bark. Water lightly at first and then, after growth is well underway, keep the plant evenly moist. Pinch vigorously through the middle of July; begin regular fertilizing and pruning and limit the summer growth to a few robust, well-pinched shoots for a more massive bloom. Set the poinsettia out in the garden as above if possible. Take cuttings from new growth. Protect the plant from artificial nighttime light during the fall and keep it a bit drier from November until the blooms appear in order to harden the final growth.

PROPAGATION: Cuttings taken from June to August result in fine blooming plants for the following winter. Take cuttings that are 4–6 inches long, dip them in rooting powder, and set them in vermiculite or in a mixture of peat moss and sand. Shade the cuttings from bright light and provide ample humidity until they are well rooted. Pot them individually or several per pot and pot-on as they become crowded. Mist young plants until they are hardy, and pinch from the very beginning through July. Sink the pots in the garden or grow the plants indoors if you are able to satisfy their uncompromising requirements (abundant light, no chills, no drafts, no drops in humidity, even temperature of 60°–70°). The parent plant may be cut back to 12 inches after supplying the propagating box; if the cuttings are taken in June and the older plant cut back and then pinched vigorously through the middle of July, the original plant will bloom impressively the following winter despite its generosity.

Pouch flower, see **Pocketbook Plant**

Red-pepper plant, see **Ornamental Pepper**

**Rose**               *Rosa floribunda*
You should keep your gift-plant rose well watered and provide it with a cool, sunny location. This plant should not be expected to adapt to a future life in the house, and if you wish to keep it, it should be planted in the garden.

LIGHT: Bright, but no direct sun.

TEMPERATURE: As cool as possible to prolong existing blooms.

HUMIDITY: Average house, 30 percent or more.

WATER: Evenly moist.

FERTILIZER: Frequent feedings of a well-balanced fertilizer once the plant is out in the garden.

SOIL: Standard indoor mixture with additional leaf mold (3:1).

WHEN THE BLOOMS FADE: Cut the plant back considerably, and, after all danger of local frost has passed, provide it with a sunny and well-drained garden site, morning sun preferred.

*Senecio cruentus*, see **Cineraria**

Slipperwort, see **Pocketbook Plant**

*Solanum pseudocapsicum*, see **Jerusalem Cherry**

# APPENDIX

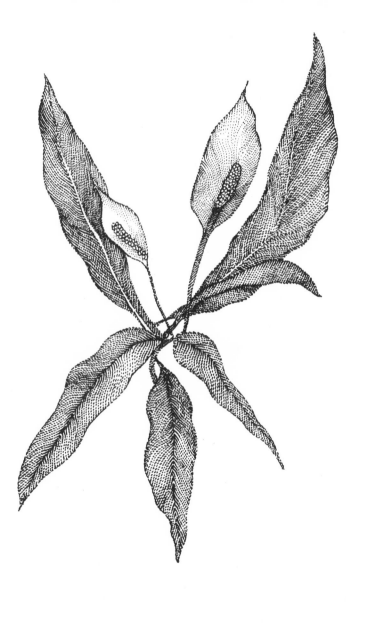

# The Plants in the Book Listed by Botanical Family

## ACANTHACEAE · Acanthus Family

| | | |
|---|---|---|
| *Aphelandra* | Zebra Plant | A. *aurantica roezlii* or A. *squarrosa louisae* |
| *Beloperone* | Shrimp Plant | B. *guttata* |
| *Fittonia* | Fittonia Nerve Plant | F. *verschaffeltii* var. |
| *Hypoestes* | Pink Polka Dot Freckle-face | H. *sanguinolenta* |
| *Thunbergia* | Black-eyed Susan | T. *alata* |

## AIZOACEAE · Fig Marigold Family

| | | |
|---|---|---|
| *Aptenia* | Ice Plant | A. *cordifolia* |
| *Conophytum* | Stone Faces Living Stones | C. *giftbergensis* or C. *minitum* C. *placitum* and others |
| *Faucaria* | Tiger Jaws | F. *tigrina* and others |
| *Fenestraria* | Window Cactus | F. *aurantiaca* and others |
| *Lithops* | Stone Faces Living Stones | L. *dinteri* or L. *hallii* or L. *karasmontana* and others |

## AMARANTHACEAE · Amaranth Family

| | | |
|---|---|---|
| *Iresine* | Blood Leaf | I. *herbstii* or I. *lindenii* |

## AMARYLLIDACEAE · Amaryllis Family

| | | |
|---|---|---|
| *Agave* | Dwarf Century Plant | *A. miradorensis* or *A. pumila* and others |
| *Clivia* | Clivia<br>Kafir Lily | *C. miniata* |
| *Hippeastrum* | Amaryllis | *H. hybrida* and var. |
| *Hymenocallis* | Spider Lily | *H. narcissiflora* and others |
| *Narcissus* | Daffodil<br>Paperwhite Daffodil<br>Poet's Narcissus | *N. pseudonarcissus*<br>*N. tazetta*<br>*N. poeticus* and others |
| *Zephyranthes* | Zephyr Lily | *Z. grandiflora* |

## APIACEAE · Parsley Family

| | | |
|---|---|---|
| *Anethum* | Dill | *A. graveolens* |
| *Carum* | Caraway | *C. carvi* |
| *Petroselinum* | Parsley | *P. crispum* |

## ARACEAE · Arum or Calla Family

| | | |
|---|---|---|
| *Aglaonema* | Chinese Evergreen | *A. modestum* or *A. simplex* |
| *Anthurium* | Anthurium<br>Tail Flower<br>Flamingo Flower | *A. andreanum* or *A. scherzerianum* |
| *Caladium* | Caladium<br>Elephant Ears | *C. bicolor* |
| *Dieffenbachia* | Dieffenbachia<br>Dumb Cane<br>Mother-in-law Plant | *D. amoena* or<br>*D. bowmannii* or<br>*D. picta* and others |
| *Monstera* | Monstera<br>Swiss-cheese Plant<br>Shingle Plant<br>Mexican Breadfruit | *M. deliciosa* |
| *Philodendron* | Philodendron | *P.* ssp. and var. |
| *Scindapsus* | Pothos<br>Devil's Ivy<br>Marble Queen | *S. pictus* var. or<br>*S. argyraeus* var.<br>*S. aureus* var. |
| *Spathiphyllum* | Spathiphyllum<br>Spathe Flower | *S. clevelandii* or<br>*S. floribundum* |
| *Syngonium* | Syngonium<br>Nephthytis | *S. podophyllum* var. |
| *Zantedeschia* | Calla Lily<br>White Calla | *Z. aethiopica*<br>and others |

## ARALIACEAE  ·  Ginseng or Aralia Family

| | | |
|---|---|---|
| *Dizygotheca* | Aralia<br>False Aralia | *D. elegantissima* |
| *Fatshedera* | Tree Ivy | *F. lizei* |
| *Fatsia* | Fatsia | *F. japonica* |
| *Hedera* | English Ivy<br>Hahn's Ivy<br>Needlepoint Ivy<br>Canary Ivy<br>Heart-leafed Ivy | *H. helix* var. |
| *Schefflera* | Schefflera<br>Umbrella Tree | *S. actinophylla* |

## ASCLEPIADACEAE  ·  Milkweed Family

| | | |
|---|---|---|
| *Ceropegia* | String of Hearts<br>Rosary Vine<br>Hearts Entangled | *C. woodii* |
| *Hoya* | Hoya<br>Wax Plant<br>Porcelain Flower | *H. bella* or<br>*H. carnosa* |

## BALSAMINACEAE  ·  Balsam Family

| | | |
|---|---|---|
| *Impatiens* | Impatiens<br>Patient Lucy<br>Patience Plant<br>Dizzy Lizzy<br>Zanzibar Balsam<br>Touch-me-not | *I. holstii* and<br>*I. sultanii* and hybrids |

## BEGONIACEAE  ·  Begonia Family

| | | |
|---|---|---|
| *Begonia* | Begonia | *B.* ssp. and var. and<br>hybrids |

## BRASSICACEAE  ·  Mustard Family

| | | |
|---|---|---|
| *Brassica* | Mustard | *B. hirta* |

## BUXACEAE  ·  Boxwood Family

| | | |
|---|---|---|
| *Buxus* | California Boxwood<br>Little-leaf Boxwood | *B. microphylla japonica* |

## CACTACEAE · Cactus Family

| | | |
|---|---|---|
| *Aporocactus* | Rat's-tail Cactus | *A. flagelliformis* |
| *Astrophytum* | Sea Urchin Cactus | *A. asterias* |
| *Cephalocereus* | Old Man Cactus | *A. senilis* |
| *Chamaecereus* | Peanut Cactus | *C. silvestrii* |
| *Echinocactus* | Barrel Cactus | *E. grusonii* and others |
| *Echinocereus* | Hedgehog Cactus | *E. baileyi* or *E. dasyacanthus* and others |
| *Epiphyllum* | Orchid Cactus<br>Night-blooming Cactus | *E. hybrida* and var. |
| *Gymnocalycium* | Chin Cactus | *G. mihanovichii* and others |
| *Hylocereus* | Night-blooming Cereus | *H. undatus* |
| *Lobivia* | Barrel Cactus | *L. aurea* or *L. haageana* and others |
| *Mammillaria* | Pincushion Cactus | *M. elongata* |
| *Opuntia* | Prickly Pear<br>Bunny Ears<br>Beaver-tail Cactus | *O. bergeriana* and others<br>*O. microdasys*<br>*O. basilaris* |
| *Rhipsalis* | Mistletoe Cactus | *R. burchelli* or *R. cassutha* or *R. paradoxa* |
| *Schlumbergera* | Christmas Cactus | *S. bridgesii* |
| *Selenicereus* | Night-blooming Cereus | *S. gradiflorus* or *S. macdonaldiae*<br>*S. pteranthus* and others |
| *Zygocactus* | Thanksgiving Cactus | *Z. truncatus* |

## CAMPANULACEAE · Bellflower Family

| | | |
|---|---|---|
| *Campanula* | Campanula<br>Star of Bethlehem<br>Italian Bellflower<br>Falling Stars | *C. isophylla* var. |

## CELASTRACEAE · Bittersweet Family

| | | |
|---|---|---|
| *Euonymus* | Euonymus | *E. japonicus* var. |

## COMMELINACEAE · Spiderwort Family

| | | |
|---|---|---|
| *Setcreasea* | Purple Heart | *S. purpurea* |

## COMMELINACEAE · Spiderwort Family

| | | |
|---|---|---|
| *Tradescantia* | Wandering Jew<br>Inch Plant | *T. albiflora* var. |
| *Zebrina* | Rainbow Wandering<br>  Jew<br>Rainbow Inch Plant | *Z. pendula* var. |

## COMPOSITAE · Composite Family

| | | |
|---|---|---|
| *Artemisia* | Tarragon | *A. drancunculus* var. |
| *Chrysanthemum* | Chrysanthemum | *C. hortorum* |
| *Gynura* | Velvet Plant<br>Purple Velvet | *G. aurantiaca* |
| *Senecio* | Cineraria | *S. cruentus* |

## CRASSULACEAE · Stonecrop Family

| | | |
|---|---|---|
| *Crassula* | Jade Plant<br>String of Pearls<br>Scarlet Paintbrush | *C. argentea*<br>*C. perfossa*<br>*C. falcata* and others |
| *Echeveria* | Hens and Chickens | *E. derenbergii* and others |
| *Kalanchoe* | Panda Plant<br>Good-luck Leaf | *K. blossfeldiana*<br>  and others |
| *Sedum* | Burro's Tail<br>Coral Beads | *S. morganianum*<br>*S. stahlii* |
| *Sempervivum* | House Leek | *S. arachnoideum* or<br>*S. montanum* or<br>*S. tectorum* var. and<br>  others |

## CYPERACEAE · Sedge Family

| | | |
|---|---|---|
| *Cyperus* | Umbrella Plant | *C. alternifolius* |

## ERICACEAE · Heath Family

| | | |
|---|---|---|
| *Rhododendron* | Azalea | *R. indicum* or<br>*R. obtusum* and hybrids |

## EUPHORBIACEAE · Spurge Family

| | | |
|---|---|---|
| *Acalypha* | Chenille Plant | *A. hispida* |
| *Codiaeum* | Croton | *C. variegatum pictum* |
| *Euphorbia* | Poinsettia | *E. pulcherrima* |

## GERANIACEAE · Geranium Family

| | | |
|---|---|---|
| *Pelargonium* | Geranium<br>House Geranium<br>Zonal Geranium | *P. hortorum* |
| | Show Geranium<br>Lady Washington<br>Martha Washington | *P. domesticum* |
| | Scented Geranium | *P. speciosa* var. |
| | Ivy Geranium<br>Hanging Geranium | *P. peltatum* |

## GESNERIACEAE · Gesneriad Family

| | | |
|---|---|---|
| *Achimenes* | Achimenes<br>Monkey-face Flower<br>Nut Orchid | *A. longiflora* or<br>*A. patens* and others |
| *Aeschynanthus* | Lipstick Vine | *A. lobbianus* or<br>*A. pulcher* |
| *Columnea* | Columnea | *C.* ssp. |
| *Episcia* | Episcia<br>Flame Violet | *E. reptans*<br> and others |
| *Gloxinera* | Gloxinera | *Rechsteineria* X *Sinningia* |
| *Kohleria* | Kohleria | *K. amabilis* or<br>*K. lindeniana* |
| *Nautilocalyx* | Nautilocalyx | *N.* ssp. |
| *Rechsteineria* | Rechsteineria | *R. cardinalis* or<br>*R. leucotricha* and others |
| *Saintpaulia* | African Violet | *S.* ssp. and var. and<br> hybrids |
| *Sinningia* | Gloxinia | *S. barbata* or<br>*S. pusilla* or<br>*S. regina* and others |
| *Smithiantha* | Temple Bells | *S. cinnabarina* or<br>*S. multiflora* or<br>*S. zebrina* vars. and<br> hybrids |
| *Streptocarpus* | Cape Primrose | *S. rexii* or<br>*S. saxorum* and others |

## GRAMINEAE · Grass Family

| | | |
|---|---|---|
| *Bambusa* | Bamboo | *B. nana* |

## IRIDACEAE · Iris Family

| | | |
|---|---|---|
| *Crocus* | Dutch Crocus | *C. moesicus* |
| *Freesia* | Freesia | *F. hybrida* and var. |
| *Neomarica* | Walking Iris | *N. gracilis* or |
| | Apostle Plant | *N. northiana* or |
| | | *N. caerulea* |

## LABIATAE · Mint Family

| | | |
|---|---|---|
| *Coleus* | Coleus | *C. blumei* |
| | Painted Nettle | |
| *Marjorana* | Marjoram | *M. hortensis* |
| *Mentha* | Mint | *M.* var. |
| | Orange Mint or | *M. citrata* |
| | Bergamot | |
| | Peppermint or | *M. piperita* |
| | American Mint | |
| | Corsican Mint | *M. requienii* |
| | Wooly Apple Mint | *M. rotundifolia* |
| | Pineapple Mint | *M. variegata* |
| | Spearmint | *M. spicata* |
| *Ocimum* | Sweet Basil | *O. basilicum* var. |
| | Purple Basil | |
| | Lemon-scented Basil | |
| | Lettuce-leafed Basil | |
| *Origanum* | Oregano | *O. vulgare* |
| *Plectranthus* | Swedish Ivy | *P. australis* |
| | Creeping Charlie | |
| *Rosmarinus* | Rosemary | *R. officinalis* |
| *Salvia* | Sage | *S. officinalis* |
| *Thymus* | Thyme | *T. vulgaris* |

## LAURACEAE · Laurel Family

| | | |
|---|---|---|
| *Laurus* | Bay | *L. nobilis* |

## LILIACEAE · Lily Family

| | | |
|---|---|---|
| *Agapanthus* | African Lily | *A. africanus* or |
| | Lily of the Nile | *A. orientalis albus* |
| *Allium* | Chives | *A. schoenoprasum* |
| *Aloe* | Aloe | *A. arborescens* or |
| | | *A. alobusa* or |
| | | *A. nobilis* or |
| | | *A. variegata* and others |

## LILIACEAE · Lilly Family

| | | |
|---|---|---|
| *Asparagus* | Asparagus Fern | *A. sprengeri* |
| | Emerald Feather | *A. plumosus* |
| *Aspidistra* | Aspidistra | *A. elatior* |
| | Cast-iron Plant | |
| *Chlorophytum* | Spider Plant | *C. elatum* |
| | Airplane Plant | |
| *Convallaria* | Lily of the Valley | *C. majalis* |
| *Cordyline* | Hawaiian Ti Plant | *C. terminalis* var. |
| *Dracaena* | Dracaena | *D. fragrans* or |
| | | *D. marginata* or |
| | | *D. sanderiana* |
| *Gloriosa* | Gloriosa Lily | *G. rothschildiana* |
| *Haworthia* | Zebra Haworthia | *H. fasciata* and others |
| | Wart Plant | |
| *Hyacinthus* | Hyacinth | *H. orientalis* var. and |
| | | hybrids |
| *Lilium* | Easter Lily | *L. longiflorum* |
| *Muscari* | Grape Hyacinth | *M. armeniacum* |
| *Sansevieria* | Snake Plant | *S. trifasciata* |
| | Mother-in-law's Tongue | *S. hahnii* |
| *Scilla* | Scilla | *S. tubergeniana* |
| | Persian Squill | |

## MALVACEAE · Mallow Family

| | | |
|---|---|---|
| *Abutilon* | Flowering Maple | *A.* var. and hybrids |
| | Parlor Maple | |

## MARANTACEAE · Arrowroot Family

| | | |
|---|---|---|
| *Maranta* | Maranta | *M. leuconeura* var. |
| | Prayer Plant | |
| | Old Rabbit Tracks | |

## MELASTOMATACEAE · Meadow Beauty Family

| | | |
|---|---|---|
| *Schizocentron* | Spanish Shawl | *S. elegans* |

## MORACEAE · Fig Family

| | | |
|---|---|---|
| *Ficus* | Rubber Plant | *F. elastica* |

## MORACEAE · Fig Family

| | | |
|---|---|---|
| | Fiddle-leaf Fig | *F. lyrata* or *F. pandurata* |
| | Creeping Fig | *F. pumila* and *F. radicans* |
| | Weeping Fig | *F. benjamina* |
| | Java Fig | |

## NYCTAGINACEAE · Four o'Clock Family

| | | |
|---|---|---|
| *Bougainvillea* | Bougainvillea | *B.* ssp. and hybrids |

## ONAGRACEAE · Evening Primrose Family

| | | |
|---|---|---|
| *Fuchsia* | Fuchsia | *F. speciosa* hybrids |
| | Lady's Eardrops | |

## OXALIDACEAE · Wood Sorrel Family

| | | |
|---|---|---|
| *Oxalis* | Oxalis | *O.* ssp. and var. |
| | Wood Sorrel | |
| | Bermuda Buttercup | |

## PALMACEAE · Palm Family

| | | |
|---|---|---|
| *Caryota* | Fishtail Palm | *C.* ssp. |
| *Chamaedorea* | Parlor Palm | *C. elegans bella* |
| *Chamaerops* | European Fan Palm | *C. humilis* |
| *Chrysalidocarpus* | Butterfly Palm | *C. (Areca) lutescens* |
| *Howea* | Kentia Palm | *H. (Kentia) belmoreana* or |
| | Sentry Palm | *H.* or *K. forsteriana* |
| | Paradise Palm | |
| *Livistona* | Chinese Fan Palm | *L. chinensis* |
| *Neanthe bella* | Parlor Palm | *N. bella* ssp. |
| | Neanthe Bella | |
| *Syagrus* | Cocos Palm | *S. weddelliana* |
| | Weddell Palm | |

## PANDANACEA · Screw Pine Family

| | | |
|---|---|---|
| *Pandanus* | Screw Pine | *P. baptistii* or *P. utilis* or *P. veitchii* and others |

## PASSIFLORACEAE · Passion Flower Family

| *Passiflora* | Passion Flower | *P.* ssp. |

## PINACEAE · Pine Family

| *Araucaria* | Norfolk Island Pine | *A. excelsa* |

## PIPERACEAE · Pepper Family

| *Peperomia* | Peperomia<br>Watermelon Begonia | *P. argyreia* or<br>*P. sandersii* ssp. and var. |

## PITTOSPORACEAE · Pittosporum Family

| *Pittosporum* | Pittosporum | *P. tobira* and<br>*P. variegatum* |

## PODOCARPACEAE · Podocarpus Family

| *Podocarpus* | Podocarpus<br>Southern Yew<br>Japanese Yew | *P. macrophylla maki* or<br>*P. nagi* or<br>*P. neriifolia* |

## POLYPODIACEAE · Fern Family

| *Adiantum* | Maidenhair Fern | *A.* var. |
| *Asplenium* | Bird's-nest Fern<br>Mother Fern | *A. nidus*<br>*A. bulbiferum* or<br>*A. viviparum* |
| *Cyrtomium* | Holly Fern | *C. falcatum*<br>*rochefordianum* |
| *Davallia* | Rabbit's-foot Fern | *D. bullata mariesii* or<br>*D. fejeensis* and others |
| *Nephrolepsis* | Boston Fern<br>Drapery Fern<br>Sword Fern | *N. exaltata bostoniensis*<br>and var.<br>*N. exaltata* |
| *Pellaea* | Button Fern | *P. rotundifolia* |
| *Platycerium* | Staghorn Fern | *P. bifurcatum* |
| *Polypodium* | Hare's-foot Fern<br>Bear's-paw Fern | *P. aureum* and others |
| *Polystichum* | Leather Fern | *P. adiantiforme* |
| *Pteris* | Table Fern<br>Pteris Fern<br>Brake Fern | *P. cretica* or<br>*P. serrulata* and var. |

## PRIMULACEAE · Primrose Family

| | | |
|---|---|---|
| *Cyclamen* | Cyclamen | *C. persicum* |
| | Persian Violet | *C. persicum giganteum* |
| *Primula* | Primrose | *P.* ssp. and var. |
| | Chinese Primrose | *P. sinensis* |
| | Fairy Primrose | *P. malacoides* |
| | Poison Primrose | *P. obconica* |

## ROSACEAE · Rose Family

| | | |
|---|---|---|
| *Rosa* | Rose | *R. chinensis minima* or |
| | Miniature Rose | *R. roulettii* and others |
| | Pygmy Rose | |
| | Fairy Rose | |
| | Rose | *R. floribunda* |

## RUBIACEAE · Madder Family

| | | |
|---|---|---|
| *Gardenia* | Gardenia | *G. jasminoides* |
| *Ixora* | Ixora | *I. coccinea* and |
| | Flame of the Woods | hybrids |
| *Manettia* | Manettia | *M. bicolor* or |
| | Firecracker Vine | *M. inflata* |
| | Candy-corn Plant | |

## SAXIFRAGACEAE · Saxifraga Family

| | | |
|---|---|---|
| *Hydrangea* | Hydrangea | *H. macrophylla* |
| *Saxifraga* | Saxifraga | *S. sarmentosa* |
| | Strawberry Begonia | |
| | Strawberry Geranium | |
| | Mother of Thousands | |
| *Tolmiea* | Piggyback Plant | *T. menziesii* |
| | Pick-a-back Plant | |

## SCROPHULARIACEAE · Slipperwort Family

| | | |
|---|---|---|
| *Calceolaria* | Pocketbook Plant | *C. crenatiflora* |
| | Lady's Pocketbook | *C. herbeo hybrida* |
| | Pouch Flower | |
| | Slipperwort | |

## SELAGINELLACEAE · Selaginella Family

| | | |
|---|---|---|
| *Selaginella* | Selaginella | *S. emmeliana* |

### SELAGINELLACEAE · Selaginella Family

| | | |
|---|---|---|
| | Sweat Plant | |
| | Spreading Club Moss | *S. kraussiana brownii* |
| | Resurrection Plant | *S. lepidophylla* |

### SOLANACEAE · Nightshade Family

| | | |
|---|---|---|
| *Browallia* | Browallia | *B. speciosa major* and |
| | Sapphire Flower | others |
| *Capsicum* | Ornamental Pepper | *C. annuum* or |
| | Red-pepper Plant | *C. frutescens* var. |
| | Christmas Pepper | |
| *Solanum* | Jerusalem Cherry | *S. pseudocapsicum* |

### THEACEAE · Tea Family

| | | |
|---|---|---|
| *Camellia* | Camellia | *C. japonica* or |
| | | *C. reticulata* |

### URTICACEAE · Nettle Family

| | | |
|---|---|---|
| *Helxine* | Baby Tears | *H. soleirolii* |
| | Irish Moss | |
| *Pilea* | Aluminum Plant | *P. cadierei* |
| | Artillery Plant | *P. microphylla* |
| | Friendship Plant | *P. involucrata* |
| | Panimiga | |

### VERBENACEAE · Verbena Family

| | | |
|---|---|---|
| *Clerodendrum* | Glory Bower | *C. fragrans* or |
| | Bag Flower | *C. thomsonae* or others |
| | Bleeding Heart Vine | |

### VITACEAE · Grape Family

| | | |
|---|---|---|
| *Cissus* | Kangaroo Ivy | *C. antarctica* |
| | Kangaroo Vine | |
| | Grape Ivy | *C. rhombifolia* |

# What Grows Well Where?

---

## Super-easy Plants to Grow

C   cooler temperatures preferred

Baby Tears
Cacti
C   Cast-iron Plant
Chinese Evergreen
Coleus
Dieffenbachia
Dracaena
C   English Ivy

Fiddle-leaf Fig
Impatiens
Monstera
Nephthytis
Palms
Philodendrons
Piggyback Plant
Pothos

Rubber Plant
Snake Plant
Spathiphyllum
Spider Plant
Swedish Ivy
Succulents
C   Walking Iris
Wandering Jew

---

## Background or "Permanent" Evergreen Plants

C   cooler temperatures preferred

C   Cast-iron Plant
Chinese Fan Palm
Dieffenbachia
Dracaena
C   English Ivy
Fiddle-leaf Fig
Golden Feather Palm

Grape Ivy
Hoya
Kangaroo Ivy
Kentia Palm
Monstera
Parlor Palm
Philodendrons

C   Pittosporum
Pothos
Rubber Plant
Snake Plant
Swedish Ivy
C   Walking Iris

253

## For Sunny Spots

C   cooler temperatures preferred

|   | | | | | |
|---|---|---|---|---|---|
| | African Lily | | Crocus | | Pink Polka Dot |
| | Amaryllis | | Croton | C | Pittosporum |
| | Asparagus Fern | | Daffodil | | Poinsettia (winter) |
| C | Azalea | C | Easter Lily | | Purple Heart |
| | Bamboo | | Flowering Maple (winter) | C | Rose |
| | Begonias (winter) | | Freesia | C | Saxifraga |
| | Black-eyed Susan Vine | C | Gardenia (winter) | | Scilla |
| C | Blood Leaf | C | Geranium | | Snake Plant |
| C | Browallia | | Glory Bower | C | Spanish Shawl |
| | Bougainvillea | | Grape Hyacinth | | Succulents |
| | Cacti (except Orchid, | | Hoya (winter) | C | Tree Ivy |
| | Thanksgiving, and | | Hyacinth | | Tulip |
| | Christmas) | C | Hydrangea | C | Walking Iris |
| | Caladium | | Impatiens (winter) | | *Plus* herbs |
| | Calla Lily | | Ixora | | *Plus* annuals; such as |
| C | Camellia (winter) | | Jerusalem Cherry | | Nasturtium, Sweet |
| | Campanula (winter) | | Lily of the Valley | | Alyssum, Marigold, |
| | Chenille Plant (winter) | | Narcissus | | Petunia, Forget-me- |
| C | Chrysanthemum | | Ornamental Pepper | | not, Pansy, Lobelia, |
| C | Cineraria (winter) | C | Oxalis (winter) | | Morning Glory |
| | Coleus | | Passion Flower | | |

## Semisunny to Semishady Places

\*       on the shadier side
\*\*     on the brighter side
\*\*\*   worth trying in a broad range
C       cooler temperatures preferred

|   |   | | | | | |   |   |
|---|---|---|---|---|---|---|---|---|
| \*\*\* | Achimenes | C \*\* | Blood Leaf | | C \*\* | Cineraria |
| \*\* | African Lily | C \*\* | Browallia | | C \*\*\* | Clivia |
| \*\* | African Violet | \*\*\* | Caladium | | \*\* | Coleus |
| \*\*\* | Aluminum Plant | \*\* | Cacti | | \*\* | Columnea |
| \* | Anthurium | \*\* | Calla Lily | | \*\*\* | Creeping Fig |
| \*\*\* | Aralia | C \*\* | Camellia | | \*\* | Crocus |
| \*\*\* | Asparagus Fern | \*\* | Campanula | | \*\* | Croton |
| C \*\* | Azalea | C \*\*\* | Cast-iron Plant | | C \*\*\* | Cyclamen |
| \* | Baby Tears | \*\* | Chenille Plant | | \*\* | Daffodil |
| \*\* | Bamboo | \* | Chinese Evergreen | | \*\* | Dieffenbachia |
| \*\*\* | Begonia | \*\* | Christmas Cactus | | \*\*\* | Dracaena |
| \*\* | Black-eyed Susan | C \*\* | Chrysanthemum | | \*\* | Easter Lily |

## Semisunny to Semishady Places

| | | |
|---|---|---|
| C *** English Ivy | ** Manettia | ** Scilla |
| *** Episcia | *** Maranta | * Selaginella |
| C ** Fatsia | *** Monstera | *** Shrimp Plant |
| *** Ferns | ** Narcissus | *** Snake Plant |
| *** Fiddle-leaf Fig | C *** Norfolk Island Pine | C ** Spanish Shawl |
| * Fittonia | ** Orchid Cactus | *** Spathiphyllum |
| ** Flowering Maple | ** Ornamental Pepper | ** Spider Lily |
| *** Friendship Plant | C ** Oxalis | *** Spider Plant |
| C ** Fuchsia | * Palms | *** String of Hearts |
| C ** Gardenia | ** Passion Flower | ** Succulents |
| C ** Geranium | *** Peperomias | *** Swedish Ivy |
| ** Gloriosa Lily | *** Philodendrons | *** Syngonium |
| ** Glory Bower | *** Piggyback Plant | ** Thanksgiving Cactus |
| ** Grape Hyacinth | ** Pink Polka Dot | C *** Tree Ivy |
| *** Grape Ivy | C *** Pittosporum | ** Tulip |
| ** Hoya | C ** Pocketbook Plant | *** Umbrella Tree |
| ** Hyacinth | C *** Podocarpus | ** Velvet Plant |
| ** Hydrangea | ** Poinsettia | C *** Walking Iris |
| ** Jerusalem Cherry | *** Pothos | *** Wandering Jew |
| *** Kangaroo Ivy | ** Purple Heart | *** Weeping Fig |
| ** Impatiens | ** Rose | ** Zebra Plant |
| ** Ixora | *** Rubber Plant | ** Zephyr Lily |
| ** Lily of the Valley | C * Saxifraga | |
| ** Lipstick Vine | *** Schefflera | |

## For Dim or Almost-dim Locations

C cooler temperatures preferred

| | | |
|---|---|---|
| Anthurium | Fiddle-leaf Fig | C Saxifraga |
| Asparagus Fern | Monstera | Schefflera |
| C Cast-iron Plant | C Norfolk Island Pine | Snake Plant |
| Chinese Evergreen | Palms | Spathiphyllum |
| C Clivia | Philodendrons | Spider Plant |
| Dieffenbachia | C Pittosporum | Swedish Ivy |
| Dracaena | C Podocarpus | Syngonium |
| C English Ivy | Pothos | C Tree Ivy |
| Ferns | Rubber Plant | Umbrella Plant |

## For Dish Gardens and Planters

C  cooler temperatures preferred

African Violet
Aralia (young)
Artillery Plant
Asparagus Fern
Baby Tears
Begonia
C  Blood Leaf
Boxwood (dwarf and
    young)
Cacti
Caladium (miniature)
Chinese Evergreen
    (young)
Coleus

Dracaena (young)
C  English Ivy
Episcia
Euonymus (young)
Ferns (young)
Friendship Plant
C  Geranium (miniature)
Impatiens
Maranta
Palms (Neanthe bella,
    Cocos, and young
    Phoenix)
Peperomias
Philodendrons (young)

Pink Polka Dot
C  Podocarpus (young)
Pothos
C  Rose (miniature)
C  Saxifraga
Snake Plant (small)
Spider Plant (young)
String of Hearts
Succulents
Swedish Ivy
Syngonium
Wandering Jew

## For Terrariums

C  cooler temperatures preferred

African Violet
Artillery Plant
Asparagus Fern
    (A. *plumosus*)
Baby Tears
Begonia
Caladium (miniature)
C  Camellia
Chinese Evergreen
    (young)
Creeping Fig
Croton
Dieffenbachia
    (young)

Dracaena (young)
C  English Ivy
Episcia
Euonymus
Ferns
Fittonia
Friendship Plant
Grape Ivy
Impatiens
Maranta
Palms (Neanthe bella,
    Cocos, and young
    Phoenix)
Peperomias

Philodendrons (young
    and small)
Pink Polka Dot
C  Pittosporum (young)
Pothos
C  Saxifraga
Selaginella
Shrimp Plant (young)
Swedish Ivy
Wandering Jew

# Suppliers

## Plants, Seeds, Fertilizer, and Equipment

Abbey Gardens
176 Toro Canyon Road
Carpinteria, California 93013

*Cacti and succulents*
Catalogue, $1.00

Alberts & Merkel Brothers, Inc.
2210 South Federal Highway
Boynton Beach, Florida 33435

*Orchids, bromeliads, and other tropicals*
Brochure of orchids, $.50
List of current foliage plants, $.50

Antonelli Brothers
2545 Capitola Road
Santa Cruz, California 95062

*Tuberous begonias, gesneriads, sedums, ferns, fuchsias, and other house plants*
Catalogue available

Bolduc's Greenhill Nursery
2131 Vallejo Street
St. Helena, California 94574

*Exotic ferns*
List of current plants, send stamped, self-addressed envelope

Buell's Greenhouses
Eastford, Connecticut 06242

*African violets, gloxinias, and other gesneriads*
Catalogue, send $.25 and long, stamped, self-addressed envelope

Burgess Seed and Plant Company
Galesburg, Michigan 49053

*Seeds, houseplants, and equipment*
Garden catalogue available
New catalogue of house plants available

W. Atlee Burpee Company
300 Park
Warminster, Pennsylvania 18974

*Seeds, bulbs, house plants, and supplies*
Catalogue available

Cactus Gem Nursery
P. O. Box 327
Aromas, California 95004

*Cacti and succulents*
List of current plants available

257

P. DeJager and Sons, Inc.
188 Asbury Street
South Hamilton, Massachusetts 01982

*Bulbs*
Catalogue available

Henry Field, Seed & Nursery Company
Shenandoah, Iowa 51602

*Seeds, nursery stock, and equipment*
Catalogue available

Howard B. French
Tozier Drive
Pittsfield, Vermont 05762

*Imported bulbs*
Catalogue available

Gurney Seed and Nursery Company
Yankton, South Dakota 57078

*Seeds, nursery equipment, and house plants*
Catalogue available

The House Plant Corner
P. O. Box 5000
Cambridge, Maryland 21613

*House plants, supplies, and equipment*
Catalogue, $.25

Ilgenfritz Orchids
Blossom Lane
P. O. Box 1114
Monroe, Michigan 48161

*Orchids*
List of current plants available

Kartuz Greenhouses
92 Chestnut Street
Wilmington, Massachusetts 01887

*Gesneriads, begonias, and other house plants*
Catalogue, $1.00

Leslie's Wild Flower Nursery
30 Summer Street
Methuen, Massachusetts 01844

*Wild flower seed*
Catalogue, $.25, deductible from first order

Logee's Greenhouses
55 North Street
Danielson, Connecticut 06239

*Begonias and other house plants*
Catalogue, $1.50

McComb Greenhouses
New Straitsville, Ohio 43766

*Cacti, ferns, gesneriads, bromeliads, and other house plants*
Catalogue, $.35

Rod McLellan Company
1450 El Camino Real
South San Francisco, California 94080

*Orchids, other house plants, and supplies*
Catalogue, $.50

Mellinger's Nursery, Inc.
2310 W.S. Range Road
North Lima, Ohio 44452

*Bonsai, terrariums, and supplies*
Catalogue available, stamps appreciated

Nichols Garden Nursery
1190 West Pacific Highway
Albany, Oregon 97321

*Seeds*
Catalogue, $.25

George W. Park Seed Company, Inc.
Greenwood, South Carolina 29647

*Seeds, house plants, supplies, and equipment*
Catalogue available

Robert B. Peters Company, Inc.
2833 Pennsylvania Street
Allentown, Pennsylvania 18104

*Fertilizers*
Catalogue available

Plantabbs
Lutherville, Maryland 21093

*Fertilizers and propagation equipment*
Catalogue available

Putney Nursery, Inc.
Putney, Vermont 05346

*Wild flowers, perennials, herbs, and ferns*
Catalogue available

Sudbury Soil Tests
Sudbury Laboratory, Inc.
Box 1383
Sudbury, Massachusetts 10776

*Soil-testing kits*
Brochure and information booklet available

## Artificial Light

General Electric Company
Lamp Division—Nela Park
Cleveland, Ohio 44112

*Lamps*
Information bulletins available

GTE Sylvania, Inc.
Public Affairs Department
Sylvania Lighting Center
Danvers, Massachusetts 01923

*Lamps and equipment*
Information bulletins available

The House Plant Corner
P. O. Box 5000
Cambridge, Maryland 21613

*Supplies and equipment*
Catalogue, $.25

George W. Park Seed Company, Inc.
Greenwood, South Carolina 29647

*Lamps, supplies, and equipment*
Catalogue available

Shoplite
566 Franklin Avenue
Nutley, New Jersey 07110

*Fixtures, lamps, and equipment*
Catalogue and booklet, $.35
Catalogue only, $.25

Tube Craft, Inc.
1311 W. 80th Street
Cleveland, Ohio 44102

*Lamps, indoor carts, equipment, and supplies*
Catalogue available

Westinghouse Electric Company
Westinghouse Lamp Division
Bloomfield, New Jersey 07003

*Lamps*
Information bulletins available

## Greenhouses

Aluminum Greenhouses
14615 Lorain Avenue
Cleveland, Ohio 44111

Catalogue upon written request

Garden of Eden Greenhouse Center
875 East Jericho Turnpike
Huntington Station, New York 11746

*Carry several lines*
Catalogue available

Lord & Burnham
Division Burnham Corporation
Irvington-on-Hudson, New York 10533

Catalogue available

J. A. Nearing
Box 348, Dept. FS
10788 Tucker Street
Beltsville, Maryland 20705

Catalogue available

| | |
|---|---|
| Peter Reimuller, The Greenhouseman<br>980 17th Avenue<br>Santa Cruz, California 95062 | Catalogue available |
| Sturdi-built Manufacturing Company<br>11304 S.W. Boones Ferry Road<br>Portland, Oregon 97219 | Catalogue available |
| Texas Greenhouse Company, Inc.<br>2717 St. Louis Avenue<br>Fort Worth, Texas 76110 | Catalogue available |

# Bibliography

## Indoor Plants

BAYLIS, MAGGIE. *House Plants for the Purple Thumb*. San Francisco, Cal.: 101 Productions, 1973.

BRILMAYER, BERNICE. *All About Begonias*. Garden City, N.Y.: Doubleday & Co., 1960.

CHIDAMIAN, CLAUDE. *The Book of Cacti and Other Succulents*. Garden City, N.Y.: Doubleday & Co., 1958.

CRUSO, THALASSA. *Making Things Grow*. New York: Alfred A. Knopf, 1969.

FREE, MONTAGUE. *All About House Plants*. Garden City, N.Y.: American Garden Guild and Doubleday & Co., 1964.

GRAF, ALFRED BYRD. *Exotica III*. Rutherford, N.J.: Roehrs Company, 1963.

HAAGE, WALTHER. *Cacti and Succulents*. New York: E. P. Dutton & Co., 1963.

KRAMER, JACK. *Flowering House Plants Month By Month*. New York: Cornerstone Library, 1967. New material 1973. Reprinted 1974.

KRAMER, JACK. *1000 Beautiful House Plants and How to Grow Them*. New York: William Morrow & Co., 1969.

McDONALD, ELVIN. *The World Book of House Plants*. New York: World Publishing Co., 1963.

SCHULTZ, PEGGY, ed. *Gesneriads and How to Grow Them*. Kansas City, Mo.: Diversity Books, 1967.

TRUEX, PHILIP. *The City Gardener*. New York: Alfred A. Knopf, 1964.

WILSON, HELEN VAN PELT, ed. *1001 African Violet Questions Answered by 12 Experts*. Princeton, N.J.: D. Van Nostrand Co., 1958.

## Greenhouses

CROCKETT, JAMES UNDERWOOD. *Greenhouse Gardening as a Hobby*. Garden City, N.Y.: Doubleday & Co., 1961.

SCHULZ, PEGGY. *How to Make Money from Your Home Greenhouse*. Princeton, N.J.: D. Van Nostrand Co., 1959.

## Artificial Light

CHERRY, ELAINE C. *Flourescent Light Gardening*. Princeton, N.J.: D. Van Nostrand Co., 1965.

KRANZ, FREDERICK H. AND JACQUELINE L. *Gardening Under Lights*. New York: The Viking Press, 1957. Revised ed. 1971.

MCDONALD, ELVIN. *The Complete Book of Gardening Under Lights*. Garden City, N.Y.: Doubleday & Co., 1965.

## Bonsai

CHIDAMIAN, CLAUDE. *Bonsai, Miniature Trees*. Princeton, N.J.: D. Van Nostrand Co., 1955.

HULL, GEORGE, F. *Bonsai for Americans*. Garden City, N.Y.:Doubleday & Co., 1964.

YASHIRODA, KAN. *Bonsai, Japanese Miniature Trees*. Newton, Mass.: Charles T. Branford Co., 1960.

## Conventional Botany

BAILEY, L. H. *How Plants Get Their Names*. New York: Dover Publications, 1963.

RICKETT, HAROLD WILLIAM. *Botany for Gardeners*. New York: Macmillan Co., 1957.

SCIENTIFIC AMERICAN, EDITORS OF. *Plant Life*. New York: Simon & Schuster, 1949–57.

SINNOLT, EDMUND W. *Botany: Principles and Problems*. New York: McGraw-Hill Book Co., 1955. 6th ed. 1963.

WENT, FRITZ W., AND EDITORS OF *Life*. *The Plants*. New York: Time Inc., 1963.

## Other Directions

BIRD, CHRISTOPHER, AND TOMPKINS, PETER. *The Secret Life of Plants*. New York: Harper & Row, 1973.

HICKS, CLIFFORD B. "Growing Corn to Music." *Popular Mechanics*, May 1963, 119:118–121.

MARTIN, RICHARD. "Be Kind to Plants—Or You Could Cause A Violet to Shrink." *Wall Street Journal*, January 28, 1972, pp. 1, 10.

McGRAW, WALTER. "Plants Are Only Human." *Argosy*, June 1969, pp. 24–27.

PARKHURST, D. F. AND PEARMAN, G. I. "Tree Seedling Growth: Effects of Shaking." *Science*, February 25, 1972.

ROBBINS, JANICE AND ROBBINS, CHARLES. "Startling New Research from the Man Who 'Talks' to Plants." *National Wildlife*, October–November 1971, 9:6, 21–24.

STONG, C. L. "Stimulating Plant Growth with Ultrasonic Vibrations." *Scientific American: Amateur Scientist*, 1966, 215:100–102.

# Index